DEWEY FOR A NEW AGE OF FASCISM

RHETORIC AND DEMOCRATIC DELIBERATION
VOLUME 22

EDITED BY CHERYL GLENN AND STEPHEN BROWNE
THE PENNSYLVANIA STATE UNIVERSITY

Cofounding Editor: J. Michael Hogan

Editorial Board:

Robert Asen (University of Wisconsin–Madison)
Debra Hawhee (The Pennsylvania State University)
J. Michael Hogan (The Pennsylvania State University)
Peter Levine (Tufts University)
Steven J. Mailloux (University of California, Irvine)
Krista Ratcliffe (Marquette University)
Karen Tracy (University of Colorado, Boulder)
Kirt Wilson (The Pennsylvania State University)
David Zarefsky (Northwestern University)

Rhetoric and Democratic Deliberation focuses on the interplay of public discourse, politics, and democratic action. Engaging with diverse theoretical, cultural, and critical perspectives, books published in this series offer fresh perspectives on rhetoric as it relates to education, social movements, and governments throughout the world.

A complete list of books in this series is located at the back of this volume.

DEWEY FOR A NEW AGE OF FASCISM

TEACHING DEMOCRATIC HABITS

NATHAN CRICK

The Pennsylvania State University Press | University Park, Pennsylvania

This volume is published with the generous support
of the Center for Democratic Deliberation at
The Pennsylvania State University.

Library of Congress Cataloging-in-Publication Data
Names: Crick, Nathan, author.
Title: Dewey for a new age of fascism : teaching
   democratic habits / Nathan Crick.
Description: University Park, Pennsylvania : The
   Pennsylvania State University Press, [2019] | Series:
   Rhetoric and democratic deliberation ; vol. 22. |
   Includes bibliographical references and index.
Summary: "Drawing from the writings of John Dewey,
   identifies the core attitudes of fascism, sets forth
   an idea of democracy as communicative practice,
   and defines the values and methods of humanistic
   logic, aesthetics, and rhetoric"—Provided by
   publisher.
Identifiers: LCCN 2019025287 | ISBN 9780271084817
   (cloth)
Subjects: LCSH: Dewey, John, 1859–1952—Political
   and social views. | Democracy and education. |
   Humanism. | Fascism.
Classification: LC71.C745 2019
LC record available at https://lccn.loc.gov/2019025287

Copyright © 2019 Nathan Crick
All rights reserved
Printed in the United States of America.
Published by The Pennsylvania State University Press,
University Park, PA 16802-1003

The Pennsylvania State University Press is a member
of the Association of University Presses.

It is the policy of The Pennsylvania State University
Press to use acid-free paper. Publications on
uncoated stock satisfy the minimum requirements
of American National Standard for Information
Sciences—Permanence of Paper for Printed Library
Material, ANSI Z39.48-1992.

To Pam,

my partner in humanism,

teaching together in the castle

CONTENTS

Acknowledgments | ix

Introduction | 1

Part 1 **The Challenge of Fascist Antihumanism**

1 Ragged Individualism | 11

2 Animist Nationalism | 28

3 Totalitarian Propaganda | 45

Part 2 **The Politics of Democratic Humanism**

4 The Art of Individuality | 63

5 Renascent Liberalism | 83

6 Intelligence and Social Movements | 100

Part 3 **The Pedagogy of Democratic Humanism**

7 Logic | 123

8 Aesthetics | 148

9 Rhetoric | 177

Conclusion: Teaching Democratic Humanism | 199

Notes | 209

Bibliography | 221

Index | 231

ACKNOWLEDGMENTS

The pond next to my parent's house.
Wooden planks nailed into the sides of trees, forming a ladder.
My father's workbench, the bin of loose metal objects.
X-ACTO knives and balsa wood.
My mother's spaghetti sauce with fresh canned tomatoes.
The family tape recorder.
In the orange Datsun 240Z at night, gazing up through the back window at the stars.
My sister's stuffed dogs.
Joe as Dungeon Master.
When the older boys were talking about *The Lord of the Rings* on the porch.
The BASIC programming guide for an IBM PC Jr.
Rain on the bonfire at Little Beach.
The piano.
Wooden backboard, soft rim, dirt basketball court, losing to my brother, again.
Tortellini and croquet at the Conti villa.
Evening jazz band with Ernie DeNapoli.
The moment Sydney Carton sacrificed himself in *The Tale of Two Cities*.
Reading *Dubliners* in John Miller's class.
When Elizabeth Cohen took Marty Haskin seriously as a person.
The Italians from FIAT.
Thanksgiving dinner with the Americans in Norwich, England.
Practicing with the UEA Aardvarks on Sunday mornings after eggs and beans.
Stream of consciousness emails to and from n.swanson.
The river continuum concept.
The beesting news story from Norm Sims.
Writing editorials in the offices of *The Daily Collegian*.
My white 1996 Nissan pickup truck.
The pages of Thom Randall's *Adirondack Journal*.
The clammy basement at Mill Street.
Poetry on an old typewriter.
The *Giants of the Gobi* dig site at OMSI.
Christmas Day in Portland, 1996, walking the empty streets with Pam.

INTRODUCTION

A free education is incompatible with fascism. Education is likely to be one of the great battlegrounds upon which is waged an intense and desperate struggle for power.
—JOHN DEWEY AND GOODWIN WATSON, "THE FORWARD VIEW"

To teach democratic humanism is not simply to apply a method in a classroom; it is to dedicate oneself to giving students the capacities—that is to say, power—to realize their individual potentialities in cooperation with diverse others in a free society. But it is also to accept the responsibility that comes with actively struggling against those forces that constantly work to undermine the free movement of creative and sympathetic intelligence. Writing in 1937 with psychologist and fellow educational reformer Goodwin Watson, John Dewey gave a name to these collective forces of reaction when they combined into a movement; that name was "fascism." For them, fascism did not represent a party, regime, or threat from an aggressive foreign power; it represented a nexus of modern attitudes committed to imposing a fixed hierarchy of values not only upon a social order but upon human nature itself. Consequently, Dewey and Watson identified that the greatest struggle with fascism tended to occur within their own country, in its habits and institutions. For instance, they saw how "Americans, when they look at some of the totalitarian states, prize highly the greater freedom of this country, but in spite of this violations of civil liberties and assaults upon educational freedom seem to be increasing."[1] For them, the only way to resist the slide into fascism, whether it be slow or rapid, was through an education that is grounded in the virtues of democratic humanism and fully cognizant of the struggle in which it was engaged.

This book represents a contribution to this struggle. In framing a pedagogical inquiry in terms of a vigorous response to the threat of fascism, it also follows the lead of John J. McDermott, who in the tradition of William James and John Dewey has called on educators of all stripes to "seek nothing less than to enable a wide variety of peoples, rooted in virtually every racial, ethnic, religious, and political tradition, to form a community in which each person lives out the uniqueness of his or her heritage and persuasion in the spirit of harmony and justice."[2] But this ambitious goal is formed with a keen awareness of what he calls the "subtle foe" of fascism.[3] For McDermott, fascism "is the major social and political virus of our century, garbled alternately as statism, nationalism, ethnocentrism, racism, and the religiously hegemonic. It is a fuse which lurks everywhere, inclusive of our souls, were we honest to so admit."[4] Although always taking on the garb of some particular culture, it originates in the universal and characteristically modern desire for "scapegoating as a self-denying cover for internal, spiritual emptiness," bolstering its authority with false promises and short-term resolutions. And here is why it remains such a threat:[5] "If it comes, it will be as an eruption from within our self-preening, self-deceiving confidence in our own 'practice' of democracy."[6] For McDermott, there is only one course before us: to "reinvigorate the advice of Dewey, building slowly, from the ground up, face-to-face, and with empathy for one another."[7] That is the task of democratic humanism.

If the threat of fascism still seems somehow distant, a product of some bygone era and irrelevant to our own time, it is worth turning for a moment to the way that Dewey diagnosed his own age in the decades leading up to what would become World War II. One origin point stands out. Writing in 1928, he envisioned himself as a kind of Robinson Crusoe who "sat down to make a debit-credit list of his blessings and his troubles . . . in order to cheer himself up."[8] Only Dewey found that his list did not bring himself a great deal of cheer. Everywhere he looked, he found "inner tension and conflict. If ever there was a house of civilization divided within itself and against itself, it is our own today."[9] In official public life, "we seem to find everywhere a hardness, a tightness, a clamping down of the lid, a regimentation and standardization, a devotion to efficiency and prosperity of a mechanical and quantitative sort." In domestic politics, "there is an extraordinary apathy, indicated not only by abstention from the polls, but in the seemingly calm indifference with which the public takes the revelation of corruption in high places." In political speech, "it goes without saying that never before in our history have there been such flagrant violations of what one would have supposed to be fundamental in the American system." And in social life, "never have the forces of bigotry and intolerance been so well organized and so active."[10] When he thought about "fascism," then, he did not restrict himself to the now-familiar images of European fascism from the mid-twentieth century. Similarly, we should think about fascism in broader terms, as a movement of reactionary resistance to change that nonetheless purports to be revolutionary in seeking to bring about a "rebirth" of some mythic past as a means to cure a nation's ills and restore some identity that is seen to be under threat.[11]

It is worth noting, however, that fascist movements almost always appear alongside their opposite—movements of democratic humanism. Indeed, the two are intrinsically linked insofar as it takes the appearance of one side to spark a self-recognition and countermovement of the other. As Dewey indicates in his remarks earlier, when culture moves along by habit, passionate movements of reform or reaction tend to be pushed to the margins and lose their vigor. It is only in times of crisis when they surge back to the center and become active agents of conscious change, for better or worse. It is no accident that when Dewey performed his Robinson Crusoe exercise in 1928, he counted not only losses on one side but also what appeared to be significant gains on the other. Despite political apathy and corruption, "there was never previously so much publicity, so much investigation and exposure having a genuinely scientific quality." In the face of growing intolerance, "the forces of reaction are also producing a more conscious and determined liberal attitude." Organized censorship and repression too "has its counterpart in spontaneously and private exploration and exhibition of shortcomings and evils." And if "we are more nationalistic than at any previous time, we are also, as far as intellectual and moral currents are concerned, more internationally inclined." Dewey concluded that "if our outward scene is one of externally imposed organization, behind and beneath there is working the force of liberated individuality, experimenting in their own ways to find and realize their own ends."[12] The conflict that Dewey perceived in 1928 is analogous to the same conflict reemerging today.

What does Dewey mean by "democratic humanism"? For Steven C. Rockefeller, Dewey's democratic humanism was the final manifestation of an early religious faith that valued the democratic way of life as "the embodiment of a spirit of sympathy, open communication, and cooperation joined together with experimentalism and imaginative vision, leading to freedom and ongoing growth for all."[13] More specifically, by "humanism," Dewey means a faith in the possibilities of an adaptable human nature to intelligently define the aims and develop the methods that serve a realizable human good. By "democratic," Dewey means a commitment to developing these aims and methods through open communication and by the voluntary participation by all who share in the indirect consequences of public action. Therefore, democratic humanism represents the faith that open communication, voluntary participation, and cooperative intelligence are the means by which to expand human life and to develop the aims, methods, and attitudes that can best adapt human nature to meet the challenges of a constantly changing world. Not to be missed in the definition is the stress that Dewey places upon the *adaptability* of human nature. By this, Dewey means neither that human nature is fixed and unchangeable (as conservativism might suggest) nor that it is infinitely flexible (as the revolutionary might believe). Rather, Dewey puts forward the view of human nature whose most distinguishing characteristic is its capacity to take on habits: "Habit, not original human nature, keeps things moving most of the time."[14] Focusing on *habitual* human nature thus challenges the pessimism of the conservative while tempering the optimism of the revolutionary. Moreover, it places great emphasis on the ways in which our environment—natural, technological, and social—conditions our habits and either suppresses or makes possible certain forms of individuality and associated life. Dewey's democratic humanism is thus not a restatement of popular clichés about striving after our dreams; it is instead a recognition that actual social change is a long and difficult task of altering recalcitrant habits and developing new ones.

It is at this most central point, our understanding of human nature, that we see the significance of education within the struggle between democratic humanism and what is more accurately termed *fascist antihumanism*. To frame the conflict as one between democracy and fascism is misleading because it implies a competition between two forms of state rather than between two competing attitudes toward human nature and toward history, for at the root of any fascist movement or regime is the attitude of fascist antihumanism that rank orders human beings according to mythic categories, each with their own fixed nature, while at the same time advocating the use of force and violence to radically remake society all at once according to some mystical ideal of union. The fascist antihumanist clings to fixed essences and dreams of total revolutions as a way of avoiding having to deal intelligently with the fact of change—and worse still, does everything in his power to intentionally thwart efforts at adaptation. In contradistinction, the democratic humanist accepts the fact that we all share the same adaptable human nature, that this human nature must change with changing times, and that this change should be managed through communication and collaboration. For Dewey, the problem of change "is ultimately that of education in its widest sense. Consequently, whatever represses and distorts the processes of education that might bring about a change in human dispositions with the minimum of waste puts a premium upon the forces that bring society to a state of deadlock, and thereby encourages the use of violence as a means of social change."[15] It is only through an education grounded in the belief that the adaptability of human nature makes it possible to cooperatively develop intelligent means to adjust to the reality of change that the ever-present seduction of fascist antihumanism can be actively resisted and overcome.[16]

Identifying the threat of fascism as something inherent in *attitudes* more than in *regimes* not only emphasizes the central role that education and teaching have in meeting this challenge, but it also forces us to engage in the hardest task of all—self-criticism. It is a relatively straightforward matter to resist fascism if the latter is only identified with the threat of an aggressive, militaristic foreign regime and their jackbooted soldiers, barbed wire, and concentration camps; it is quite another matter to identify fascist tendencies in one's own culture and history. This fact makes it all the more remarkable that when Dewey addressed the challenge that Mussolini and Hitler posed in 1938, he criticized the hypocrisy of those very nations who felt called upon to "oppose and resist the advance of fascist, totalitarian, authoritarian states."[17] He goes on,

> What do we mean when we assume that we, in common with certain other nations, are really democratic, that we have already so accomplished the ends and purposes of democracy that all we have to do is to stand up and resist the encroachments of non-democratic states? We are unfortunately familiar with the tragic racial intolerance of Germany and now of Italy. Are we entirely free from that racial intolerance, so that we can pride ourselves upon having achieved a complete democracy? Our treatment of the Negroes, anti-Semitism, the growing (at least I fear it is growing) serious opposition to the alien immigrant within our gates, is, I think, a sufficient answer to that question.[18]

The very next year, in his 1939 *Freedom and Culture*, Dewey drew the logical conclusion: "The serious threat to our democracy is not the existence of foreign totalitarian states. It is the existence within our own personal attitudes and within our own institutions of conditions similar to those which have given a victory to external authority, discipline, uniformity and dependence upon The Leader in foreign countries. The battlefield is also accordingly here—within ourselves and our institutions."[19] Dewey never denied the imperative of resisting the advance of fascist regimes, although he was admittedly wary of the domestic impact of a full military mobilization. Given his experience in the First World War, he was all too aware of how fascism at home was often the product of resisting fascism abroad. The fact was that although a fascist regime might be destroyed by military force, the spread of fascist antihumanism could only be confronted by a committed and long-term education in a culture of democratic humanism.

To the extent that there is a single overarching aim of the pedagogy of democratic humanism, it is equivalent to McDermott's idea of "making relations." For McDermott, the central pedagogical vice of our time is captured in the symbol of the standardized test, which represents the dominance of "conceptual boxes" over the infinite conductivity, depth, and meaning of perceptual experience. Reflecting the reactionary and fearful attitude of fascist antihumanism, so much institutional education seems determined to block the "run of the imagination, opting rather for a world made up of boxes, separate one from the other, each defined and named, impervious to the rash of potential relations that yield themselves only to the reflection born of experienced perception." As a consequence, schools that have succumbed to this virus have become dead places in which "the classroom is a morgue and the children are cadavers, passive witnesses to an anatomical dissection on behalf of a fixed curriculum." It is against this creep of intellectual paralysis within the creative faculties of our human nature that McDermott suggests a curriculum in which the making of relations is its primary task—"namely, taking these inherited conditionings and turning them from conceptual rocks into something more diaphanous, crossed and re-crossed with variant images, attitudes, and styles." In short, to engage in the making of relations means "the forging of a distinctively personal experience in the doings and under goings which constitute our experience." In such a pedagogy, there is no limit to the expansiveness of meaning, for "in the hands of those who can make and remake relations, even negative events become the nutrition for creative life."[20]

The pedagogy of democratic humanism follows McDermott's lead by combining the three arts tasked with making and remaking relations in intellectual, perceptual, and practical experience—logic, aesthetics, and rhetoric—into what one might call the "new trivium" for the modern age. So the old medieval trivium of grammar, logic, and rhetoric is usurped with new and different versions of arts designed not to rationalize a fixed order of things but to think, feel, and act creatively in a world of becoming. Logic teaches the art of inquiry into the world around us, the method by which we define problems and discover the means to their resolution. Aesthetics teaches the art of form, the method by which we realize the meanings of nature and communicate them to others through the medium of the senses. Rhetoric teaches the art of deliberation, the method by which we constitute shared situations and move others to action based on a passionate commitment to rational judgment. The attitudes developed through training in these arts make our actions more intelligent, our experiences more meaningful, and our relationships more just. They are the naturalistic analogues to Plato's great triad of the true, the beautiful, and the good. They are the artistic extensions of thought, feeling, and action. They are the means by which we cultivate every aspect of the human personality and engage it meaningfully in a shared world.

The calling of the teacher in this pedagogical vision is to create spaces of freedom in which individuals can teach the arts of democratic humanism for the purpose of enabling others to act intelligently within a plurality, build a common world, and resist what Isabelle Stengers calls "the coming barbarism."[21] To return to the overarching aim of education as defined by McDermott, this would mean above all taking seriously the art of making relations. Following the same Jamesian path, Stengers writes that we should today give "primordial importance to the making of relations, the construction of what he would call a pluriverse, even identifying the relation making capacity as synonymous with civilization."[22] What the pedagogy of democratic humanism stresses is that there is more than one way to make relations. The majority of our most meaningful relations, in fact, are established through our sense of aesthetic taste during those moments in which we share with others a feeling of common liking for something in our environment. Yet our place in the larger cosmos is understood through our system of logical relations that binds together parts of our experience into a loosely coherent whole. Rhetoric, meanwhile, often brings us together with strangers to act in concert for some common aim and, in doing so, disrupts and reforms relations with often radical and unexpected novelty. The common aim of the arts of democratic humanism is thus to cultivate in every individual the art of making and remaking relations in a pluriverse of constant becoming.

To return to Dewey's address to teachers in 1937, education remains today, throughout the world, a battleground in the struggle not only for power but over the meaning of power itself. For those seduced by the lure of fascist antihumanism, power is the capacity for one group, fused together into a monolithic unity through propaganda, to resist adaptation to change and, if necessary, impose its will upon another to recover the purity of some mythic past. The fascist sees the world outside and the diverse people who inhabit it as an enemy to fear and objects to control, respectively. Consequently, intelligence, creativity, and empathy are all stunted, dominated, and channeled toward a single end—namely, the crystallization of a single personality immune to history. This is the threat of our time and perhaps the threat of all time. To teach democratic humanism is thus to commit oneself to cultivating a different understanding of power. For the democratic humanist, power is the creative capacity for individuals to recognize, cultivate, and actualize human potentialities within a pluralistic communicative environment that balances difference with cooperation. Power is the possession of the intellectual freedom and bodily liberty to encounter and inquire into the infinite complexity of a world alongside others without subordination or fear. Power is having the wisdom to perceive and the courage to challenge the vices of wastefulness, injustice, and ignorance that so often pervade our practices and institutions. Democratic humanism rejects the block universe of fascism and embraces the universal potential shared by all human beings in order to help others envision and make real their own sense of creative individuality.

PART I
THE CHALLENGE OF FASCIST ANTIHUMANISM

I

RAGGED INDIVIDUALISM

So far, all is for the best in the best of all possible cultures: our rugged—or is it ragged?—individualism.

—JOHN DEWEY, *INDIVIDUALISM OLD AND NEW*

On almost any day, one can find some popular pundit asserting with great pride and vigor that Americans live in the best of all possible worlds. When pressed to defend this claim, they will almost inevitably point to the latest manifestation of that "hero of romance" that embodies the American Dream: *Economic Man*.[1] This is no Dickensian Scrooge, who seeks only to withdraw to the "counting room, there to engage in a prosaic grubbing into musty ledgers."[2] No, this is an individual for whom "the adventure was its own justification," that adventure being the constant and ambitious pursuit of wealth and creative acquisition.[3] Indeed, this individual is seen as a hero precisely because his (it has been, and continues to be, portrayed almost always as a man) personal ambition also serves the public good. His wants and desires are celebrated as a form of "glorified power; at their magic touch the world was to be transformed; they were, when unshackled from legal artifice and political despotism, the sure source of prosperity and continual progress; the earthly savior of mankind."[4] And perhaps even more astoundingly, this individual is even blessed by the mind of God with foresight into what is good not only for himself but for everyone else because of an innate ability to perceive the consequences of all his actions: "All the work of the world, from the most ordinary to the most extraordinary, is presided over by this omniscient deity of calculating reason, who through his uniform presence in each separate individual is summed up by integral calculus into a virtually omniscient mind."[5] The conspicuous success of Economic Man due to his reliance on unfailing, godlike intuitions thus apparently proves to all of us that the best of all possible worlds is one in which we are left to our own devices to acquire the sign (in this case, the possession of money) that we have been uniquely blessed by God.

Yet it is a curious irony that when pressed to define the character of this modern individual, one almost always is given a picture of the "rugged individual" whose imagery is best captured not by moneyed capital but by Western films. In the American economic romance, our hero is born a nineteenth-century, sturdy pioneer who just so happens to own an international conglomerate in pharmaceuticals, while those who are left behind have the bad fortune to not be blessed by God. There is, of course, no arguing with a romance: "One is either inside the romance or outside it. It is true and is the standard of truth, if you are inside; it is silly or insane, if you are outside." Yet true or not, this romance illuminates our current situation by expressing and perpetuating a conception of individualism and human nature that has become so pervasive as to have become common sense. John Dewey sums up this conception: "Our tradition in economics and industry is that of rugged individualism. We are taught to believe that all start equal in the economic race without any external handicaps being imposed on any persons and that reward and victory go to those of superior personal energy, ability, industry, and thrift, while, barring the exceptional cases of physical disease and accident, those who fall behind do so because of individual defects. We are taught that in this equal struggle between individuals all the great virtues of initiative, self-respect, self-help, standing on one's own feet, moral independence, and the rest are acquired."[6] Furthermore, critics have noted throughout modern history that when "there seem to be those who seem to be left out of its distribution, there is always the assurance that the ways of Providence are proverbially mysterious."[7] In other words, an individualism that conforms to the needs of our money culture teaches that each of us is born with a human nature already outfitted to pursue personal economic interest above all other interests and that what we consider "virtues" are actually just byproducts of acting unfettered on this primary drive. Paradoxically, our individualism teaches us that isolation, competition, intuition, and self-interest are the means to attain a well-rounded soul and a just society.

A treatise on the pedagogy of democratic humanism begins with Dewey's critique of individualism precisely because the romantic version of Economic Man has been consistently used as an ideological rationale for educational policies and pedagogies that severely constrain (or even make impossible) humanistic forms of education. For instance, Stanley Aronowitz identifies 1976 as the year when the ideology of rugged individualism arrived in New

York City "and with it a huge wet blanket descended over public education." This wet blanket of rugged individualism came in the form of what he calls "neoliberal policies—that is, privatized services" grounded in so-called market-driven concepts. These policies viewed democratic experiments in education as wasteful and inefficient when judged by the corporate logic of profit and productivity, and soon after, "the only new ideas that received any hearing were those having to do with cost-cutting, administrative control of teachers and students, crime prevention, and the concept that schooling was about job preparation for private business."[8] This state of affairs has continued unabated into the present day; equally true, therefore, is Aronowitz's claim that without a sustained resistance to these trends, "the powerless will remain at the mercy of the system of control and subordination."[9] The result, more appropriately termed a "ragged" individualism, renders people dependent, alienated, and alone at the very moment when learning to work intelligently and sympathetically alongside others in a complex and expanding environment is necessary to confront the challenges of what Dewey calls "the machine age."

One of the tragedies of Dewey's legacy is that his work and reputation have been used to advance and justify the very form of education he so often criticized and condemned. As Aronowitz explains, the most corrosive of these applications have occurred when so-called progressives "misread John Dewey's educational philosophy as meaning that the past need not be studied too seriously, [and] have offered little resistance to the gradual vocationalizing and dumbing down of the mass education curriculum"; in other words, they interpreted Dewey's emphasis on experience and practice as a call for reducing curricular requirements and promoting "practical, work oriented programs for high school students." The end result was that progressives joined with conservative reformers "to justify a relentless instrumentalism in curriculum design: In the name of anti-traditionalism and nationalism, high schools do not teach philosophy or social history—principally the role of social movements and making history—or treat world literature as a legitimate object of study."[10] When Dewey talked about instrumentalism, of course, he did not mean that all value was determined by whether a concept or method served as an instrument for careerist ambitions and material gain; he meant that it was evaluated according to its effects, including that which it had upon the entire spectrum of human values. Yet by narrowing the meaning of instrumentalism to the sphere of the economic, "educational thought has lost, even renounced, Dewey's program directed to the reconstruction of experience."[11]

For Aronowitz, any genuine progressive reform must not slip into the trap of evaluating schools only according to equality of access and test score rankings, important as those factors might be when considered as part of a whole. As he rightly points out, "Even conservatives who favor vouchers and other forms of public funding for private and parochial schools have justified privatizing instruction on the grounds of access." But such debates leave unaddressed the rugged individualist assumption that we desire access to only the kind of education that accepts "work as a mode of life: one lives to work, rather than the reverse."[12] As Dewey argued his entire career, universal access to public education is the foundation on which we built democratic social life, yet he also stressed that it was an education for life *in its entirety*, not just one facet of life. According to Aronowitz, to accomplish this ambitious aim requires that schools "relieve themselves of their ties to corporate interests and reconstruct the curriculum along the lines of genuine intellectual endeavor."[13] Specifically, it requires that "schools fulfill their responsibility to students and their communities when, at every level, they offer a program of systematic, critical learning that simultaneously provide students with access to the rich traditions of so-called Western thought, history, and the arts, including literature, and open parallel vistas of Africa, Asia, and Latin America."[14] For as Aronowitz concludes, true education "may be defined as the collective and individual reflection on the totality of life experiences," not just the experiences of one's local group. It is only when schools cease to operate under the stifling confines of "ragged" individualism that they have the freedom to begin this necessary experiment.[15] But to accomplish this task first requires us to emancipate ourselves from the romantic mythology that rationalizes and perpetuates these antihumanist policies.

The American ideal of the rugged individual paints an inspiring picture. In American history, popular culture, and economic theory, one encounters an "unceasing glorification of the virtues of initiative, independence, choice and responsibility."[16] Dewey acknowledges some historical bases for this ideal, both economic and political, as it existed for certain populations (primarily white men) in the early decades of the country. As Dewey narrates, "When our country was in process of creation, the men who transported goods carried them with horses and wagons which they owned themselves." Not only did they make their products with their own hands, with their own tools, in their own neighborhoods; they "worked with a few neighbors whom they knew personally and who had a common stake in their local community.

This was the time when rugged individualism had a meaning and it was the time when democratic institutions were born."[17] The rugged individualism of the colonial period was easily transported to the West after the War of 1812, as Americans met the Western frontier with the killing, suppression, and expulsion of native peoples: "With free land, a sparse and scattered population, largely rural, and a continent to subdue, there was room for everyone—not merely physical room, but room for energy and personal initiative, room to carve out a career, seemingly boundless opportunity for all who had the vigor, wit, and industry to take advantage of it."[18]

These frontier origins of rugged individualism, once the violence and racism of its foundations were forgotten or romanticized, would eventually form the basis of that most enduring of myths: the "American Dream." This was a dream initially reserved only for a few and realized at the great expense of many, but in time it became "the distinctively American idea of freedom of opportunity for all alike, unhampered by differences in status, birth and family antecedents, and finally, in the name at least, of race and sex."[19] This dream promised that the rugged individual would achieve success as long as he or she possessed the initiative to take risks, the independence to go it alone, the judgment to make the right choices, the responsibility to acknowledge one's failures, and the opportunity to take credit for one's accomplishments. If one were to ask how to acquire such virtues, this myth also provided an easy answer: the rugged individual comes to possess them in the very act of striving for success. The environment would be both a source of education (by providing obstacles to be overcome) as well as a source of personal fulfillment (by providing economic and social rewards). All people were born into the world as individuals and became *rugged* individuals through trial and error while competing against other individuals.

It was Thomas Jefferson who provided to the myth of the American dream a particularly democratic aura. Although he himself was a Virginia plantation owner and slave master, the typical Jeffersonian hero was an independent small farmer who possessed a natural virtue, acquired from his autonomous labor with the land, which made him an ideal citizen capable of contributing to the governance of his local community. Jefferson's eighteenth-century democratic ideal was rooted in a preindustrial agrarian society that "placed the self-centered person in a small self-contained community."[20] Wrestling with Jefferson's legacy remains absolutely essential if we are to preserve what is best in Jefferson while acknowledging his blindnesses. Writing in 1940, Dewey argued that in the face of totalitarianism, it is doubtful "whether defense of democracy against the attacks to which it is subjected does not depend upon taking once more the position Jefferson took about his moral basis and purpose, even though we have to find another set of words in which to formulate the moral idea served by democracy."[21] It was Dewey's lifelong goal to formulate and define this set of words so that we might face our present circumstances with a new set of tools.

Thus, what we must first do is confront the poverty of our current terminology. It was clear to Dewey that the constellation of meanings, both intellectual and practical, that circled around the phrase "rugged individualism" systematically undermined any possibility of political or economic reconstruction. Dewey consistently stressed that he did not reject the "ends" of rugged individualism (which is to say the creation of individuals with the virtues of initiative, independence, choice, and responsibility); rather, his aim was to promote "the growth of individuals who shall be rugged in fact and not merely in abstract theory."[22] Despite his constant critiques of the ideology behind the term, he confessed, "I am one who believes that we need more, not fewer, 'rugged individuals' and it is in the name of rugged individualism that I challenge the argument."[23] Like Supreme Court Justice Louis Brandeis, Dewey saw that "many things which have been justified on the basis of 'rugged individualism' are to be condemned as hostile to the development of free individuals."[24] The issue concerned not the ends of rugged individualism but the inadequate means it used to achieve those ends and the erroneous moral and philosophical foundations used to rationalize those means.

Consistent with Jefferson's own fears, the conditions from which the conception of pioneer individualism arose had already begun to disappear by the time of his death in 1826, as already the first steamships and railroads were breaking down barriers of time and space. But more important than even the increase in pace of travel was the expansion of the scale of industry. Dewey uses the railroad as a symbol of the radical societal and economic shift toward centralization and expansion during the nineteenth century. There is no space for rugged individualism when it comes to building and running a railway system. To realize the transcontinental railroad in the 1860s, for instance, "corporations with issuance of bonds and stocks that bring about the accumulation of large capital drawn from a great variety of individuals were necessities if we were to use steam and electricity instead of depending upon horses and wagons." To see the contrast between the old rugged individualism and the corporate structure of modernity, one need only compare the "old-fashioned wagon-works with the big automobile factories in Detroit" or the "old forge and blacksmith shop in which ironwares were produced with the mills and factories of the United States Steel or Bethlehem

Corporations of today." This shift can be encompassed in the larger shift in emphasis from "personally managed production" to production in which the personal element is subordinate to the "aggregation of impersonal capital."[25] The industrious artisan entrepreneur celebrated by Russell Conwell's "Acres of Diamonds" became replaced by later monopoly capitalists such as Andrew Carnegie and Nelson Rockefeller.

The name Dewey gives to this new era of modernity is "money culture." This does not imply that its opposite is a culture *without* money or industry: "Industry and business conducted for money profit are nothing new; they are not the product of our own age and culture; they come to us from a long past." However, that long past was one in which industry was conducted personally by the hand and in the home, a past in which money represented hard currency that functioned as a means of interpersonal exchange of goods produced by that labor. What changed this dynamic was largely one thing—the introduction of the *machine*. In short, "our law and politics and the incidents of human association depend upon a novel combination of the machine and money, and the result is the pecuniary culture characteristic of our civilization." This money culture has resulted in crowding out "the spiritual factor of our tradition, equal opportunity and free association and intercommunication," and in its place there has been "a perversion of the whole ideal of individualism" that has "become the source and justification of inequalities and oppressions."[26] In our modern money culture, money no longer functions as a concrete medium of exchange between individual artisans, laborers, and professionals who trade on their own industry; rather, money becomes an abstract field of relationships that structures the movements of capital, governs the operations of industry, and renders human individuals and their personal choices largely irrelevant to the goal of accumulation.

By "machine," then, Dewey obviously does not mean a tool such as a hammer or a needle, which operates only through the direct exertion of human energy and toward an end determined by its particular user. A machine, for Dewey, has three distinct characteristics: First, a machine is a complex mechanism that supplements, or even replaces, "the energy of human muscle and nerve by the inanimate energies of heat, electricity, chemical reaction."[27] Second, a machine's workings are the products of science, such that the machine is built with an "intellectual apparatus" already "physically incarnate" inside the machine itself. It is for this reason that Dewey makes the claim that "the machine is the authentically embodied Logos of modern life."[28] In the time of the pre-Socratic philosophers of ancient Greece, Logos was the transcendent rationality of the world order embedded in the very nature of things; in the modern age, it is the machine itself that embodies this order through its processes, networks, and algorithms. Lastly, and most importantly, a machine inverts the relationship between the user and the used. In the age of pioneer individualism, individuals used the ax to build their homes; in the machine age, the laborer is used by the machine to manufacture a product: "The machine worker, unlike the older hand worker, is following blindly the intelligence of others instead of his own knowledge of materials, tools, and processes."[29] The fact that machines have become more advanced and the old assembly lines obsolete has not changed this relationship today.[30]

The introduction and spread of the machine also radically transform the way money functions in culture. Unlike precious metals and gemstones, money functions as a symbol rather than a concrete thing with intrinsic value. Gold and emeralds are always physical objects first; it is as money that they are "substitutes, representations, and surrogates, which embody relationships."[31] Money thus forms a kind of language, a medium of communication that allows people with vastly different experiences (and even perhaps different languages) to exchange goods and services that, ideally at least, promote each other's personal interests. Yet the rise of the machine opens the possibility for a few individuals to dictate the techniques, control the working conditions, and define the productive aims of its labor force. In this situation, money becomes a means of accumulating capital for the purpose of leveraging power over thousands—if not millions—of people. The competition over goods or markets that dominated pioneer conditions becomes a "competition for power—competition for power over other men." Money thus becomes an extension of the machine and a way of exerting its power. Dewey goes on:

> Instead of using the machines (and science has its tools and machines as much as the factory) to find out the things which may be useful to all people and then giving them to all those who are interested, there is the attempt at the private control of the land from which all our food and natural resources come; there is the struggle of men against each other for command of power that comes through owning the machines; there is the struggle in competition for the command of money, the means of credit, without which modern life cannot be carried on. And the competition, instead of being rivalry and emulation, is this brutal struggle for the control of power, the command of things

that will enable those who have them to regulate and impose upon the lives of others.[32]

To say that American culture has become a "money culture" is thus a way of saying that money has become the sole sign of one's power and measure of one's status in that system. To be sure, other goods that we prize—such as friendship, family, spirituality, education, happiness, and creativity—still exist as goods, but they are goods that have become viewed as things to acquire because of the purchasing power afforded to us through the acquisition of money. To lack money is therefore to render oneself utterly helpless to determine either the means or ends of one's life and to become merely a disposable extension of the machine itself.

Finally, it should hardly come as a surprise that the qualities most characteristic of money culture are consistent with those of the machine: "quantification, mechanization, and standardization." "Quantification" refers not only to a fetish for numbers and accumulation, a natural byproduct of money culture; it also includes an "attendant disregard of quality." Quantity, in short, becomes equivalent with that which is real and substantial—the mark of reality being that which can be exchanged—while quality is something ephemeral and subjective. "Mechanization" refers to the tendency to translate every activity or practice into an algorithm, so that it is the technique, rather than the product, that becomes the true accomplishment. Mechanization thus refers to the "almost universal habit of esteeming technique as an end, not as a means, so that organic and intellectual life is also 'rationalized.'" Finally, "standardization" refers to the dominant effect of quantification and mechanization—the creation of uniformity not only in material objects but also in subjective thought and emotion. With standardization, "differences and distinctions are ignored and overridden; agreement, similarity, is the ideal. There is not only absence of social discrimination but of intellectual; critical thinking is conspicuous by its absence."[33] The result of these three qualities is a culture whose practices are designed to produce an impersonal but highly profitable homogeneity.

Here is where the romantic corrective enters, culminating in the heroic mythology of Economic Man. For the irony is that the moment one turns away from actual practice and toward popular culture, this very same culture imagines itself as being populated with individuals who reject materialistic determinism in favor of an idealistic sentimentality: "Our whole theory is that man plans and uses machines for his own humane and moral purposes, instead of being borne wherever the machine carries him. Instead of materialism, our idealism is probably the loudest and most frequently professed philosophy the world has ever heard. We praise even our most successful men, not for their ruthless and self-centered energy in getting ahead, but because of their love of flowers, children, and dogs, or their kindness to aged relatives." The enemies in our movies and television shows always put profit ahead of people, proving that "nothing gives us Americans the horrors more than to hear that some misguided creature in some low part of the earth preaches what we practice—and practice much more efficiently than anyone else—namely economic determinism." Meanwhile, our heroes consistently make sacrifices and are "surcharged with altruism and bursting with the desire to 'serve' others."[34] Encountering these representations abroad, one would think that Americans despise the ruthless pursuit of money, condemn materialism, and want nothing more than to live self-sacrificing religious lives for the growth of one's soul and the good of one's community.

One can, of course, attribute much of this disjunction between representation and reality to the impulse to wax nostalgic about the past as a way of shielding oneself from the present. This impulse toward romanticism is always with us and has long been a staple of popular literature even before the advent of television. But writing in 1930, Dewey situates this romantic impulse in a particular historical moment: "It is evident enough that the rapid industrialization of our civilization took us unawares. Being mentally and morally unprepared, our older creeds have become ingrowing; the more we depart from them in fact, the more loudly we proclaim them. In effect we treat them as magic formulae. By repeating them often enough we hope to ward off the evils of the new situation, or at least to prevent ourselves from seeing them."[35] Given the rapidity, scope, and intensity of a change that overwhelms our minds, "it is not surprising that men have protected themselves from the impact of such vast change by resorting to what psycho-analysis has taught us to call rationalizations, in other words, protective fantasies."[36] And in an age of mass culture, in which profit is made from the immediate satisfaction of emotional needs, the entertainment industry is fully prepared to take advantage of the situation by giving narrative form to those fantasies. Dewey writes, "Where is the wilderness which now beckons creative energy and affords untold opportunity to initiative and vigor? Where is the pioneer who goes forth rejoicing, even in the midst of privation, to its conquest? The wilderness exists in the movie and the novel, and the children of the pioneers, who live in the midst of surroundings artificially made over by the machine, enjoy pioneer life idly in the vicarious film."[37]

Yet the perpetuation of these fantasies into the twenty-first century cannot be attributed to emotional reactions alone; these fantasies endure because their structure is built on an ideological foundation with long historical roots. The historical roots are found in the eighteenth-century liberalism of John Locke, whose principles were given powerful rhetorical expression in Thomas Paine's *Common Sense* and the U.S. Declaration of Independence. These were revolutionary documents written in the defense of freedom, when the "freedom for which our forefathers fought was primarily freedom from a fairly gross and obvious form of oppression, that of arbitrary political power exercised from a distance centre." Naturally, then, the chief enemy of liberty was viewed as governmental power, and "freedom came to be almost identified with jealous fear of an opposition to any and every extension of government action."[38] Perhaps even more powerfully, the old liberalism of Locke bolstered this revolutionary defense of freedom with a philosophy of human nature, in which the clash between citizen and state was really just one manifestation of the more fundamental tension between individual and society. In fact, the state in its ideal form would not be used to *further* organized social action but would actually function to actively defend the individual *from* society. The old liberalism thus "defined the individual in terms of liberties of thought and action already possessed by him in some mysterious ready-made fashion, in which it was the sole business of the state to safeguard."[39] When the conditions of colonial America reached a point in which these liberties were felt to be a reality, the liberalism of Locke realized its revolutionary potential and found its greatest supporter in Jefferson.

The ideology that underwrites rugged individualism emerged from this early liberalism once the revolutionary aims of the leading elites had been accomplished. By the middle of the nineteenth century, "the economic and political changes for which [the leading elites] strove were so largely accomplished that they had become in turn the vested interest, and their doctrines, especially in the form of *laissez-faire* liberalism, now provided the intellectual justification of the *status quo*."[40] The transformation of Locke's revolutionary liberalism into a conservative laissez-faire ideology was a relatively easy task. With representative democracy now a given, the focus turned toward economic rather than political liberty, and the tension between individual rights and social control hardened into a firm opposition: "Economists developed the principle of the free economic activity of individuals; since this freedom was identified with absence of governmental action, conceived as an interference with natural liberty, the result was the formulation of *laissez faire* liberalism."[41] The old revolutionary maxim that government exists to secure the rights of the people and must be based on the consent of the governed became used to resist any move made by society or the state to limit or regulate private control of the forces of production. The battle cry of the farmers at Lexington and Concord had become the ideological cover first for slave owners to cry "liberty" when the state wished to transform their property into persons and later for U.S. Steel to deny the constitutionality of labor laws and violently suppress striking workers.

Yet laissez-faire liberalism always had a romantic response to criticisms that its system produced not equality or liberty but disparity and oppression: the glorification of "individualism." In effect, laissez-faire liberals developed "a double system of justifying apologetics." On one front, "they fell back upon the natural inequalities of individuals in psychological and moral make-up, asserting the inequality of fortune and economic status is the 'natural' and justifiable consequence of the free play of these inherent differences." This rationalization took its most extreme form in the social Darwinism of the nineteenth century and was given its fullest expression by Herbert Spencer, who erected it into a principle of cosmic justice. For those wishing a more sentimental justification, "the other line of defense is unceasing glorification of the virtues of initiative, independence, choice and responsibility, virtues that center in and proceed from individuals as such." Yet this line of defense was no less deterministic than the first one, for these individuals were described as being born for success just as much as the less fortunate class of human beings were destined for failure. In either case, "the underlying philosophy and psychology of earlier liberalism led to a conception of individuality as something ready-made, already possessed, and needing only the removal of certain legal restrictions to come into full play."[42] Paradoxically, in this new romance of individualism, the more obstacles and hardships an individual had to overcome, the more blessed they were for having the opportunity to prove their innate virtues (excluding, of course, legal restrictions on property, which seemed to limit the full flowering of individuality). Today, our laissez-faire individualism really means rugged individualism for a few and ragged dependence for the many.

But Dewey's critique of rugged individualism goes further than a critique of economic inequality. It goes to the heart of what it means to be a human being. Although designed to provide an ideological rationalization for the concentration of wealth in a few private hands, laissez-faire individualism and its romantic accompanying protective fantasies have in the process created something akin to a mass psychosis—a collective break with reality. The machine age is characterized by quantification, mechanization, and standardization and looks at human beings as appendages to industrial processes; consequently, a notion of individuality arises that celebrates personality as something inherent in each person and unrelated to our social ties and cultural environment. But this condition merely makes human beings all the more open to exploitation by economic machines while producing something other than well-rounded, virtuous, and emotionally stable souls: "Individuals who are not bound together in associations, whether domestic, economic, religious, political, artistic or educational, are monstrosities."[43] In place of encouraging the cultivation of social life and action out of which individuality grows, one finds instead romantic stories of plucky individuals making it big or heroic capitalists spreading the wealth.

The cumulative effect on social psychology of the two continuous and pervasive influences—the impacts of the machine age and laissez-faire ideology—is not to produce rugged individuals in a community but "lost" individuals in a crowd. Lacking the stable relations that constitute social life, the human individual will naturally try to form them elsewhere, for "the individual cannot remain intellectually a vacuum. If his ideas and beliefs are not the spontaneous function of a communal life in which he shares, a seeming consensus will be secured as a substitute by artificial and mechanical means." Consequently, the individual will engage in a "desperate effort to fill the void by external agencies and which obtain a factitious agreement."[44] That is to say, the lost individual will become "found" once she inserts herself into a crowd, which has been provided for her by the very techniques and technologies that have alienated her from genuine society.

The ironic result is the production of mass conformity in the name of rugged individualism. At first this seems counterfactual, as nothing is more publicly celebrated in America than individuality or more ridiculed than conformity. But this is because these words have been drained of their meaning. It is thought that conformity is due to an overreliance of the individual upon society, while separateness is the mark of individuality. In fact, the opposite is often the case. This is precisely because society is not a substance but a system of relations, which means that being in society includes "the give and take of participation, of a sharing that increases, that expands and deepens, the capacity and significance of interacting factors." When one lacks society—even the society of just one meaningful other—one lacks relationships, which in turn deprives one of the opportunity to expand and deepen one's own sense of participation in the world. Relations one may have, but they become artificial, fleeting, and superficial relations provided by the techniques of mass society, which include not only entertainment and news but now also religion and politics. These methods "produce mass credulity, and this jumps from one thing to another according to the dominant suggestions of the day." It is this instability and flux that we often mistake for individuality, when in fact it is better named its opposite—conformity; for "conformity is a name for the absence of vital interplay; the arrest and benumbing of communication." The superficial appearance of individuality is simply due to our willingness to continually shift from one interest to another as our whims dictate (or are dictated to) over time, but if one looks across space, one sees nothing but sameness at any single moment: "We think and feel alike—but only for a month or a season. Then comes some other sensational event or personage to exercise a hypnotizing uniformity of response. At a given time, taken in cross-section, conformity is the rule. In a time span, taken longitudinally, instability and flux dominate." Ironically, it is our very eagerness to throw ourselves into the flux of change that is a symptom of our lack of stable habits and virtues that characterize genuine individuality. The temporary satisfaction that comes from "artificially induced uniformity of thought and sentiment is a symptom of an inner void."[45]

Given the characteristics of alienation, conformity, and helplessness that continue to pervade so much of mass society, it is no wonder that we would take shelter in the protective fantasy that we remain the inheritors of Jeffersonian rugged individualism. At his most eloquent, Jefferson was the greatest humanist of his time, expressing what Dewey called a "faith in common human nature, in its potentialities in general and in its power in particular to respond to reason and truth."[46] It is based on the faith that Jefferson advocated for the possibility to periodically revise the Constitution to adapt to changing conditions. Jefferson believed it was the "right of the people to govern themselves in their own way and in their ability to exercise the right wisely."[47] But he was also one of the greatest hypocrites of his time, unabashedly owning other men and women as property and refusing to give them their freedom even at his death—a detail that not only reflects on his own character but warns of the dangers of glorifying the past. Yet in his writings, he nonetheless presents an attractive vision of democracy from the ground up, celebrating the natural virtue that comes from the independent farmer's ability to control his own destiny. For the modern individual thrown into a mass society who must adapt herself to being just one of a quantity of laborers adapting themselves to the standardized techniques of global industry, who must often abandon close relationships in favor of superficial connections mediated through technology, and who often has little time to try to understand—let alone alter—the causal relationships of global politics and economy that directly influence her life, it comes naturally to imagine oneself back in a simpler time, when the center of one's world was one's own shop and home. The result is an uncomfortable vacillation between nostalgic yearning for the good old days long gone and the aggressive assertion that the rugged individualism of those same good old days is alive and well in one's own character—if only one is given the opportunity to express it.

The tragic result of all these psychological contortions is that the early, incomplete colonial humanism of Jefferson gradually morphs into its opposite, a modern antihumanism eager to subordinate and regiment humanity in general in the name of promoting the transcendence of the exceptional individual or chosen group. For this transformation to happen, three moves are necessary. First, and most importantly, his faith in a *common* human nature that is shared by all people must be narrowed and restricted to a belief in a *differentiated* human nature that creates different categories and orders. For instance, this belief was already implicit in Jefferson when he excluded slaves from his humanism and made secondary the rights and liberties of women. Second, recognition of an *adaptable* human nature that acknowledges a multiplicity of impulses and capacities that change with historical circumstances must be replaced with the recognition of a *fixed* human nature in which certain powers and virtues are innate in certain populations and serve ends that are often outside human experience. For instance, Jefferson, in the legacy of eighteenth-century rationalism, often privileged "reason" as an a priori faculty that allowed any individual to perceive what was right and just, a position that supported his radical claim that certain things are "self-evident." Lastly, belief in his perception that we possess a *social* human nature requiring the formation of relationships with others to create virtuous character must be replaced by a belief in a *solipsistic* human nature viewing individuals as essentially autonomous units for which society is at best a means to an end and at worst a corrupting influence. A precursor of this position is also found in Jefferson's conception of the individual as primarily a bearer of natural rights that were given to any person by virtue of being born. Antihumanism thus isolates the individual from society and grants that individual certain innate powers and virtues that exist to serve not the common human good but the desires of the privileged few or the one.

Modern antihumanism is the culmination of these transformations when wedded to the economic ideology of laissez-faire "rugged" individualism. Looked at from a distance, this ideology seems to have all the marks of humanism—a celebration of virtue, the encouragement of equal opportunity, and a focus on achieving realizable human aims. However, as with almost all corruptions of idealistic philosophies, the transformation of rugged individualism into something darker occurs as soon as the need to rationalize unintended consequences leads its advocates to tap into widespread anxieties, fears, and resentments to attribute blame. Why do only a few prosper while a majority suffer? Clearly it is because the economic system is rewarding a natural aristocracy and passing moral judgment on those born to be parasites. Why do we privilege economic success as a sign of virtue while neglecting the development of arts, sciences, and culture? Because the drive to accumulate wealth in a competitive environment is innate in human nature and cannot be suppressed. Why do we not encourage organized social action and intelligent government policies to remediate poverty and form a more just society? Because any initiative that comes from society is an invasion of the innate rights of the human individual and promotes dependence on society rather than rugged individualism. Most of us are by now familiar with this cycle of logic, for it is embedded in our cultural consciousness, but this does not make it any less antihumanistic. At its foundation is the presumption that we are all born alone in the world, that the pursuit of happiness is granted only to a few, but that we live in the best of all possible worlds because it allows us to pursue the one thing we all desire—wealth—even at the price of widespread human suffering.

This form of antihumanism, which calls itself "individualism," is not fascist in itself, but it lays the foundation for fascism by creating a social order in which people feel not only helpless and alone but also resentful and superior to others. As Dewey argues, "The movement that goes by the name of *Individualism* is very largely responsible for the chaos now found in human associations—the chaos which is at the root of the present debasement of human beings."[48] Fascism, as we will see, is the final manifestation of this chaos and brings the debasement of human beings to its culmination, while being at the same time a chaos fostered by the dogmas of laissez-faire individualism. For what this form of individualism has fostered in society is not just conformity but intolerance, and "an antihumanist attitude is the very essence of every form of intolerance."[49] Ironically, the ideology of individualism preached tolerance in the name of free markets while at the same time fostering intolerance toward any group that would assert its rights to access those markets, thus denying them even that limited economic freedom. The response to these demands has always been the same: to proclaim the inalienable rights of individuals to be free from social control and to struggle—succeeding or failing on their own—for a narrowly economic goal, all while proudly intolerant of anyone who would demand "unearned" rewards and thus corrupt the moral economy of laissez-faire capitalism. In the daily lives of those lost individuals in a crowd, none of this provides any material support, but for some, it does provide a base emotional satisfaction that, unlike the parasitic many, at least *they* are enduring their suffering as rugged individuals. And this presumption allows the sentiment to grow that perhaps their rugged individualism also makes them just a little more human.

2

ANIMIST NATIONALISM

The Nation by which millions swear and for which they demand the sacrifice of all other loyalties is a myth; it has no being outside of emotion and fantasy.
—JOHN DEWEY, "THE FRUITS OF NATIONALISM"

In 1927, when President Calvin Coolidge announced a new, aggressive interpretation of international law, Dewey was prepared to call out the policy for what it was—an instrument of nationalist aggression. Coolidge had cited examples from Mexico, Nicaragua, and China in which the properties of American citizens and corporations were taken without proper compensation as warrant for declaring that the United States had a new right and imperative to enforce the demands of liberty and justice abroad, with force if necessary. In Dewey's interpretation, "The gist of his revolutionary edition of international law (if he says what he means and knows what he means) is that any property right or property interest of any private citizen or any corporation in a foreign country (doubtless with the tacit understanding that it is not one of the Great Powers) is a National Interest to be protected when necessary by national force." What troubled Dewey about this proposition was not so much its specific policy consequences, although these might be significant; it was the underlying presumption that something called a "National Interest" could be offended or suffer injustice because a foreign government confiscated a banana farm owned by the United Fruit Company. Conversely, Dewey imagines the likelihood that "if a large gold field were located just over the border of Alaska, thousands of American breasts would swell with pride, as thousands would be depressed if it happened to lie in British territory."[1] In reality, neither of these things much benefit the lives of ordinary people—and indeed, for some they might actually be harmful—and yet there is nothing more common than feeling pride when one's "national honor" is being celebrated or defended in some far-off place for reasons one does not quite understand. Dewey explains, "Men who pride themselves upon being 'practical' and 'concrete' would be incensed beyond measure if they were told that the nation to which they yield such unquestioning loyalty is an abstraction, a fiction.... Individual persons may be insulted and may feel their honor to be at stake. But the erection of a national territorial State into a Person who has a touchy and testy Honor to be defended and avenged at the cost of death and destruction is as sheer a case of animism as is found in the records of any savage tribe."[2]

It is in this "animistic" understanding of nationalism—that is to say, nationalism not as a political structure but as a unifying, animating spirit—that makes nationalism a central component of fascist antihumanism. That is to say, if nationalism was used to "signify public spirit as opposed to narrow selfish interests" or its accompanying patriotism was used "as a synonym for intense loyalty to the good of the community of which one is a member," then nationalism would be completely consistent with democracy, whether local or global, for in that case, nationalism would be a necessary political recognition that the attainment of one's individual good is bound up with pursuing the good of a larger whole. But nationalism takes on a fascist character when "unquestioned emotional loyalty, so supreme as to be religious in quality, has invaded the whole of life." In this case, nationalism does not represent a complex interaction between the parts of a dynamic whole but rather a direct absorption of fragmented individuals into an undifferentiated cult of irrationality—namely, one that takes on the identity of a single personality who speaks with the voice of some charismatic "Leader" and tells tales of mythic origins and ultimate destinies. This kind of nationalism has no necessary connection with a government or state and in fact often arises in direct opposition to it; rather, it lives within attitudes of people who would sacrifice the actual good of individuals for the supernatural good of some personified abstraction.

Paradoxically, fascist antihumanism manages to make such effective use of two such seemingly contradictory attitudes as those of rugged individualism and animist nationalism. Dewey stressed that "it cannot be said too often in the present state of opinion that this seemingly sudden outbreak of totalitarian collectivism was in fact the breaking through the surface, into overt manifestation, of underlying phases of the previous individualism."[3] What Dewey meant was that both rugged individualism and totalitarian collectivism were "monistic" ways of understanding human collectives in the same singular, undifferentiated fashion as they did human individuals. In each case, identity is treated as a rigid block unit rather than a flexible and interconnected part of a pluralistic community. The only difference is that in totalitarian collectivism, the unit is larger than that of rugged individualism. Consequently, it is far easier for an isolated individual, detached from any meaningful social relations, to insert himself or herself into a fascist movement without ever changing any essential attitudes. For Dewey, the relationship between individualism and nationalism shows fascism to be a particularly virulent outgrowth of nationalism in times of social division, political breakdown, and economic crisis that, in turn, inevitably pressure schools to promote their mythic histories.

As with the myth of rugged individualism, therefore, the teacher committed to the ideals of democratic humanism must be prepared to encounter resistance from those caught up in nationalist passions, particularly when those individuals are fellow administrators and teachers, for only occasionally do confrontations about some "national honor" occur between two nation-states on the military battlefield; more often than not, they occur *within* the boundaries of a single nation-state and on the battlefields of everyday social life. Writer, teacher, and black intellectual bell hooks recalls two such battlefields in an autobiographical essay included in her book *Teaching to Transgress: Education as the Practice of Freedom*. The first was the battlefield of the high school of her youth, a previously all-white school to which she was bused under a desegregation policy with other black students. They were forced to wait in the gymnasium before the white students arrived in order to (according to the administration) reduce hostility and conflict, but such efforts did nothing to reduce the de facto racial lines in place: "The white school was desegregated, but in the classroom, in the cafeteria, and in most social spaces racial apartheid prevailed."[4] The second battlefield was the university in which she taught as a professor. She recalls an encounter with a new white male colleague who "went on a tirade at the mere mention of my Toni Morrison seminar, emphasizing that *Song of Solomon* was a weak rewrite of Hemingway's *For Whom the Bell Tolls*." For her, this incident revealed "how deep-seated is the fear that the de-centering of Western civilization, of the white male canon, is really an act of cultural genocide."[5] Her experience thus vividly demonstrates the degree to which the struggles for "national honor" seep into the educational system, as both our habits of association and our canonical texts are influenced by abstract loyalties to mythic identities that are far deeper and stronger than one's legal nationality. For her, there is nothing more appealing for a threatened and alienated member of a former dominant group than to be seduced by the fascist call "to bring order to the chaos, to return to an (idealized) past."[6]

In the school environment, dominant forms of nationalism usually operate by appealing to the taken-for-granted superiority of some methods, principles, or canon when confronted with an appeal to an alternative or multicultural perspective. Once again, bell hooks recalls an experience at Oberlin College when she participated in a group of seminars, open to all professors, which focused on transformative pedagogy. What she found was that whenever she spoke of how her own experience in racially segregated schools informed her pedagogical practices, "many of the professors present at the first meeting were disturbed by our overt discussion of political standpoints. Again and again, it was necessary to remind everyone that no education is politically neutral." The professors had assumed that by teaching the inherited Western canon dominated by "great white men," they had left politics behind. They were teaching the classics, and the classics for them were value-neutral, whereas the teaching of Toni Morrison clearly served a special interest that was informed by political correctness. As she sums up her experience, "We found again and again that almost everyone, especially the old guard, were more disturbed by the overt recognition of the role our political perspectives play in shaping pedagogy than by their passive acceptance of ways of teaching and learning that reflect biases, particularly a white supremacist standpoint."[7] Importantly, her aim was not to reject the value of those works or, in her own words, to "replace one dictatorship of knowing with another."[8] It was rather to acknowledge that no body of work comes with an implicit sanction of its authority simply because it resonates with some nationalist tradition cloaked in the language of "Western civilization," yet this is often what is done.

Against this monovocality of nationalist pedagogy, hooks recommends an approach to education that emphasizes what she calls "coming to voice." This does not mean allowing anyone to speak about any subject whenever they want and validating their opinions without any standard of judgment; such a free-form, undisciplined classroom rarely leads to structured learning. As hooks explains, "Coming to voice is not just the act of telling one's experience. It is using that telling strategically—to come to voice so that you can also speak freely about other subjects."[9] Coming to voice then requires a keen awareness of the context in which that voice is expressed, including not only the academic information of the course but also—and perhaps most important—the social context of the other students in the course. It requires a strategic orientation so that the words one says to others stimulate something in their own experiences that in turn opens up the possibility for new points of connection, conversation, and experience. In other words, coming to voice is a performative act that carries with it a rhetorical orientation. As she explains, "In our everyday lives we speak differently to diverse audiences. We communicate best by choosing that way of speaking that is informed by the particularity and uniqueness of whom we are speaking with." Consequently, in a multicultural world that is not confined within artificial nationalist boundaries, "the engaged voice must never be fixed and absolute but always changing, always evolving in dialogue with the world beyond itself."[10] Dewey's critique of nationalism thus provides educators tools for recognizing and overcoming the passions that would resist the experience of coming to voice—an experience absolutely foundational for the pedagogy of democratic humanism.

No matter one's political affiliation, it is difficult not to be struck by the superficiality, restlessness, discontent, and destructiveness of mass society when we are allowed a moment to reflect on our times. What Dewey said at the turn of the twentieth century seems as true today as ever: "Only an acute maladjustment between individuals and the social conditions under which they live can account for such widespread pathological phenomena. Feverish love of anything as long as it is a change which is distracting, impatience, unsettlement, nervous discontentment, and desire for excitement, are not native to human nature. They are so abnormal as to demand explanation in some deep-seated cause."[11] For many idealistic critics, this cause is not hard to find; it is "materialism," which is a catchall term for the stultifying influence that naturalism in science, technology, and society has had on the development of the human spirit. Their creed "holds to a complete gulf between nature and man in his true being, and finds in the irruptions of nature into human life the source of all the evils and all the woes that beset mankind." The solution to these problems would thus be to find the redemption of humanity in idealized visions of the cultural past that would "yoke the religious emotions of mankind to the promotions of the ideal phases of human life." By isolating oneself from the messy, complex, and often indirect horizontal relationships that an individual forms in "material" society, one then forms a clear, simple, and direct vertical relationship with some ideal and typically supernatural essence that promises the ecstasy of transcendence and the promise of true virtue.[12]

The creed that Dewey was describing in these passages actually went by the name "Humanism"—in this case, the one Paul Elmer Moore and Irving Babbitt advanced in their book called *New Humanism*. For them, Humanism (with a capital *H*) was so called because they wished to distinguish the realm of the authentically *human* from the realm of the inauthentically *natural*. For them, to be authentically human was to make use of something called the "transcendental imagination," to free oneself from the bonds of the material world and thereby achieve union with a supernatural essence—in their case, that of a Christian God. For Dewey, of course, this is the exact opposite of what genuine humanism means. For him, true humanism takes seriously "the problem of integrating science in its bearings upon life, and of rendering at the servant instead of the master of human destiny."[13] But such humanism lacks the immediate emotional satisfaction of a Humanism that allows one to lash out at modernity in all its forms and turn one's head toward the heavens in expectation of an immediate transcendent union with something greater than oneself. Capital-*H* Humanism allows anyone who wishes to launch into a scathing critique of modern society because it undermines our sense of "humanity," corrupts the "human spirit," calls into question "what it means to be human," or violates our "human rights"—even though the exact meanings of these terms are usually left undefined. But what is most certainly clear for the so-called Humanist is that the materialist culture of modernity is a hollow shell that must be transcended.

Yet there is a paradox at the heart of this so-called Humanism that reveals an important neurosis at the heart of modern culture—in particular its religious culture. Moore and Babbitt wish to put forward a new form of spiritual transcendence, and yet the particular religious quality they share is continuous with the very laissez-faire individualism they reject. Popular religious movements commonly condemn materialistic individualism, "but in noting the historic course of the rise and bankruptcy of the individualistic movement, no mistake is greater than to overlook the substantial moral support given to Individualism in its laissez-faire Liberal career by the heritage bequeathed from certain religious traditions." All of these religious traditions "taught that men as inherently singular or individual souls have intrinsic connection only with a supernatural being, while they have connection with one another only through the extraneous medium of this supernatural relationship."[14] If the doctrine of laissez-faire individualism is taken seriously, what justifies economic competition is not the outcome of particular interactions but rather the ultimate course of all events guided by the inscrutable cosmic justice of the "invisible hand." To condemn the justice of one supernatural order in the name of the virtues of some other supernatural order may change our allegiance but does not change the structure of our associations. We remain strangers to each other except through the medium of a shared supernatural relationship, with some external characteristic becoming a sign of an inner possession of shared spiritual grace.

It must also be admitted, however, that this desire for transcendence often lies dormant. During times of relative political stability, economic security, and cultural continuity, a purely economic individualism may be functionally held together by the techniques of the machine age. If people do not acquire satisfaction or prosperity from their jobs, at least most are able to work. If culture does not provide them a rich resource of meaningful relationships with others, at least it provides an entertainment industry to distract and stimulate them. If political parties do not actually govern, at least they are able to reiterate old platforms, parties, and issues in a way that generates an appearance of responsibility. Periodically, individuals might step out of the routine of their lives and give voice to frustrations—and perhaps yearn for some higher connection with an ideal, whether that ideal be called Humanism or some other thing—but these outbursts will be absorbed by the culture industry, and people will return to their ordinary existences. And for the most part, whatever political ideology an individual professes, they will in practice adhere to a vague liberalism, which "is hardly more than a temper of mind, vaguely called forward-looking, but quite uncertain as to where to look and what to look forward to."[15] But there will be a sense at least that history is progressing and that the lives of one's children may be better than one's own.

But then there are times of crisis in which the faith of this vague liberalism suddenly evaporates. No longer is it enough to revel in outbursts of frustration or appeal to individual transcendence; something collective must be done. It is these points at which nationalism appears with a resurgent vigor that often seems to come from nowhere. Historically, the specific empirical causes of these crises were many and varied—economic depression, political paralysis, population migrations, technological innovation, climate change, or destructive war, to name just a few. However, the one effect that remained the same was the production of a sense of "national frustration and humiliation" that lead masses of people "to welcome any kind of government that promised to restore national self-respect."[16] Individuals who may have promoted their own rugged individualism one morning woke up the next as patriots dedicated to the cause of blood and soil. For Dewey, this is no contradiction. The cause of our "excited and rapacious nationalism" is rather a "situation in which corporateness has gone so far as to detach individuals from their old local ties and allegiances but not far enough to give them a new center and order of life." Consequently, "the balked demand for genuine cooperativeness and reciprocal solidarity in daily life finds an outlet in nationalistic sentiment. Men have a pathetic instinct toward the adventure of living and struggling together; if the daily community does not feed this impulse, the romantic imagination pictures a grandiose nation in which all are one."[17] Nationalism is thus ironically the strongest and most violent in nations in which individuals find themselves the most lost; the sudden casting off of the veneer of "rugged individualism" thus reveals both its fundamental shallowness and its quasi-religious basis.

Nationalism is thus the fruit of an underlying religious individualism that surges into view when a perceived threat to identity leads a mass of individuals to seek an emotional and active union with a spirit of "the nation" that is forcefully actualized through the machinery of propaganda. Nationalism thus shares a similar motivational structure as that of Moore and Babbitt's "Humanism" insofar as it condemns the decadence of modernity, rejects the influence of "society," and promises a transcendent connection with some supernatural ideal; it differs by associating this ideal not with an *abstract* and *universal* notion of the "Human" but with a very *concrete* and *particular* grouping of humanity identified as a nation. Unlike competing forms of transcendence, whether religious or aesthetic, nationalism promises to subordinate any and all such forms within a single resurgent cultural identity, complete with its own tribal god whose essence is expressed through art, passed on through blood, and communicated through the voice of a Leader. It is for this reason that sudden converts to nationalism often overflow with protestations of their "love" for their country; nationalism maximizes "the satisfaction that comes from a sense of union with others, a feeling capable of being intensified till it becomes a mystical sense of fusion with others and being mistaken for love on a high level of manifestation."[18] But it is because this mystical fusion with others relies on a shared sense of connecting with some higher national spirit—rather than a more political nationalism grounded in historical traditions and geographical boundaries—that gives this kind of nationalism its animistic character.

What does Dewey mean by "animism"? Animism in its most elementary form is "the attribution of desire and intent to inanimate things."[19] For instance, we commonly employ animism to describe works of art, as "when we speak of a painting as alive, and its figures, as well as architectural and sculptural forms, as manifesting movement."[20] This is the first clue to how animism applies to nationalism, especially with its traditional expression through monuments, buildings, and spectacles. The second clue comes from language itself. Animism is made possible by an act of naming. As he explains, "Since words act upon things indirectly, or as signs, and since words express the significant consequences of things (the traits for the sake of which they are used), why should not words act also directly upon things to release their latent powers? Since we 'call' things by their names, why should they not answer?"[21] Animism thus results from not simply any use of words but the use of words to designate an entity with a personal relationship to us—that is, our friend or foe. And this brings to the third essence of nationalistic animism, which is that it designates an active, animating spirit that is our ally against some opposing supernatural force. Psychologically, "it is a notorious fact that the one who hates finds the one hated an obnoxious and despicable character; to the lover his adored one is full of intrinsically delightful and wonderful qualities. The connection between such facts and the fact of animism is direct."[22] In the history of Christianity, for instance, animism is the accusation early Christians hurled at Roman pagans who invested certain objects with animistic powers that would help one's friends and hurt one's enemies.

In animist *nationalism*, the "nation" no longer represents a name for a geographically bounded, culturally continuous, and historically conditioned political regime; it represents a transcendental personality to whom I am related as lover and beloved and that in turn jealously protects me against those who would do me harm. At the same time, one must not think of it in terms of a relationship between a people and a traditional patron god, such as that of Athena to Athens. First, in the traditional model, a city, nation, or people are blessed by an external god who acts as its parent and protector. It is essentially a dualistic conception based on a firm distinction between the realms of the ideal and the actual that can never be fully crossed. In nationalism, however, the transcendental personality is the spirit of the nation *itself* unfolding its ideal in the realm of the actual. It represents "the embodiment of the divine and absolute will and ideal" in "the existing world of nature and of men." For Dewey, this personality is captured in Hegel's notion of "Spirit," or *Geist*, in which "patriotism, national feeling, national consciousness" are "transformed by deliberate nurture into a mystic cult." Second, the *Geist* that is the subject of the mystic cult of nationalism does not exist as a distinct and autonomous personality, as a parent does to a child; it exists as an immanent but teleological animating force that inhabits not only objects, such as monuments or flags, but also human beings, thus making the "human ego the authorized and creative agent of absolute purpose."[23] Thus nationalism is a peculiar kind of animism because it animates not only objects but other people—or rather, the latent "spirit" within a human body (usually transmitted through the blood and felt in the gut).

The emotional release this experience produces is dangerous to underestimate, particularly when it occurs within a period of stagnation or crisis. For instance, "common observation, especially of the young, shows that nothing is more exasperating and more resented than stirring up certain impulses and tendencies and then checking their manifestation." In ordinary times, these impulses result in typical outbursts of youthful rebellion and the embrace of the latest countercultural trends. However, there are times in which the impulses and tendencies of more than only teenagers are felt to be thwarted and checked, when whole populations feel victimized by forces they cannot control. A "period of uncertainty and insecurity, accompanied as it is by more or less unsettlement and disturbance, creates a feeling that anything would be better than what exists, together with desire for order and stability upon almost any terms." It is at these times in which "the satisfaction obtained by the sentiment of communion with others, of the breaking down of barriers, will be intense in the degree in which it has previously been denied opportunity to manifest itself."[24] Lost and frustrated individuals suddenly find themselves named the bearers of a national will, spirit, and destiny alongside chosen others.

To those outside of this experience, it might seem as if these people have willingly cast off their individuality to become one with "society"—a source of continuous puzzlement to those who do not understand how violent nationalism continually erupts in the most individualistic modern societies. In matter of fact, they are often no more "social" than before, at least insofar as the word *social* refers to the multiple layers of relationships we have with other human beings—for instance, as manifest in our social relations as "parent, citizen, employer, wage-earner, farmer, merchant, teacher, lawyer, [or] good citizen."[25] Indeed, it is actually frequent for converts to nationalism to *reduce* their level of participation in society, severing their connection with those institutions, individuals, or groups that they feel to be corrosive to their newfound sense of purpose. Far from becoming one with society, converts to nationalism feel as if they have actually embraced their true individuality and are contemptuous of those who would sacrifice their individuality in the name of sentimental social relationships or artificial social norms. In extreme cases, such as totalitarian Germany, representatives of the state can actually "claim their regime is giving the subjects of their state a 'higher' freedom than can be found in democratic states, individuals in the latter being unfree because their lives are chaotic and undisciplined."[26] The implication here is that democracies, being "social" affairs, dilute the energies of its citizens because of its pluralistic society, whereas nationalistic regimes are single-mindedly committed to actualizing the latent potential in every individual.

The name often given to this newfound sense of individuality is "personality." Of course, this term does not refer in any way to the kind of personality celebrated in popular culture—a unique (but social) person with idiosyncratic (but attractive) tastes, different (but harmless) perspectives, and rare (but entertaining) talents. For the nationalist, this latter type of personality is the epitome of shallowness, conformity, and cowardice—a person who wants only to impress and please as many people as possible while offending no one. The nationalistic personality rejects these sentiments. It wishes to challenge the "leveling idea of the supremacy of mere numbers," which is seen to be social democracy, and embrace the "differences in the inborn capacities and the achievements of different peoples." Personality is thus the name not of merely external characteristics that are the products of fashion and industry; personality is something internal and innate, an "active or vital energy" that spurs the will from deep within.[27] In other words, to possess a personality is to be completely identified with the transcendental personality of the *Geist* and to commit oneself to being its creative agent of absolute purpose in the world through revelatory action.

For many, the "higher freedom" that this idea of personality offers represents a significant and attractive alternative to laissez-faire individualism, in which the "so-called 'free enterprise' in business and finance was taken to be identical with the very essence of freedom." In other words, laissez-faire individualism conceives of initiative, vigor, and independence as being "limited to exercise in the economic area," while "the meaning of their exercise in connection with the cultural resources of civilization, in such matters as companionship, science and art, is all but ignored."[28] The emancipatory quality of nationalism is that it subordinates the economic to a more primary motivation—the realization of the national spirit in all its forms. This does not eliminate the economic impulses—and indeed may only mask them in the long run—but for a while, at least it makes the realization of cultural resources a priority and bestows a sense of self-respect and honor on all those who feel they can play a part in that realization. For instance, when looking back on the First World War, when millions of people suffered for years for a "cause," Dewey concluded that participating in this nationalistic sentiment had "been a strong factor in reconciling 'humbler' folk to enforced deprivation of material benefits, so that, at least for a time, a sense of honorable equality more than compensates for less to eat, harder and longer hours of work—since it is psychologically true that man does not live by bread alone."[29] In sum, the "higher freedom" of nationalism is both negative and positive. Negatively, it liberates people from a fixation on economic rationality; positively, it enables them to actively promote what they see as their unique cultural civilization in all spheres of life without restriction.

Yet it is equally important that, in almost every other sense, animist nationalism actually carries to the extremes, with only subtle modifications, the fundamental tendencies of laissez-faire individualism it purports to reject. First, despite altering its nature, it nonetheless remains committed to the "search for *the* meaning of life and *the* purpose of the universe."[30] The demotion of economic success and the promotion of national pride do not alter the assumption that only certain purposes are innate in human nature. Second, despite providing a "yearning for emotional fusion," it nonetheless leaves individuals as alienated from sustained and meaningful social relations as in a regime of ragged individualism.[31] As before, a semblance of community is found in "the envy and admiration of the crowd, but the crowd is also composed of private individuals who are equally lost to a sense of social bearings and uses."[32] The emotional satisfaction that accompanies achieving a national destiny does not do away with the more difficult task of intelligently negotiating the relationship between means and ends. Third, despite protestations of unity and shared purpose, animist nationalism actually exaggerates the ruthless competitiveness of laissez-faire capitalism that pits individual against individual. The only difference is that it replaces individuals with nationalities as the competitive agents. The result is a "doctrine of national sovereignty," which in effect is "a direct proclamation of the unlimited and unquestionable right of a political state to do what it wants to do in respect to other nations and to do it as and when it pleases."[33] But this is nothing more than the principles of unrestricted laissez-faire individualism applied to competitive nations in a political sphere.

It is from within this extreme doctrine of "national sovereignty" that the fascist character of antihumanism takes root. Animist nationalism already continues and exaggerates the antihumanist attitudes already present in laissez-faire individualism—namely, by subordinating the plurality of human aims to a single national purpose, separating the individual from his or her natural and social environment, and classifying certain human beings as innately superior and inferior to others according to their "national" identities. But this animist nationalism becomes explicitly fascist when, faced with recalcitrance, it transforms its idealism into violence directed against enemies both internal and external. Fascism as an explicit political movement, in other words, represents the sudden unleashing of violent energies driven positively by a sense of destiny and negatively by a hatred for all who would seek to resist it. This fascist aspect of antihumanism manifest is easily identified by three qualities: (1) the explicit support of racism and bigotry, (2) the appearance of a charismatic Leader, and (3) the valorization of violence. These three qualities always appear together not by accident but by a clear emotional logic.

The racist character of fascism grows naturally out of antihumanism's discriminatory tendency to classify certain classes of human beings as having distinct qualities, innate virtues, and ultimate destinies that separate them from the rest of humanity. Of course, this racism always sees itself as an expression of patriotism, understood as "a synonym for intense loyalty to the good of the community of which one is a member; for willingness to sacrifice, even to the uttermost, in its behalf." Thus fascism begins as soon as "an unquestioned emotional loyalty, so supreme as to be religious in quality, has invaded the whole of life." But no sooner does the euphoria of patriotism appear than alongside it arises suspicion and antagonism to all those who do not share a similar loyalty. Internally, one begins "by shaming heretics and intimidating dissidents," and externally "the test and mark of public spirit becomes intolerant disregard of all other nations." Ultimately, "patriotism degenerates into a hateful conviction of intrinsic superiority."[34] What begins as pride in certain shared cultural characteristics and historical traditions becomes hardened into a belief in innate racial characteristics that are distinct to certain populations by blood.

It is at this point that Dewey's insight into nationalism's "animist" tendencies can explain the fascination of fascist discourse with talk of blood and soil. In the fascist mind, of course, they are not racists at all, if by racist one means treating another person unfairly simply because of the color of their skin or some other external marker. They will say that their patriotism and their intolerance for other groups have nothing to do with superficial appearances but rather involve some inner "spirit" that animates them from within, and "what is more 'inner' than 'blood'"?[35] Speaking of Nazi rhetoric, for instance, Dewey observes that "blood, race, instinct, passion, in the vocabulary of Hitler, are names for life, for the vital; and they are a name for what move men to act *en masse*." Consequently, "he employs 'blood, race, and soil' in a mystical sense, if one defines 'mystical' to mean the complete submergence of fact and idea in an overpowering emotion supposed to reveal higher truth than cold intelligence can compass."[36] This logic is purely animistic, with a sense in which by naming another person as a "patriot" or member of a common "race," one imbues them with that mystical vital force that spreads throughout their body and cannot be rationally articulated or explained. It may even begin purely as a source of personal pride. But the logic of racism unfolds naturally once this antihumanistic sentiment is expressed to criticize other groups:

> It may start by being directed at a particular group, and be supported in name by assigning special reasons why that group is not worthy of confidence, respect, and decent human treatment. But the underlying attitude is one of fundamental distrust of human nature. Hence it spreads from distrust and hatred of a particular group until it may undermine the conviction that any group of persons has any intrinsic right for esteem or recognition—which, then, if it be given, is for some special and external grounds, such as usefulness to our particular interests and ambitions. There is no physical acid which has the corrosive power possessed by intolerance directed against persons because they belong to a group that bears a certain name. Its corrosive potency gains with what it feeds on. An anti-humanist attitude is the essence of every form of intolerance. Movements that begin by stirring up hostility against a group of people end by denying to them all human qualities.[37]

Unfortunately, the sentiments of fascist antihumanism are all too easy aroused in times of social crisis, particularly when given voice by a charismatic Leader. At first, this Leader is almost always seen as what Dewey calls a "rabble-rouser." Their initial appearance usually coincides with a growing distrust in government, when complaints about incompetence and inefficiency are "increased by the general belief that they, with the courts and with administrative bodies, are favorable to special interests, by association and by education and at times by corruption."[38] This pervasive distrust, often completely legitimate, "gives both the rabble-rouser and the would-be dictator their opportunities. The former speaks in words for the oppressed mass against oppression." But as soon as criticism turns to blame, the scapegoating begins. Alongside the increase in patriotism comes the identification and targeting of enemies. Consequently, "the power of the rabblerouser, especially in the totalitarian direction, is mainly due to his power to create a factitious sense of direct union and communal solidarity—if only by arousing the emotion of common intolerance and hate."[39] Thus we have the not-infrequent phenomenon of a savior turning tyrant. The rabble-rouser may speak in the name of democratic patriotism, but "in historic fact he has usually been an agent, willing or unknowing, of a new form of oppression. As Huey Long is reported to have said, Fascism would come in this country under the name of protecting democracy from its enemies."[40]

Yet when Dewey talks about the phenomena of "The Leader," he means more than a rabble-rouser—although a "Leader" may begin as one. Dewey capitalizes this term for a reason. A common misunderstanding of fascism is that its Leaders come to power in the same way as traditional authoritarians—by rewarding loyal followers and enforcing obedience on everyone else through the sword. While that certainly applies, the motivational power of fascism is not so crassly instrumental. Fascism derives its power from its mysticism, from that animistic sense of being one with a transcendent personality. Consequently, the Leader is never seen as a mere individual; he is rather the embodiment of Personality who speaks with the voice of the Nation or the Race. Dewey finds it significant, for instance, that Hitler frequently claimed "he was entrusted by God, or Destiny, or Nature (he uses different words at different times) with a mission from on high to awaken the slumbering German genius to consciousness of its own being and its intrinsic strength. Hitler believed or claimed to believe that he was divinely called to evoke what slumbered in German blood."[41] A rabble-rouser remains simply a person insofar as an audience perceives him to be a means of resisting oppression or targeting one's enemies; he becomes a Leader the moment he becomes fully identified with the spirit and destiny of a nation that speaks not the language of reason but the language of intuition.

The culmination of fascist racism and its embrace of a charismatic Leader is the celebration of violence as the preferred method of achieving nationalistic aims. This is in no way to deny the pervasiveness of force in all cultures, democratic or otherwise, as an acceptable method of attaining goals, most notably by using the police and the military. Nor is it to create a false opposition between law and force. Dewey acknowledges, for instance, that "force is the only thing in the world which affects anything, and literally to substitute law for force would be as intelligent as to try to run an engine on the mathematical formula which states its most efficient running." By "force," then, Dewey refers to anything that can directly affect changes in some other object. Thus when "we justify the use of force in the name of justice when dealing with criminals," force refers to the physical apprehension and isolation of a criminal, whereas justice refers more to the abstract idea akin to a mathematical formula. However, in Dewey's terminology, force becomes "violence" when it ceases to intelligently support and be subordinate to a clearly defined and justified end. For example, in the face of our "infantilely barbaric penal methods," which do not function at all as "an effective and economical means of securing specific results, we are using violence to relieve our immediate impulses and to save ourselves the labor of thought and construction."[42] For Dewey, the sheer presence of the use of force does not condemn it; force is necessary for any society to function. He does, however, condemn violence, which has as its primary appeal the sheer exhilaration of its expression.

The place of violence in fascist antihumanism is unique not because of its existence (a degree of wasteful violence is present in all societies) but because of its almost spiritual character. Violence in fascist societies becomes not just a crude means to an end but a direct expression of the animist will as it seeks to make manifest an ideal in the immediate present without the need for the mediation of intelligence. For instance, everyone agreed by 1942 that there was "no ground for doubt of the position of the doctrine of sheer force in the scheme of Hitler." However, most critics did not go further than condemning the "fanatical ruthlessness, brutal intimidation, and cruel persecution" of his regime. What they did not quite grasp was that this violence was not just a brute manifestation of typical gangsterism; it was more accurately described as an expression of the highest idealism. From the perspective of Hitler—and of all fascists—the quest for national greatness "was 'spiritual' (*geistige*) and that therefore its redemption must also first of all be spiritual. A rebirth of idealistic faith was the primary necessity. In his *Mein Kampf* Hitler along with glorification of force expressly states its subordination (military and economic like) to ideas and ideals." Violence was therefore an important part of the "purifying" process that would bring "the German people from weakness to strength."[43] To enact violence was thus to perform a spiritual task; it was to overcome the constraints of the will and allow the full expression of one's personality in direct action.

However, despite being cloaked in an aura of idealism, the actual violence was not subordinated to any intelligent end; it was glorified as an end in itself. As a consequence, fascist regimes historically articulate the highest and most glorious ends but then implement the most wasteful and violent policies. For as Dewey constantly emphasized throughout his work, "you may set up ends that are intrinsically desirable, but what you actually get will depend upon the means you use to attain them. The most important thing about the means employed for attainment is the ratio of intelligence to force that characterizes them. Sheer violence signifies force used with the minimum of intelligence."[44] It bears repeating, however, that the reason fascist regimes rely on violence is because of their combination of idealism and antihumanism. Believing that they are "organs, agents of the divine absolute spirit, and are realizing its purposes," they do not need to rely on such crude and time-wasting methods as the scientific study of nature or political deliberation about the relationship between means and ends; they believe that "reason operates unconsciously" and that the most authentic human beings "act according to their impulses, passions, desires and private egotisms."[45] Consequently, the attitude of fascist antihumanism does not merely ignore scientific inquiry and overlook the importance of democratic deliberation; it consciously rejects the development and deployment of intelligence in all spheres, eager to use whatever force at its disposal to serve the redemptive purposes of violence.

Finally, it is in this pairing of idealism and violence, resulting in a complete subordination of all material resources and technological powers to higher "spiritual" interests of the race, that we find the triumphant transformation of lost individuality into the fascist personality. In laissez-faire individualism, spiritual interests were degraded to mere commodities to be bought and sold within a competitive economic marketplace, leaving individuals feeling at the whim of the imperatives of the machine age and their economic overlords. With the appearance of fascism, this same individual now steps into the field triumphant, a bearer of a newfound inner personality of a spiritual race that proudly proclaims, through the voice of its Leader, complete dominance over the machine age and the subordination of all petty interests to the destiny of the nation. In the name of rejecting modernity and recovering some past greatness still latent in the blood and soil of a people, it harnesses all the tools of modernity to thrust boldly into the future some nostalgic vision of the past. And so in the name of expressing their true and authentic selves, fascist antihumanists willingly become mere cogs in a violent, technological machine, more fully dominated than at any other time in their existence and yet satisfied—if but for a moment—that they have manifested their "Humanity."

3

TOTALITARIAN PROPAGANDA

We live exposed to the greatest flood of mass suggestion that any people has ever experienced.... There are individuals who resist; but for a time at least, sentiment can be manufactured by mass methods for almost any person or any cause.
—JOHN DEWEY, *INDIVIDUALISM OLD AND NEW*

Dewey coined the phrase "New Paternalism" in December 1918, a month after the Allies signed an armistice with Germany ending the First World War. It appeared as the title of an essay in *New Republic*, later reprinted under the title "Propaganda." His aim was not necessarily to criticize the jingoistic war propaganda of the *state* in its effort to mobilize the public against Germany and its allies. He was writing at a time when the reaction *against* the heavy-handed state paternalism of the war effort had been "prompt, widespread and highly organized." Censorship was already relaxing, letters were no longer being freely opened, the Espionage Act was allowed to lapse, and Secret Service agents were being discouraged from exercising their "kindly supervision of telegraph and telephone lines." His concern was rather the replacement of the old state paternalism with a new kind of paternalism of economic elites, for what the war had accomplished was to demonstrate for the new overlords how easy it was to control not only the whole industrial field but also the sphere of public opinion, essentially taking over the centralized mechanisms of industrial and economic control established by the government: "They proved that a few fortresses in our day absolutely command the whole industrial field." The postwar elites clearly wished to retain the breadth of the state's influence over public opinion, even after it returned to full control by private hands. Thus even as some interests aggressively wished to shake off state control after the war, "strangely enough there is one form of paternalism stimulated by the war for the continuation of which the same interests are anxiously eager, namely, intellectual paternalism."[1] The price of liberating our bodies from direct control by the state—whether in industry, the military, or prisons—was to hand over our minds and our sentiments to be carefully managed from inside the fortresses of capital.

None of this occurred at its outset for any sinister or conspiratorial reason. Dewey called this phenomenon "intellectual paternalism" in order to recognize the complex motivations that inspired the new propagandists. First, the propagandists recognized that "the development of political democracy has made necessary the semblance at least of consultation of public opinion. The beliefs of the masses cannot be openly ignored." Second, they reacted to the very real condition that "the immense size of a democracy like our own would make the development of community of sentiment and persuasion impossible unless there were definite and centralized agencies for communication and propagation of facts and ideas." The solution to this problem was to reject the heavy-handed techniques of state propaganda and enforced indoctrination and instead start from "the fact that democracies are controlled through their opinions, that opinions are formed by the material upon which they feed, and that propaganda disguised as the distribution of news is the cheapest and most effective way of developing the required tone of public sentiment." After the war had made the world safe for democracy, these new propagandists would "make democracy safe for the world by a careful editing and expurgation of the facts upon which it bases the opinions which in the end decide social action." As the masses could not "yet be trusted to think for themselves," the directions of thought, as well as its factual foundation, would be provided for them.[2] Undoubtedly, those responsible for spreading false rumors about Germany to undermine the armistice saw themselves as merely massaging the facts as a means of helping Americans make the right decision in the national interest.

Dewey made all these observations in 1918. By the time he warned the public about the manufacture of sentiment by mass methods in 1930, the power of the postwar telegraph press to influence opinion had been long overshadowed by the combined forces of the movie, the motorcar, and, most importantly, the radio, which was the first truly "mass" medium that could reach millions of people with the same message simultaneously. And today, of course, all these technologies feel archaic compared to the electronic and digital media that we now feel to be extensions of our own bodies and minds. Yet what Dewey observed about the psychological and social impacts of propaganda remains as true today as in the early twentieth century, even if the technological means of producing, disseminating, and receiving messages have changed. The mass consumer readership of large, centralized newspaper conglomerates may have been replaced by active networked users of social media applications, but that has not inhibited—and in fact, in many cases has exacerbated—the ability of propagandists to manufacture the sentiments of huge segments of the population and to provide a sacred canopy of meaning to shield them from having to deal intelligently with "the vastness of economic and political conditions."[3] This is not to deny the necessary role that the news media must play to cultivate shared communities of sentiment to deal with complex problems. It is rather to point out that propaganda reverses this causal logic and sees the presence of complex problems as an opportunity to manufacture sentiments—especially those sentiments built on pride, insecurity, and fear.

Propaganda is also perhaps the greatest obstacle to fulfilling the ideals of democratic humanism in the classroom. Spread effortlessly through modern digital communication, propaganda masquerades as education and even as community, isolating individuals into narrowly defined groups and inoculating them against new ideas and relations. Educator Paulo Freire saw these effects of propaganda firsthand. For him, the most insidious effect of propaganda as a tool of education is not primarily, as it is commonly assumed, to indoctrinate a population in a single world view; it is rather to debase the very words that make a coherent world view possible. This is because a word, for Freire, is more than just an instrument for conveying information; it is a means of facilitating reflection and action, each informing the other. Consequently, for him, "there is no true word that is not at the same time a praxis [action]. Thus, to speak a true word is to transform the world." Propaganda severs reflection and action and turns words into empty vessels, "unauthentic words." According to Freire, "An unauthentic word, one which is unable to transform reality, results when dichotomy is imposed upon its constituent elements. When the word is deprived of its dimension of action, reflection automatically suffers as well; and the word is changed into idle chatter, *verbalism*, into an alienated and alienating 'blah.'"[4] This occurs, to be sure, with self-conscious propaganda such as that described by Dewey, in which names and facts and events part ways and no longer refer in a coherent way to anything predictable, tangible, or meaningful. But it also occurs when words no longer matter, when nouns and verbs are strung together to refer to nothing other than themselves, completely detached from the realm of reflection and action, which is to say the realm of lived experience. Thus when the time comes to act, words are of no use; one must simply await the appearance of the next meaningless command.

Perhaps even more insidiously, there lurks the ever-present temptation to use propaganda—even when seen as a form of resistance—as a pedagogical tool to meet the challenges of the modern age. Acting as the educational Oedipus who would strive to see and know all as a method of confronting complex problems, even well-meaning teachers might seek to empower students by using the most direct and authoritative methods to fill their minds with enlightenment. Yet the unavoidable fate would be to produce the opposite result; it would be, in the words of Paulo Freire, to "turn women and men into automatons—the very negation of their ontological vocation to be more fully human."[5] But for Freire, this is the inevitable outcome of employing what he calls the "banking" concept of education, in which teaching "becomes an act of depositing, in which the students are the depositories and the teacher is the depositor," and "in which the scope of action allowed to the students extends only so far as receiving, filing, and storing the deposits."[6] Within the system of teaching, propaganda finds its habitation. A teacher might be sincere and well-meaning, genuinely eager to empower students with his or her carefully chosen subject matter, yet if he or she lacks trust in the students' capacity to reason for themselves, the teacher will inevitably abandon "dialogue, reflection, and communication, and will fall into using slogans, communiqués, monologues, and instructions."[7] Propaganda will fill the void, and the banking method will be pressed into service, and this will all be done for the greater good.

The answer to the challenge of propaganda, for Freire, is therefore not a campaign of counterpropaganda, which adopts the same methods but uses different content; it is to engage in dialogue through what he calls "problem-posing" education. In the banking concept of education, a teacher stands as an absolute authority over the passive minds of the students who are assembled within the experiential void of the classroom walls. In problem-posing education, a teacher approaches students within the context of their own experience in their environment, stimulating them to reflect upon and act within a real situation. Consequently, Freire argues, "problem-posing education bases itself on creativity and stimulates true reflection and action upon reality, thereby responding to the vocation of persons as beings who are authentic only when engaged in inquiry and creative transformation."[8] Similarly, whereas the monologue is the preferred method of banking education, dialogue is the natural counterpart in problem-posing education, for dialogue embodies a genuine encounter between human beings. Dialogue, he writes, "is the encounter in which the united reflection and action of the dialoguers are addressed to the world which is to be transformed and humanized." It is, in short, "an encounter among women and men who name the world."[9] This is also Dewey's vision of the activity of education, an activity that stands in direct contradiction to the banking methods of propaganda.

In 1943, a Hollywood film debuted that purported to dramatize the real-life experiences of former Soviet ambassador Joseph E. Davies during the early years of World War II. Soon after, a review of the movie appeared in the *New York Times*: "The film *Mission to Moscow* is the first instance in our country of totalitarian propaganda for mass consumption—a propaganda which falsifies history through distortion, omission or pure invention of facts, and whose effect can only be to confuse the public in its thought and its loyalties." This accusation was the opening salvo in an editorial that Dewey coauthored with Suzanne La Follette, who had served with him in 1937 on the "Commission of Inquiry into the Charges Made against Leon Trotsky in the Moscow Trials" (a.k.a. the Dewey Commission). Given the fact that their commission, "after painstaking investigation, concluded that the Moscow trials were frame-ups," it is understandable that they would react so strongly to a movie that, in the interest of bolstering American support for a highly problematic ally during the war, re-creates an almost entirely fictional account of the same trials as if they had successfully rooted out a fifth column while adhering to the highest standards of justice. Such a farcical account, they argued, "may serve the interests of Soviet propaganda. It does not serve the interests of 'truth about Russia.'"[10]

The movie had actually been based on a popular best seller by Davies of the same name, which Dewey had forcefully criticized even before the film had been produced. As Dewey wryly commented in his review of the book, the title should have been "Before and After the Miraculous Revelation." This is because although the *actions* of the story revolve around the years 1936 to 1938, when Davies had been the Soviet ambassador, the *meaning* of those actions was only realized after a moment of revelation many years later. For Dewey, "the story reminds the reader of the experience, on the road to Damascus, of the doubter who became an apostle of the Church. In the case of Ex-Ambassador Davies, the holder of the Moscow Mission became a missionary." During his actual time as ambassador, Davies had actually often expressed great reservations about the actions of the Soviet regime, particularly their violent purges and show trials, noting at one point that "the Terror here is a horrifying fact. There is a fear that reaches down and haunts all sections of the community."[11] However, years later, after the Soviets had become allies, a revelation came to him about what the purges had all been about: "Three years, practically to a day, after Mr. Davies had left Moscow, he discovered a meaning for what went on there which totally escaped him while he was on the ground. . . . A flash, the flash, revealed to him that the purges, the whole terror (as he frankly called it when he was in the midst of what was going on) was revealed to him. The statesmanlike and farsighted Stalin was protecting his country from the fifth columnists, traitors, saboteurs, those who years afterwards played havoc with defense against the Nazis in all other European countries."[12] The book was an effort to justify the terror as a farsighted political necessity and to reveal the Soviet allies to be committed to democracy and freedom. The movie then put this narrative on screen, distorting even further the narrative of the book by creating fictional trials and oversimplifying an already simplistic story.

This particular artifact provides an ideal example through which to crystallize Dewey's views about propaganda into a succinct definition. Dewey never claimed to be as sophisticated a critic of propaganda as a journalist like Walter Lippmann, and his essay on "The New Paternalism" is his only sustained theoretical analysis of its methods. However, the problem of propaganda appears in passing references numerous times in his later writings, from which a more comprehensive interpretation can be pieced together, especially when supplemented by his more specific writings on *Mission to Moscow*. This single artifact elicited not one but four articles from Dewey, a solo-authored and vicious critique of Davies's original book published in *New Leader*, and four letters to the *New York Times*—three of them coauthored with La Follette. These texts not only offer the most sustained and detailed propaganda criticism Dewey ever penned, but they were directed toward a propaganda artifact that, being an independent Hollywood film, perfectly represented the workings of modern democratic propaganda through the medium of the for-profit news and entertainment industries.

The definition that will be subsequently analyzed and defended is as follows: *Propaganda is the organized and sustained manipulation of industrial media by press and publicity agents to generate an ephemeral and confused pseudopublic opinion by a constant and subtle distortion of fact, an aggressive stimulation of impulse, and the repetition of a single, though changing, totalizing point of view.* Propaganda, for Dewey, is primarily a form of social control that can only be understood as an expression of power rather than as a subset of communication. Although it certainly makes use of communication, specifically mass communication, its production of messages is best seen as an end product of a more complex machinery of control. For instance, when

Dewey uses terms like *communication, persuasion, argumentation, deliberation*, or *art*, he refers more specifically to an interaction between individuals in which they are primarily responsible for the production and reception of messages, however mediated they might be. Propaganda cares nothing for the individual and is interested only in movements of mass opinion. In other words, propaganda is the regulatory arm of the machine age, a direct result of the need to manage public opinion in order to smooth the transition to a technologically managed society that maximizes profit and control for the few at the expense of the many. All this becomes clear in Dewey's critique of *Mission to Moscow*.

The most outstanding characteristic of *Mission to Moscow* is the fact that it was not directly state-produced propaganda but was first a commercial success as a book published by Simon and Schuster (selling seven hundred thousand copies and being translated into thirteen languages) and then a Hollywood movie (less successful) produced by Warner Brothers studios. Consequently, although both artifacts were indirectly supported by the federal government, they were produced by private entertainment industries with a profit motive. When Dewey first attacked the book's distortions, therefore, he could not distinguish one motive from another: "Whether the misrepresentation comes from zeal in behalf of large sales, or from the belief that the cause of the allies is thereby furthered, I have no way of knowing."[13] But this is not so much an assertion about the specific artifact as about a general state of affairs. Since propaganda in a modern democracy almost always is disseminated through private media, the true motives of any message are almost impossible to discern and almost equally difficult to change: "The causes which require large corporate capital to carry on modern business" result in "the fact that all economic conditions tending toward centralization and concentration of the means of production and distribution affect the public press, whether individuals so desire or not."[14] Any message that gains public presence can almost never be detached from the causes of economic centralization and concentration and the financial motives that result from them.

In fact, the most ubiquitous propaganda in modern society is not explicitly "political" in a conventional sense but simply concentrates on promoting the myth of rugged individualism that rationalizes the injustices of the machine age. The result is, as Dewey explains, that "our prevailing mentality, our 'ideology,' is said to be that of the 'business mind' which has become so deplorably pervasive." In the absence of a political crisis, therefore, the popular propaganda of entertainment fills the available media with traditional romantic propaganda such as the American Dream. For instance, "even statistically and in so-called prosperous times, the proportion of economic failures to successes is at least ten to one, and it requires a continual stream of propaganda of success stories to prevent the rise of widespread doubts as to the soundness of the system."[15] All this is as much a result of propaganda as nationalistic support for a war effort; it represents a sustained use of industrial media by financial interests to maintain the economic status quo that supports them.

Second, although purported to be a true and disinterested report of the facts by a single individual, *Mission to Moscow* was actually a product of press and publicity agents working through multiple industrial media outlets to disseminate a specific narrative of events. Dewey first alludes to this influence when he speculates that "the representation of President Roosevelt talking to Mr. Davies of the film seems to suggest that it is at least semi-official."[16] But no better proof that the film had been produced in large part at the request of publicity agents was the fact that the one who responded to Dewey's letter in the *New York Times* was neither Davies nor the film producer but rather Arthur Upham Pope, the chair for the Committee for National Morale created by President Roosevelt to study ways of encouraging domestic support for the war. In the first of two responses, Pope offers a point-by-point defense of the film's historical realism and its celebration of Russia's "stupendous effort and immeasurable sacrifice for the common welfare of the nation and her will to a collective peace."[17] Although never admitting there was any collusion between the government and Warner Brothers, Pope's full-throated support of the movie and utter contempt for Dewey and La Follette betrays a vested interest. Indeed, he admits as much in the conclusion of his second letter: "No one asks Professor Dewey or Miss La Follette to keep silent, as they charge, but every one's freedom of speech is necessarily somewhat curtailed in wartime, and in moments of national stress and peril the common will must be protected from divisive conflicts."[18] The not-so-subtle threat betrays Pope's status as an agent of the Roosevelt administration. Press and publicity agents, in short, give propaganda its organizational character. Loosely speaking, publicity agents create pseudoevents to capture public attention, while press agents supply narratives for those events that provide the talking points and moral lessons. For instance, Pope acted the publicity agent insofar as he encouraged the production of the film but then turned press agent the moment he started writing letters for the *New York Times*.

But once again, one should not be distracted by the specific agenda of this or that interest. Looked at more broadly, the entire industry of press and publicity agents is an expression of singular economic power. Dewey remarks that "power is power and must act, and it must act according to the nature of the machinery through which it operates. In this case, the machinery is business for private profit through private control of banking, land, industry, reinforced by command of the press, press agents and other means of publicity and propaganda."[19] Consequently, even if two businesses are in direct competition with one another for the same market, they nonetheless employ the same methods through the same media: "Hence we have today a multitude of agencies which skillfully manipulate and color the news and information, which circulate, and which artfully instill, under the guise of disinterested publicity, ideas favorable to hidden interests."[20] This creates an environment in which, no matter what the specific message might be at any one time, the social impact is the same: "We are ruled by headlines, publicity agents and 'counsellors of public relations.'"[21] A film like *Mission to Moscow* is unique only for having called attention to this fact.

That propaganda represents an organized and sustained effort by publicity agents in support of specific interests naturally culminates in its third characteristic, which is a narrow enthusiasm for a single perspective at the expense of all others. Dewey notes, for instance, the stark contrast between the actual reports sent back by Davies while he was working as a Soviet ambassador, which commented on the widespread feeling of fear and terror, with "the make-believe Russia of the film." Whenever possible in the movie, Stalin is portrayed as a statesman of great honor and forethought, and "wherever Mr. Davies goes he encounters a happy confidence in the regime." In contradistinction, everything that opposed the Soviet regime in any way is caricatured and ridiculed. This includes not only demonizing all the victims of the Soviet show trials but representing "Stalin as having been driven into Hitler's arms by the Franco-British policy of appeasement." Indeed, Dewey even notes that "the sinister totalitarian critique of the parliamentary system is introduced in the film," and "the traditional isolationism of some American members of Congress before the war is represented as equivalent to pro-nazism."[22] All this was the product of a single, concerted effort to modify, include, and invent "opinions, characters, events, dates, with no regard for anything except the picture of Russia and Joseph E. Davies which Mr. Davies and the Warner Brothers want the American people to accept as the truth."[23]

This subordination of all matters of fact, form, and presentation to a single interest characterizes a uniquely propagandistic aesthetic that subordinates diverse expression to singular purpose. Propaganda involves the limitation of creative impulse and the "overweighing of certain values at the expense of others until, except for those in a similar state of one-sided enthusiasm, weariness rather than refreshment sets in."[24] For the propagandist, however, this weariness can be held at bay by keeping the young in a state of one-sided enthusiasm by attempting, as he saw in Russia, to "prostitute the schools, the radio and the press to the inculcation of one single point of view and the suppression of everything else."[25] And in politics, particularly the politics of nationalism, propaganda takes its most aggressive form, in which "by constant reiteration, by shaming heretics and intimidating dissidents, by glowing admiration if not adoration of the faithful, by all agencies of education and propaganda (now, alas, so hard to distinguish) the phrases in which these defenses and appeals are couched become substitutes for thought."[26] The point is that all propaganda has inherently totalitarian tendencies insofar as it seeks not to insert its view within a plurality of opinion but to dominate all opinion with a single perspective.

The counterpart of this single-mindedness is deflection, the employment of strategies of distortion, omission, and the violation of language itself as a means of conforming the factual world to one's opinion. For instance, the movie highlights testimony about "alleged meetings with Trotsky abroad" but omits the fact that this testimony was "immediately challenged in the world press and conclusively disproved by evidence offered in rebuttal before the international commission of inquiry." It claims that Stalin had always been (despite the pact they signed) an enemy of Hitler but omits any "mention of the Soviet Government's demand for a negotiated peace after Stalin and Hitler had divided Poland." The film claims to be a faithful reproduction of the experience of Ambassador Davies, but in fact it "falsifies not only the trials but Mr. Davies's own reports on them to the State Department and his comments in letters to individuals." The film at one point shows Marshal Mikhail Tukhachevsky "having his day in court," when in fact he was "secretly executed in June, 1937, after no trial at all."[27] And perhaps worst of all, these omissions and falsifications are justified in the film "by pleading the rights of 'fictional technique'" despite the fact that the movie firmly declares that it will provide "the truth about Russia." However, Dewey and La Follette argue that "if a film is offered as objective truth, then its distortions of truth must be called by their right name. A work cannot honestly be presented as truth and defended as fiction."[28] But it is precisely this confusion and reversal of meanings that is produced by propaganda.

The larger concern for Dewey is not that propaganda falsifies accepted facts and distorts experienced reality; it is that it does so with the express purpose of undermining the integrity of our symbolic system and calling into question the entire idea of what it means to be a "fact." Of course, as a pragmatist, Dewey is not appealing to a facile realism; he is recognizing that symbols only carry pragmatic meaning insofar as they promise to culminate in some common experience recognizable by a language community. However, as technology makes possible mass communication about political matters far distant from the experience of any individual and as political parties make use of this technology to influence political action, the inevitable outcome is that "words not only take the place of realities but are themselves debauched."[29] In this environment, in which the imperatives of mass party politics combine with a mass communication industry dominated by economic interests, symbols find their meaning not in their connection with reality but in their relationship to the latest idealized aim promoted by this or that party. Consequently, "favorable and unfavorable presentation of individuals, laudation and ridicule, subtle suggestion of points of view, deliberate falsification of facts and deliberate invention of half-truth or whole falsities, inculcate by methods, of which those subject to them are not even aware, the particular tenets which are needed to support private and covert policies."[30] Lying becomes not merely a means to an end but an end in itself, for it produces an inability to ever really discern what is true from what is false.

Propaganda compensates its audience for this constant deception, however, with its fifth characteristic of being able to arouse passionate and violent emotions. What it lacks in accuracy it makes up for in enthusiasm, even if the price one pays for this enthusiasm is high. It is bad enough, Dewey writes, that Davies's book, through distortion and omission, creates a "false idealization of Russia" and "lends itself to creation of dangerous illusions." But it also has a corrupting emotional impact: "Surrender to emotional hysteria during war time may result in creating a dangerously false picture of those who at the time are on our side as well as create a hysteria of hate for all who are on the other side."[31] This very impact is evident on Ambassador Davies himself, who after his "revelation" decided that terror, violence, and oppression were worthy and virtuous methods when faced with an enemy as despicable as Trotsky and his fifth column. By demonizing an enemy and arousing emotions to a fever pitch, actions that formerly elicited disgust became patriotic sacrifices for a cause.

This means that the satisfaction of this aesthetic is primarily emotional rather than cognitive; like most advertising, it emphasizes "the role of wants, impulse, habit, and emotion" while denying "any efficacy whatever to ideas, to intelligence."[32] Propaganda arouses a very specific set of emotions that are highly polarized, such that extreme pleasure and extreme pain look at each other across a chasm. This is particularly obvious in wartime, in which "all the emotional reactions have to be excited." For instance, to provoke pain, "propaganda and atrocity stories are enlisted." But wartime also must keep up morale, and "morale is largely a matter of keeping emotions at a certain pitch; and unfortunately fear, hatred, suspicion, are among the emotions most easily aroused."[33] No one learned this lesson better than Hitler. In his analysis of *Mein Kampf,* Dewey stressed Hitler's manipulation of emotions:

> Hitler's contempt for intellectual measures and for science, except when used as an effective technical instrument in propaganda, are the obverse side of his belief in the power of emotion to reach the masses, and of his conviction that when "intellectuals" are emotionally stirred they fade into the mass. For it is characteristic of intense emotion to rule out discrimination; emotion is an all or none state. We fear and hate all over; the emotions are inherently totalitarian. When they are once kept excited they control belief and every semblance of intellectual operation. Indifference, apathy, Hitler called his chief foe; excitement, and always some new source of excitement, is the consistent quality in his inconsistent policies. Since emotion is total, it knows only black and white, not intermediate shades. Hence the ideal value of Germanic blood needed for effective presentation an extreme and wholly dark opposite.[34]

It is important to emphasize that Dewey is not denying the importance of emotion in judgment; indeed, he often stresses the importance of emotion in all aspects of our lives, including our intellectual lives. What he stresses here is the effect of *intense* emotion that taps into fear and hate, overwhelms reflective thought, and colors all experience either black or white. It is this *class* of emotions, not emotion itself, that gives propaganda its peculiar force.

Finally, the cumulative and lasting effect of propaganda on society can perhaps best be captured in one word—*confusion*. Dewey and La Follette, for instance, began their first letter about *Mission to Moscow* with the accusation that the movie's "effect can only be to confuse the public in its thought and its loyalties." But they also closed the letter the same way, only this time expressed with even stronger language and by drawing a controversial comparison. They write, "*Mission to Moscow* is a major defeat for the democratic cause. In putting out this picture the producers, far from rendering the patriotic service on which Mr. Davies compliments them, have assailed the very foundations of freedom. For truth and freedom are indivisible, as Hitler knew when he expounded his method of confusing public opinion through propaganda. The picture *Mission to Moscow* makes skillful use of the Hitler technique." This technique is, to be sure, to spread ideological indoctrination, to arouse extreme emotions, to distort facts, and to rally a mass public to support a violent cause, but it is also to throw into confusion every fact, every loyalty, every virtue, and every meaning of every word. For instance, just after the movie was released, the Soviet government announced it had "executed as 'Nazi agents' the two Polish Jews, Ehrlich and Alter, internationally known leaders of Socialist labor whom it had arrested when it invaded Poland." And yet because of propaganda like this movie, no outcry was made in America despite the fact that these men clearly were enemies, not allies, of the Nazis. But when propaganda throws the public into a complete state of confusion, it is virtually impossible to take a moral stand when there is no firm ground to stand upon. Consequently, "the picture *Mission to Moscow* and similar propaganda have helped to create a certain moral callousness in our public mind which is profoundly un-American."[35]

The fact that the primary effect of propaganda is confusion—rather than dogmatism, manipulation, commitment, indoctrination, or "belief"—is an important and often overlooked insight. One of the reasons it is overlooked is that its *immediate* effect is not confusion but confidence, such that an entire nation might be made to enthusiastically support a military ally who had just months prior been an enemy. But by "confusion," Dewey does not mean an immediate feeling of emotional bewilderment but rather a habitual inability to think consistently, to relate the past to the future, or to investigate the relationship of means to ends. Propaganda cultivates a readiness to react impulsively to stimuli in the moment but not to reflect on the meaning of events as they unfold in time. As proof of this confusion, Dewey points to the "meaninglessness of present political platforms, parties and issues." In large part due to the capacity for propaganda to constantly rationalize changing positions through the debauchery of language, "on the whole our politics, as far as they are not covertly manipulated in behalf of the pecuniary advantage of groups, are in a state of confusion; issues are improvised from week to week with a constant shift of allegiance. It is impossible for individuals to find themselves politically with surety and efficiency under such conditions. Political apathy broken by recurrent sensations and spasms is the natural outcome."[36]

Propaganda, in other words, is not intended to create a solid constituency of believers who hold to a firm ideological commitment to principles over the long term; it is rather to generate a loyal base of followers able to discard or embrace any belief insofar as their actions fulfill an emotional commitment to a vaguely defined cause. It is a specific characteristic of fascism to debase language so that even a culture's highest symbols, noblest ideals, and most virtuous narratives can be stripped of their meaning and turned into weapons of oppression. For instance, in fully developed fascism, the striving to actualize human potentiality becomes translated into a mythic quest to unleash the already-existing power of the will that is said to be innate by virtue of blood and soil. The freedom of the mind becomes a freedom from having to consider any ideas outside of a preapproved and bounded set of clichés and doctrines, usually incoherent, that mark one as belonging to a chosen sect. Wisdom and courage, meanwhile, become celebrated respectively as the ability to perceive higher and lower orders of humanity and the manly virtue to rid oneself of things such as compassion, understanding, or doubt that inhibit acts of discrimination and violence. And the flourishing of individuality, in its final and tragic irony, becomes identified with the power to repeat ideological slogans and talking points on command.

The specific product of propaganda is thus not a *public* opinion but a *pseudo*public opinion whose function is to keep the public in darkness. By "pseudo-public opinion," Dewey means a public opinion that consists primarily of an emotional allegiance or opposition to the latest set of largely vacuous partisan symbols. This is partly the tragic consequence that Dewey sees of rapid technological development, particularly of the mass media: "The very agencies that a century and a half ago were looked upon as those that were sure to advance the cause of democratic freedom, are those which now make it possible to create pseudo-public opinion and to undermine democracy from within."[37] Once harnessed by vested political and economic interests, communication media once thought to herald an age of egalitarianism and the light of reason introduce nationalism and the darkness of irrationality. For example, "the propaganda of the Soviet Union, Italy, Germany and Japan is easily identified by the fact that in every important matter the words used have to be read in reverse. They are selected and weighed with no reference to anything but their effect upon others." By way of contrast, in everyday practical life, one is able to judge probabilities based on experience and deliberate using symbols that have a meaningful relationship to objects in one's environment. Propaganda, however, yanks words completely out of context and produces "complete inversions of truth [that] are astonishingly confusing. They produce a state of daze that endures long enough to enable its creators to accomplish their will while darkness still prevails."[38] For the fact is that propagandists never want their actual interests to come to light: "Sinister class interests flourish better in the dark."[39]

Propaganda is the darkness that falls over society once it gives itself over to fascist antihumanism. Propaganda feeds off of the intense emotions that divide human beings into irreconcilable and antagonistic classes, sects, races, and nations and flatters its consumers that they are the sheep among goats. Propaganda arouses these emotions by debauching symbols and turning them into mere signals that direct actions in support of this ally or against this enemy. Propaganda undermines the legitimacy of fact and reason until the very capacity for intelligence is slowly eroded away and reflective thought becomes idle fantasy. Propaganda speaks the language of pride, honor, individuality, loyalty, and personality at the same time that it harnesses all the capacities of the machine age to turn populations into mere appendages of vested interests. And in periods of crisis, propaganda harnesses all the surplus energy that remains and channels it toward the fascist aim of totalitarian dominance of one group over another. But perhaps the saving virtue of those crises is that it becomes so dark that one recognizes the darkness for what it is and asks for the first time if, perhaps, light is possible.

PART 2
THE POLITICS OF
DEMOCRATIC HUMANISM

4

THE ART OF INDIVIDUALITY

> Since individuality is a distinctive way of feeling the impacts of the world and of showing a preferential bias in response to these impacts, it develops into shape and form only through interaction with actual conditions; it is no more complete in itself than is a painter's tube of paint without relation to a canvas.
>
> —JOHN DEWEY, *INDIVIDUALISM OLD AND NEW*

In 1894, Dewey left Ann Arbor, Michigan, to take a job at the University of Chicago. For many months, he stayed in boarding houses in the city as he tried to find a home for his family and spent his free time writing many letters back to his wife, Alice, who was taking care of their three children, Fred, Evelyn, and one-year-old Morris. Dewey was particularly fond of his youngest child, named after his beloved mentor at Johns Hopkins University, George Sylvester Morris. Many of his letters to Alice are filled with loving anecdotes of how Dewey struggled to teach Morris to eat, build block towers, and pronounce words. One letter from Chicago stands out in its expression of sheer parental love. He writes,

> As for Morris himself, he is the joy of my life & the delight of my eyes and all other things which all lovers have ever said of their beloveds. I think he looks more & more like the infant Jesus in the Sistine picture—; perhaps it is on that acct, I am just beginning to appreciate the marvels of that picture—I suppose I saw it so early & so long as a "religious" picture that I never saw anything but the label till recently. Now it seems to have all the promise of all future free humanity in it.[1]

This is as pure an expression of Dewey's humanism as one can find. Looking at Morris, he thinks immediately of a work of art by Michelangelo and in doing so sees his son as an artist would. The only difference in the comparison is that Morris is his *own* work of art. His very individuality is the work that is constantly in the process of being remade in time through creative effort, interaction with materials, and a relation with an environment, and it is the promise of that creation that brings a delight to his father, who otherwise must endure bad food and poor company in a Chicago boardinghouse.

This expression of affection might be easily dismissed as the romantic dreams of a doting father, but it takes on added significance when compared with a more "democratic" observation he makes just a paragraph later in the same letter. Dewey relates to Alice some of his experiences with Hull House, a settlement house founded by Jane Addams and Ellen Gates Starr to provide social and educational services for working-class and immigrant populations in Chicago's Near West Side. One thing that struck him was the fact that the women in that neighborhood, being close to the state university, actually had the right to vote for its trustees (including two "very strong women" on the ballot) despite being denied the vote for any other public office. He writes, "Everybody is going to vote apparently, & the interesting thing is to see how the politicians—the men—are working to get the woman vote out. It settles the question as to 'whether women would vote or not.' Give 'em the ballot, & the politicians will do the rest. It also shows how wide open everything is in Chicago to see the energy & system with which women's votings clubs &c are being organized. Chicago is the greatest place in the world."[2] Although lacking the emotional sentimentality of his description of his son as the baby Jesus, Dewey's encomium to the energetic acts of self-organization and political agency by Chicago women amount to the same expression of the promise of a future free humanity. In this case, the city itself, as a synecdoche for its diverse and striving population, becomes exemplary of a work of art that warrants its own Michelangelo fresco.

In fact, the case of the women in Chicago is a far better example of what he means by individuality being understood as a product of art. The relationship between parent and child, after all, is often distorted by authoritarian tendencies in which the child becomes literally the property of the parent to be forced into a specific mold. In this case, the "art" is not a living art but a dead one, something literally fixed in place to be admired, perhaps, but never liberated. But Dewey celebrates art not as a fixed object but as a process of creative growth and of continually enriched experience. The individual as a work of art is created anew every day within the process of becoming that occurs in the transaction between an organism and its environment. There is thus an essential two-sidedness to Dewey's conception of individuality. On the one hand, it is from *within* the individual, from her energies and powers and capacities, that creative force flows. On the other hand, the flourishing of individual power requires an environment that allows those powers to be expressed, as well as tools and technologies to express those powers. The women of Chicago were given a tool (the vote) and an environment (the trustee elections) in which to express themselves, and as a result, they began constructing for themselves a new identity, a new social organization, and a new way of speaking and acting in the world that literally *made* them into different people. The only ones surprised by this phenomenon were those who denied the principles of democratic humanism at the outset.

It bears repeating that celebrating everyone's right to be an individual in the abstract does not get very far along the road to democratic humanism; rugged individualism too celebrates that right, and fascism even is known for advocating something called a "higher individualism." What matters are the methods we use to make individuality a reality. Antihumanism in its many forms, including some that masquerade with the name of "Humanism," shares a common assumption that the substance and end of individuality are already fixed in some form prior to the life and experience of any particular individual. Sometimes it exists in genetics; sometimes in fate; sometimes in a nation, ethnicity, or race; sometimes in a literary or religious tradition; sometimes in the images of advertising; and sometimes in the mind of God. Whatever the *source* of individuality, antihumanism conceives of "growth" as something teleological, as something that unfolds the power of an innate potentiality as it moves toward its ultimate form. In this case, the environment might provide the resources for that growth, but they are not formative of its ends or value. Consequently, antihumanism perceives the human being as moving *through* the world as an isolated unit.

By contrast, humanism understands individuality as constantly changing and adapting to its environment, an environment that necessarily involves being *in* and *with* an environment that is shared by others. Dewey's conception of individuality thus describes an immanent, not a teleological, process; that is to say, it is a result of the complex transaction that generates causes and aims out of the totality of the relations at any one time. Dewey's democratic humanism thus distinguishes itself from its popular competitors by being rooted in a thoroughgoing immanent naturalism. In contradistinction to the dualistic conception that defined a "Humanism" that somehow stands in opposition to nature and the world of material objects and events—usually in the name of making humanity stand "above" them—he advances a humanism that embraces our intimate interconnection with our social, technological, and natural environment. In no way does this deny space for religious faith or belief in God, as Dewey's reference to the Sistine Chapel signifies; it is only to say that however the world was created and by what or whom, human beings were created with a nature uniquely designed and adapted for the universe in which they were born. The religious faith of democratic humanism is that human nature, whatever its origin, provides us the unformed powers and possibilities through conscious transaction with our environment by which individuals form themselves into works of art always in the making. Dewey's naturalism thus provides the foundations for individual growth that form the basis of his social, political, and educational philosophy.

The method by which Dewey's idea of individuality is implemented in the classroom can be seen in the work of Stephen Fishman and Lucille McCarthy, one a teacher of philosophy and the other of English. For decades, they have experimented with classroom practices that are consistent with the attitudes and values of democratic humanism, documenting their failures and successes in order to craft a pedagogy of hope. Essential to their mission as teachers is overcoming those isolating conceptions of "rugged" individualism that render us fundamentally alienated and disconnected from our natural and social environments. As they observe in an earlier work, one of the problems is that even the most well-meaning educational reformers share "a common conception of human nature and individual liberty, both ends of the political spectrum seeing freedom as 'freedom from.'" Wedded to "our dominant individualistic creed," they "favor competition at a cost of cooperation, independence at the cost of dependence, and professional mobility at the cost of communal allegiance." For Fishman and McCarthy, Dewey offers a way out of these zero-sum games grounded in irreconcilable dualisms. For Dewey, authentic individuality is achieved within, not outside of, our relationships in a social environment. As a result, "this leads him to take a different approach to education, one which stresses the importance of learning to get along with others, not just as part of a do-gooders hope for some distant utopian democracy, but because cooperation actually satisfies a deep-seated human need."[3] Consequently, it is only by fully acknowledging the nature of this deep-seated human need that we can genuinely imagine a pedagogy of democratic humanism.

After years of applying Dewey's pedagogical symbols in the classroom, Fishman and McCarthy arrived at one overarching aim that guided their practices—teaching students the art of what they call "living in hope." Characteristic of Dewey's understanding of individuality as something that developed in relationship to an environment, what they mean by this phrase is "having an ultimate hope or goal toward which one works that gives one's life significance in relationship to nature and the human community. Living in hope means that one has a sense of belonging, purpose, faith in one's ideals, and unification." What is uniquely Deweyan about this practice, of course, is not simply having hope; this is a characteristic of any moral or educational philosophy. The emphasis falls on the term *living*. To *live* hope is to intimately feel how one's practice grows out of a sense of organic and connected life rather than an abstract image of a better future. This is why the first key to living in hope, for Fishman and McCarthy, is the possession of a sense of gratitude. Specifically, this would be a kind of gratitude that embodies a "deep piety towards nature, including our ancestors and progeny." Against the alienating assumptions of modern individualism and its bootstrap ideals of self-advancement, gratitude that grows out of a sense of democratic humanism emphasizes the virtue of continuity. We are links, it reminds us, "in a long human line, a line toward which we should feel reverence and piety. No matter how much our lives are uniquely our own, we remain fundamentally interconnected with others."[4] The pedagogy of democratic humanism thus encourages students to identify the multifarious links we have with other human beings and our natural world, constantly calling them to mind to expand our senses of selfhood in practice. As in the classrooms of Fishman and McCarthy, it employs types of assignments that satisfy curricular demands to learn new material while at the same time making students more aware of their complex relationships to the past, to others, and to their environment. In the end, Fishman and McCarthy hope students take "with them a residue from the course which continues to influence the sorts of students they are, the sorts of persons they are becoming." And that is the goal of the pedagogy of democratic humanism—to find ways to help students in the process of becoming by encouraging reflection on their relations within their wider world.[5]

On October 27, 1889, Dewey delivered an address to the Students' Christian Association (SCA) of the University of Michigan, reprinted in November under the title "The Value of Historical Christianity." At the time, Dewey still belonged to the Congregationalist church he had joined while living in Burlington, Vermont, and he felt an obligation to explain to the students the relationships among faith, knowledge, and social practice. As summarized by Rockefeller, Dewey believed at the time that "knowledge properly understood, is intimately related to the will and moral action, and the will finds its final end in desiring, knowing, and doing God's will."⁶ Unique about Dewey's address was his rejection of the notion of God as a separate, detached, supernatural being who communicates his will through commands from on high. For him, "God is no remote Being away from the world, that he is no force which works in physical Nature alone, but that he is an ever present fact in life, in history, and in our social relations." To find God, in other words, one must not look *above* oneself but *around* and inside oneself. God is the "reality of our ordinary relations with one another in life. He is the bond of the family, the bond of society. He is love, the source of all growth, all sacrifice, and all unity." And his will too can be discerned within these realities and relations in which we are embedded. Consequently, "the Spirit is not a mystery working only in miracles, in revivals, etc., but is the intelligence present in all man's science, in his inspiration for whatever is better than himself." Therefore, it is not alone, in some private spiritual connection with a distant God, that we find our salvation; it is with "union with humanity and humanity's interests."⁷

For anyone familiar with the history of American thought, one might hear familiar refrains of Ralph Waldo Emerson in Dewey's early humanism. This is no accident. Dewey had read Emerson at the University of Vermont and would be influenced by Emerson's thoughts throughout his life. In 1903, he would pronounce Emerson the "Philosopher of Democracy" in a lecture at the Emerson Memorial meeting, and in 1947, he wrote a letter in the Harvard Alumni Bulletin that Emerson "is the Founder of Humanism in religion."⁸ In short, Emerson represented for Dewey the father of democratic humanism. In Dewey's 1903 lecture, for instance, he uses Emerson to refute the Western philosophical tradition that had greedily defended a vision of truth accessible to an elite few. In this elitist tradition, truth became a "truth of philosophy, a truth of private interpretation, reached by some men, not others, and consequently true for some, but not true for all, and hence not wholly true for any." Here is the root of all antihumanism, which alienates human experience from the sources of truth and then creates a hierarchy of power and virtue based on who possesses it and who does not. But Emerson, Dewey explains, challenges this entire tradition:

> To Emerson all "truth lies on the highway." Emerson says, "We lie in the lap of immense intelligence which makes us organs of its activity and receivers of its truth," and the Idea is no longer either an academic toy nor even a gleam of poetry, but a literal report of the experience of the hour as that is enriched and reinforced for the individual through

the tale of history, the appliance of science, the gossip of conversation and the exchange of commerce. That every individual is at once the focus and the channel of mankind's long and wide endeavor, that all nature exists for the education of the human soul—such things, as we read Emerson, cease to be statements of a separated philosophy and become natural transcripts of the course of events and of the rights of man.... [H]e finds truth in the highway, in the untaught endeavor, the unexpected idea, and this removes him from their remotenesses. His ideas are not fixed upon any Reality that is beyond or behind or in any way apart, and hence they do not have to be bent. They are versions of the Here and the Now, and flow freely. The reputed transcendental worth of an overweening Beyond and Away, Emerson, jealous for spiritual democracy, finds to be the possession of the unquestionable Present.[9]

Here we find the same themes Dewey expressed in his SCA address—namely, the rejection of any separate, supernatural realm "Beyond and Away"; a definition of knowledge as something experienced and put into practice in the moving present; and a conception of individuality as something formed through active relations in nature, society, history, and commerce. The only difference is that in his lecture on Emerson, he does call the source of this truth "God."

The Emersonian roots of Dewey's democratic humanism and his notion of individuality as an ongoing work of art are important to recover in order to preserve democratic humanism's fundamentally religious character, a character that endured even after he drifted away from institutional Christianity and embraced a more explicitly humanistic conception of religion. For Dewey, in his later writings, the meaning of what it meant to be "religious" was not restricted to faith in the existence of a supernatural being; a religious attitude was present whenever one desired "the sense of a connection of man, in the way of both dependence and support, with the enveloping world that the imagination feels is a universe."[10] Elsewhere he describes religious faith "as the unification of the self through allegiance to inclusive ideal ends."[11] Put together, what he meant was that a person was religious insofar as she imagined a universe that surrounded, supported, and guided her toward some ideal unity or fulfillment. By contrast, a "religion" was thus any institutionalization of this attitude in a specific body of beliefs and practices. For Dewey, therefore, democratic humanism was a thoroughly *religious* ideal, for it presented us with a vision of an interconnected universe in which we are born, by which we grow, and through which we strive to achieve inclusive ideals that satisfy not only our own interests but the interests of those who live alongside us and who come after us. This was Emerson's faith, and it is also Dewey's faith; the name for their religion is "democracy."

In order to cast new light on Dewey's humanistic sense of individualism, this chapter will continually relate back to Dewey's usage of Emerson as a touchstone in his writings. The justification for this strategy is the fact that Dewey chose Emerson from the entire Western philosophical tradition to quote in the closing pages of *Individualism Old and New* as he attempts to clinch his argument about the need for a new conception of individuality for a new age. In fact, he quotes Emerson three times in the last two paragraphs. The first quote from Emerson establishes the problem—namely, how easy it is for Emerson to be co-opted by the proponents of rugged individualism who use him to maintain the opposition between individual and society. Emerson writes that "'society is everywhere in conspiracy against its members,'" a sentiment easily taken out of context and used to promote the fallacy that every genius is sui generis. But Dewey offers a competing quotation as a corrective. Emerson also wrote, "Accept the place the divine Providence has found for you, the society of your contemporaries, the connection of events." Against the notion that society or nature stands as something fixed and separate from individuality, Emerson in this passage recognizes that it is precisely the interconnections of natural events and social relations, particularly "as formed of moving in multiple associations," that are "means by which the possibilities of individuality can be realized." Finally, Dewey quotes Emerson. saying that "'it is vain that we look for genius to reiterate the miracles in the old arts; it is its instinct to find beauty and holiness in new and necessary facts, in the field and roadside, in the shop and mill.'" For Dewey, this is a call for us to accept "the corporate and industrial world in which we live"—but in accepting it, not to acquiesce to it. It is to envision a new individuality and a new society, one that can be beautiful rather than alienating, holy rather than profane; in this way, we will "create ourselves as we create an unknown future."[12]

Grasping the full import of Dewey's conclusion requires a more careful analysis of each of the premises that support his humanistic interpretation of individuality. The premises are as follows: First, human experience is intimately naturalistic. Second, human nature is composed primarily of active, rather than passive, powers. Third, meaningful individuality is a product of the social use of language in practice. Fourth, science and technology are extensions of the human mind and body. Finally, the art of individuality represents the conscious and ongoing creation of habits that allow individuals to creatively express power within society. All these premises lay behind Dewey's claim that Emerson's philosophy amounts to "the identity of Being, unqualified and immutable, with Character."[13] In other words, from the perspective of democratic humanism, there is no realm of existence that can be posited that is outside of human experience in nature, just as there is no transcendent aim of life that overrides the imperative to develop one's individual character—and the character of others—in society.

To begin, the most direct connection Dewey shares with Emerson is his naturalism, culminating in what he calls a "naturalistic humanism."[14] In *Nature*, Emerson had claimed that "all nature exists for the education of the human soul."[15] As we have already seen in the discussion of nationalism, there are other forms of "Humanism" that purport to glorify what it means to be human by separating it off from everything natural, material, or social—in effect, by making humanity a monster. For these sham humanists, naturalism equates to materialism, which in turn is accused of making human beings mere biological machines determined by external forces and instinctual desires. Their solution is the embodiment of the "modern" attitude: "Man is taken not only as Lord over nature but as Lord in its oldest and most discredited sense—that of a despotic monarch supposed to rule by mere fiat."[16] Dewey's understanding of naturalism rejects both of these absurdities. For him, the values that make life worth living are found *in* nature—or more specifically, in our *experience* in nature: "Naturalism finds the values in question, the worth and dignity of men and women, founded in human nature itself, in the connections, actual and potential, of human beings with one another in their natural social relationships."[17] Dewey's naturalism should best be approached from an immanent, ecological perspective, as a way of seeing individuals and societies as embedded within a network of events, relationships, and forces that are the conditions for their development and growth.

For Dewey, to be a naturalist is to bridge the dualisms between mind and body, concept and percept, value and fact, and experience and nature. Rather than imagining a "veil or screen which shuts us off from nature," with our ideals on one side and the material world on another, Dewey sees nature as something *inside* our experience. In turn, experience "is no infinitesimally thin layer or foreground of nature, but that it penetrates into it, reaching down into its depths, and in such a way that its grasp is capable of expansion; it tunnels in all directions and in so doing brings to the surface things at first hidden—as miners pile high on the surface of the earth treasures brought from below." Naturalism thus presents experience and nature as two parts of a total experience. On the one hand, "experience presents itself as the method, and the only method, for getting at nature, penetrating its secrets." On the other hand, nature as disclosed to us through experience "deepens, enriches, and directs the further development of experience."[18] This is all common sense when viewed in the context of ordinary life; this is the justification for every vacation, adventure, or exploration a person takes. It is only when it becomes a matter of explicit principle that somehow it offends.

However, Dewey's naturalism goes further than looking at human beings as any biological organism that must adapt to its environment. This understanding might lead, as its critics accuse, straight back to a material or mechanistic philosophy that leaves no place for human values, choice, intelligence, or imagination. For Dewey, however, value itself is *found* in our experience in nature; the "good" is as natural as a tree. The principle of naturalism makes us at home in the world. We not only experience things and events; we also experience values and qualities. In other words, what experience discovers in its acts of penetration, reaching, grasping, and tunneling are not simply material phenomena that are only afterward overlaid with meaning and value; we actually discover those meanings and values themselves. To the objection that naturalism deprives the world of its ideal significance—say, the beauty of the sun on a harvest, the goodness of a crop, and the pride of feeding one's family—Dewey responds as follows:

> If experience actually presents esthetic and moral traits, then these traits may also be supposed to reach down into nature, and to testify to something that belongs to nature as truly as does the mechanical structure attributed to it in physical science.... The traits possessed by the subject-matters of experience are as genuine as the characteristics of sun and electron. They are found, experienced, and are not to be shoved out of being by some trick of logic. When found, their ideal qualities are as relevant to the philosophic theory of nature as are the traits found by physical inquiry.[19]

This is not to deny the importance of reflective thought, the manipulation of symbols, or the communication of meanings that occur before, after, and during our experience in nature. Communication, as we will see in subsequent chapters, is a fundamental activity that allows us to invest our experience with greater meaning so that we might act with a more conscious purpose, a sense of control, and ultimately, an expectation for further richness. Furthermore, not everything in our abstract symbol systems can be directly experienced, nor does every experience convey to us a deep significance. Dewey's naturalism emphasizes our ecological relationship to nature as an environment and recognizes that it is ultimately our experience in nature, in one form or another, that provides the origin and consummation of all human meanings, values, and practices.

A corollary of Dewey's naturalism is that one should see the human organism as a nexus of active powers that reach out into nature with intent and purpose. Once again, this perspective comes from Emerson. Dewey mentions that Emerson had written that "the individual man is only a method, a plan of arrangement."[20] Specifically, Emerson goes on to say that man is "a selecting principle, gathering his like to him, wherever he goes," much like "the lodestone amongst splinters of steel."[21] What Emerson meant was that, following Immanuel Kant, we should see the human being as active in *creating* her own experience rather than passively receiving sense impressions, as in John Locke. This presumption of outgoing energy is already implicit in Dewey's naturalism insofar as he always speaks of experience using active verbs, much as we would describe our ordinary experience in terms of things we *did* or objects we *encountered* rather than stimuli we registered with sense organs. This is what makes experience, he says, a "double-barreled word" that includes not only *what* exists but also *how* people "act and are acted upon, the ways in which they do and suffer, desire and enjoy, see, believe, imagine." For example, experience "denotes the planted field, the sowed seeds, the reaped harvests, the changes of night and day, spring and autumn, wet and dry, heat and cold, that are observed, feared, longed for; it also denotes the one who plants and reaps, who works and rejoices, hopes, fears, plans, invokes magic or chemistry to aid him, who is downcast or triumphant."[22] In short, we only know the planted field by *planting*, appreciate the changes of day and night by *observing*, and feel triumphant or downcast by *competing*.

The foundations for this active and explicitly experimental understanding of human action, perception, and experience was first expressed in one of Dewey's most important early works, his 1896 "The Reflex Arc Concept in Psychology." In this work, Dewey challenged the conventional dualistic understanding of human experience as a form of stimulus and response, in which an external object causes a sensation in the body, which is then followed by an idea in the mind, which then culminates in a reaction. In the familiar example of a child touching a candle flame, for instance, "the ordinary interpretation would say the sensation of light is a stimulus to the grasping as a response, the burn resulting is a stimulus to withdrawing the hand as response and so on." Dewey's revolutionary suggestion was to start instead with the act. In this way, "the real beginning is with the act of seeing; it is looking, and not a sensation of light." Once the origin point shifts, the entire experience transforms from one of a passive and mechanical stimulus and response into an active and experimental process of learning. The burn, rather than being something that initiates a pain response, actually becomes a "completion, or fulfillment, of the previous eye-arm-hand coordination." It is in this way that the child is able to "learn from experience and get the ability to avoid the experience in the future." Anticipating his language in *Experience and Nature* three decades later, he says that under this model, "the so-called response is not merely *to* the stimulus; it is *into* it. The burn is the original seeing, the original optical-ocular experience enlarged and transformed in its value."[23] In other words, the burn becomes a confirmation of what occurs after the act of reaching, which in turn followed an act of seeing and all the curiosity and imagination that went into that activity.

In his later work, Dewey would describe this consistent outgoing energy in terms of impulses and habits. Every aspect of our body, mind, and character can thus be defined not in terms of its reactive capacity to stimuli but in terms of the means actively used to fulfill some desire, aim, or yearning. For instance, he explains that "the eye hungers for light, the ear for sound, the hand for surfaces, the arm for things to reach, throw and lift, the leg for distance, anger for an enemy to destroy, curiosity for something to shiver and cower before, love for a mate." Friedrich Nietzsche caused an uproar by explaining all of these activities through something called "the will to power," but for Dewey, the will to power is a "name for a quality of all activity," in which we take *activity* to refer to any mental or physical action that "terminates in added control of conditions, in an art of administering objects." Activity thus means not only physical activities such as reaching for candle flames but emotional activities such as expressing love or mental activities such as performing a mathematical operation. In each case, there is "no generalized will to power, but only the inherent pressure of every activity for an adequate manifestation."[24] What caused such a controversy for Nietzsche was the implication that this will to power had a fixed and narrow end—namely, the domination and exploitation of others—but this reading is tainted by antinaturalist assumptions that separate our impulses from our ideals. For Dewey, the will to power represented the drive for every activity, impulse, habit, or emotion to find expression and achieve its consummation in whatever form it existed during its state of development. One can develop a will to love as well as a will to dominate, a will to create as well as a will to destroy. What matters is not the presence of will but its form and direction.

The task of the humanist teacher is to recognize the existence of these impulses and to form and direct them as the coherent and conscious powers of a creative individual, powers that Dewey called "habits," for habits are not thoughtless repetitive behaviors: "Habits are arts. They involve skill of sensory and motor organs, cunning or craft, and objective materials. They assimilate objective energies, and eventuate in command of environment."[25] Habits are therefore methodical ways of acting in response to certain problems or tasks that involve physical as well as mental processes. Thus "habit does not preclude the use of thought, but it determines the channels within which it operates. Thinking is secreted in the interstices of habits." It is in this conscious production of habits that we find the relationships among art, individuality, and character. By an "art," Dewey means a *technē*, a term that in the original Greek referred both to the desire to "command practices that were rational and a reason embodied in practice."[26] Art was not something distinct from science or craft but rather was any practice that adhered to a rationally derived method as opposed to those dictated by chance, impulsiveness, or fate. For instance, "the sailor, miner, fisherman and farmer think, but their thoughts fall within the framework of accustomed occupations and relationships."[27] And as demonstrated by Dewey's examples, these habits come to represent the individual character of a person: "Character means all the desires, purposes, and habits that influence conduct. The mind of an individual, his ideas and beliefs, are a part of character, for thought enters into the formation of desires and aims."[28] And since thought too is a habit, then our entire sense of individuality—which is to say, what makes us characteristically, rather than accidentally, both common with and distinct from other people—is determined by the conscious formation of habits.

But what makes naturalism uniquely *humanistic* is the recognition that human beings are distinct from other species by their unique capacity to use *language*. For Dewey, "language is a natural function of human association; and its consequences react upon other events, physical and human, giving them meaning or significance."[29] From a naturalistic standpoint, language is not something that is grafted upon or external to nature; it is a part of nature itself and a means by which we reach deeper into its essence. Dewey writes that "when Emerson said that he would almost rather know the true name, the poet's name, for a thing, than to know the thing itself, he presumably had this irradiating and illuminating function of language in mind. The delight that children take in demanding and learning the names of everything about them indicates that meanings are becoming concrete individuals to them, so that their commerce with things is passing from the physical to the intellectual plane."[30] It is this transformative power of language to recast mere events into objects, qualities, values, relations, and friends that made Dewey proclaim that "of all affairs, communication is most wonderful" and "a wonder by the side of which transubstantiation pales."[31] To transform bread into the body of Christ is certainly a miracle, but language performs millions of such miraculous transformations every day in ways both large and small, miracles that we take for granted because their existence is part of the quotidian wonder of being a symbol-using animal.[32]

Even more wondrous than its capacity to transform events into meanings, however, is the capacity for language to transform a solitary human being into a social individual. These two words, *social* and *individual*, are put together here in order to stress that they are two parts of a whole, much in the same way as experience and nature. Indeed, it is impossible to talk about a human individual apart from her social relations formed through language. Dewey proves this through a thought experiment: "Omit language and other means of inter-communication from the account, and no intellectual development of human beings, even in their differential or individual capacities, is conceivable. Think of any human adult in a concrete way, and at once you must place him in some 'social' context and functional relationship—parent, citizen, employer, wage-earner, farmer, merchant, teacher, lawyer, good citizen, criminal—and so on indefinitely."[33] One might conceivably think of a fictional character such as Mowgli from Rudyard Kipling's *The Jungle Book* as an exception to the rule, but he too had social relationships with animals established by language. And even Daniel Defoe's *Robinson Crusoe*, with the titular character stranded alone on an island, is not a counterexample, precisely because Crusoe "did not cease to be a social individual just because he was by himself on an island. He had his memories, his expectations, his experiences, which had come from his former association with other people." Consequently, although we can point to one organic human person as being completely isolated, one "cannot define *individuality* physically or externally. It is a matter of spirit, of soul, of mind, and the way in which one enters into cooperative relations with others."[34] To be an individual is to have intercommunication with others mediated through language *in* society but, at the same time, to stand *out* from society because of one's distinct, unique, and recognizable way of acting within those relations.

The larger point is that not only are these social relations established through language but also the learning of language is itself a social process.

There is no such thing as a private language—meaning a symbol system created and used only by a single individual. This common misunderstanding is produced by thinking of language only as a way of pointing at things and giving them names, such as pointing at a hat and making the sound "hat."[35] But for a child who didn't already understand English, the "the sound h-a-t would remain . . . a seemingly inarticulate grunt, if it were not uttered in connection with an action which is participated in by a number of people." Nor does the word *hat* become particularly meaningful when a parent says "hat" every time he puts it on a baby's head. The child learns the meaning of "hat" when she has an interest in using it and when "the thing and the sound are first employed in a joint activity, as a means of setting up an active connection between the child and a grown-up."[36] For instance, if a hat was always readily available for a child, she would never have a reason to learn its name; she would simply take it. However, as soon as the child requires the action of a parent to keep her head warm, she will learn the word in the context of a shared situation whose outcome is a desired action or practice. The word *hat* becomes not only a reference to an object; it becomes an act of communicating one's experience (and its accompanying emotions, desires, memories, contexts, and purposes) to another person. But to accomplish this task requires, in turn, "getting outside of it, seeing it as another would see it, considering what points of contact it has with the life of another so that it may be got into such form that he can appreciate its meaning."[37] Absent this social process of thinking from the perspective of another within a shared situation, communication is nothing more than an instinctual usage of sounds and gestures as is found in the animal world.

Lastly, an essential part of human nature is our capacity to extend our powers into nature using science and technology. Philosophers often point out, for instance, "that man might well be called *Homo Faber*. He is distinguished as the tool-making animal." But all too often, the focus falls on the use of tools *itself*, such as the evolution of a club into a stone ax into an iron ax into a chainsaw. In this way, human beings would be seen as advanced birds or primates, both of which make use of simple tools to serve specific functions. But modern human beings use tools very differently than animals and not because of the advanced nature of the tool. Tools do not develop in a sporadic and accidental manner based on trial and error; they are designed to control and direct natural forces that are understood in terms of mechanical relationships and determinate laws that are not guided by any fixed ends.[38] When human beings stopped worshiping nature as a spiritual entity and started to see it as a material resource, it led to "the substitution of one thing for another, to the conversion of one form of energy into another; to the effecting of transformations." In other words, homo faber developed alongside homo sapiens, technology alongside science, the result of which was power. Thus "when chemical fertilizers can be used in place of animal manures, when improved grain and cattle can be purposefully bred from inferior animals and grasses, when mechanical energy can be converted into heat and electricity into mechanical energy, man gains power to manipulate nature."[39] To be human, in other words, is to be able to develop new ways of controlling nature by combining the fruits of the mind, developed through language and communication, with the work of the body, extended and amplified by technology.

Indeed, Dewey actually integrates the meaning of science within the definition of technology. For him, "'technology' signifies all the intelligent techniques by which the energies of nature and man are directed and used in satisfaction of human needs; it cannot be limited to a few outer and comparatively mechanical forms." This definition is consistent with his pragmatism. Insofar as we look at both tools and ideas as instrumental, they will both prove their value in practice. That includes obvious forms of practice and technological development, such as "the engineering arts that have produced the railway, steamship, automobile, and airplane, the telegraph, telephone, and radio, and the printing press." But these practices also include methods, ideas, and relations. Thus technological development "also includes new procedures in medicine and hygiene, the function of insurance in all its branches, and, in its potentiality if not actualization, radically new methods in education and other modes of human relationship." Today, we might divide these practices into the natural sciences and the human sciences, but for Dewey, they are both forms of technology insofar as they are designed to direct energies and satisfy human needs through conscious organization and manipulation of intellectual and physical resources. To be a homo faber is not simply to be one who wields an ax; she might also be one who investigates the stars, manages a corporation, leads a political party, advances a moral theory, or develops a vaccine.[40]

If the technological capabilities of homo faber are obvious to everyone, the implications for our understanding of human nature might not be. It is all too common, for instance, to recognize the power and influence of technology on the one hand and to completely separate it from what it means to be authentically human on the other. At any period of historical development, there always appears "the belief, sedulously propagated by some who pride themselves on superior taste, that the machine is itself the source of our troubles." This belief is then usually the critical expression of an underlying antinaturalism that sees the machine as the manifestation of the "reduction of all distinctive human values, moral, esthetic, logical, the blind mechanical conjunctions and material entities—a reduction which is in effect their complete destruction."[41] As we have already seen, sometimes this results in a retreat toward some spiritual or aesthetic "Humanism" that purports to reject all science and technology in praise of that which is truly human; other times it results in a grotesque fascism that in one breath condemns the decadence of the machine age while in the other breath urging the harnessing of technological power to forcibly restore some lost glory to the human spirit. Either way, one finds in the back of all these movements a sense that the technological capacities of homo faber are somehow a distortion, rather than an expression, of human nature.

For Dewey, however, this position *denies* rather than *affirms* human nature. Human beings are born with extraordinary capacities not only of action but of intelligence and perception. These powers are given by nature and are thus as natural and innate as any "soul" or "spirit." For Dewey, "it seems both intellectually petty and morally ungracious to feel contempt for the matrix of our being and the inescapable conditions of our lives." Antinaturalism is thus a form of self-hatred.[42] By contrast, naturalism accepts that both science and technology represent "the extension of our natural organs of approach to nature. And I do not mean merely an extension in quantitative range and penetration, as a microscope multiplies the capacities of the unaided eye, but an extension of insight and understanding through bringing relationships and interactions into view."[43] For Dewey, science is an extension of the organ of the mind just as machines are extensions of the organs of the body and the sensory organs. Both of these extensions represent technology, which in turn functions as an extension of the powers, impulses, and capacities of human beings *in* nature and *in* society.[44] Put simply, as human beings develop the technological means of extending themselves into the natural and social world for the sake of power, they also alter the capacities of human nature itself.

When it comes to the art of individuality, these four characteristics of human nature—naturalism, power, language, and technology—lead us to the conclusion that achieving individuality requires the cultivation, through conscious art, of the social attitudes, habits, and practices that direct the expression of power through the technologies that give to individuals the freedom to articulate ends and choose the means to their realization. In a roundabout way, this is what Dewey meant when he closed *Individualism Old and New* with Emerson's call to "find beauty and holiness in new and necessary facts, in the field and roadside, in the shop and mill."[45] This was a passage from the closing paragraph of the final chapter, "Art," of Emerson's first *Essays*. There, Emerson had called for a new poetry that would not retreat from technological modernity or find solace in the beautiful, as opposed to the useful, arts in the belief that the useful can never be anything other than profane. Dewey's call for a new kind of individualism is consistent with Emerson's call to reject the dualism between the useful and the beautiful such that all our creative powers can be turned to finding ways to make technology serve the beautiful and the holy, for as Emerson says, as soon as we establish this dualism, we in effect condemn ourselves to a technology that serves only mercenary impulses while imprisoning the beautiful within the sphere of the useless.

A thoroughgoing naturalism accepts, rather than denies, that individuals are constituted through their transactions with their environment, which includes both natural and social relations mediated through our tools and technologies. As seen by the persistence of conceptions of rugged individualism, even today, our culture remains entranced by the fantasy that the modern citizen is a hero of the old West with the benefits of electrical and digital technology. But the fact is that the "United States has steadily moved from an earlier pioneer individualism to a condition of dominant corporateness." By the term *corporate*, of course, Dewey does not mean a condition of belonging to a multinational corporation; he means "the tendency to combination in all phases of life," in which "associations tightly or loosely organized more and more define the opportunities, the choices and the actions of individuals."[46] These organizations, in turn, are produced not by social relations but by the influence of technology. In 1929, Dewey mentioned the influence of "the radio, the railway, telephone, telegraph, the flying machine and mass production, changing the United States from an agrarian and rural population to a city and industrial one."[47] Today, any number of newer technologies might be used to discuss the development of a national to a global economy and from a national to an international political association. Dewey's point is that our technologies—in particular, transportation and communication technologies—develop new forms of multilayered "corporate" social relationships that can be neither understood nor directed without a new definition of individuality that corresponds with the changes. That is why "the problem of constructing a new individuality consonant with the objective conditions under which we live is the deepest problem of our times." What we require is a vision of individualism in which "equality and freedom [are] expressed not merely externally and politically but through personal participation in the development of a shared culture."[48] That was true in 1930 and remains so in the twenty-first century.

The practical implications that follow from Dewey's conception of individuality as a work of art can be seen most clearly in its application in Dewey's educational philosophy, for which he is most widely known. For Dewey, "the ultimate aim of education is nothing other than the creation of human beings in the fullness of their capacities. Through the making of human beings, of men and women generous in aspiration, liberal in thought, cultivated in taste, and equipped with knowledge and competent method, society itself is constantly remade, and with this remaking the world itself is re-created."[49] Education for the democratic humanist is not stamping out a "mold" of the individual in conformity to some predetermined utopian vision or ultimate destiny, the result of which is as predictable as it is common: "Originality is gradually destroyed, confidence in one's own quality of mental operation is undermined, and a docile subjection to the opinion of others is inculcated, or else ideas run wild." In contradistinction, the democratic humanist seeks to teach others the arts that will help them become individuals with the power to adapt to changing circumstances, through thought and action, in a world constantly in the making. To be an "individual" thus has two meanings for Dewey: "In the first place, one is mentally an individual only as he has his own purpose and problem, and does his own thinking. . . . Only by a pupil's own observations, reflections, framing and testing of suggestions can what he already knows be amplified and rectified. . . . In the second place, there are variations of point of view, of appeal of objects, and of mode of attack, from person to person."[50] The goal of the educator is thus to create an individual that, following Dewey's humanism, can identify her own purposes and problems in experience, think for herself using the tools of language developed in society, and develop her own point of view and mode of attack by expressing power through available means and technologies.

But as Dewey saw in the collective actions of women in Chicago, this commitment to individuality does not work in opposition to society and to the shared needs of a community, a city, state, or nation. In fact, the art of individuality takes as a starting point the fact that we are bound together in social relations as never before; it also accepts as a moral principle that achieving genuine individuality requires creating a society in which all are free and empowered to work together rather than against one another. The tragic coda to this appeal is that Dewey's son Morris would never have the opportunity to achieve the potential that his father saw in him as a young boy—to become that work of art that his father could admire. On a trip to Europe in 1894, in which Dewey hoped to give his son the worldly experience to enrich the horizons of his imagination, Morris became sick with diphtheria and died in Italy at the age of two. His death devastated his father, but it did nothing to diminish his democratic commitments, for Morris was a victim of another failure of collective intelligence—in this case, the common struggle against disease—that resulted in cutting short another life of possibility. For the democratic humanist, it is not enough to praise individualism in the abstract; it requires attentive care to make the achievement of individuality a reality. No empty praise of ideals will accomplish this goal; its attainment requires a shared commitment to the development of the arts that give human beings the real power to craft their own individual characters alongside others in a shared environment marked by both permanence and change.

5

RENASCENT LIBERALISM

A cooperative economic and social order is the only kind of order in which there will be a genuine possibility for equality among human beings irrespective of race, color and creed, and of the other things which are now played upon to divide people in order that a few may have a monopoly of privilege, power, and influence.
—JOHN DEWEY, "ADDRESS TO THE NATIONAL ASSOCIATION FOR THE ADVANCEMENT OF COLORED PEOPLE"

On May 19, 1932, Dewey stood up in the auditorium of the Shiloh Baptist Church in Washington, DC, to address the twenty-third meeting of the National Association for the Advancement of Colored People (NAACP) in the midst of the Great Depression. Yet he came neither to lament the widespread suffering of people in the country nor to point out the unique ways that African Americans were targeted for oppression beyond acknowledging it as an undeniable fact. Rather, his purpose was to encourage his audience to see the new possibilities for political action opened up by the economic collapse, "a collapse which has demonstrated the falsity of the political and economic philosophy upon which we have been feeding." Dewey tells the story, for instance, of how he "met an engineer, a leader in his profession, a few weeks ago and he said, 'do you know I have only begun to think since 1932.'" Although the man had certainly thought a great deal about problems of engineering, he had never considered "the relation of his work, that of the engineering profession, to the whole social and economic construction before that collapse of 1929 in the way he has to do now."[1] The crisis of the Great Depression had shattered the wall that separated his comfortable life from the rest of the world and had forced him to realize the degree to which his own interests were interconnected with individuals and with publics that he had never before considered. It was this collective impulse to think—in particular, to think of one's common interests with different others—that Dewey believed opened up opportunities for political action and reform.

Two things stand out in Dewey's NAACP address that characterize his political writings in the 1930s and 1940s. The first is his sweeping condemnation of the two established parties in the United States. Although Dewey always considered himself a defender of liberalism, his liberalism had a distinctly social character that was at odds with the narrow economic liberalism that dominated both the Democratic and Republican establishments, despite slightly different coloring and emphases. For Dewey, "the real political issues of the day are economic, industrial and financial, and both of the old parties are engaged in the game of hide-and-seek, hiding their own attitude from the masses of the people; and seeking constantly favors and campaign contributions and the backing of the business and financial institutions that really control our public life." The fact that the average vote in national elections was usually less than half of the electorate was indicative of "an underlying instinct that under the existing conditions it is just the difference between tweedle-dee and tweedle-dum which of the two old parties gets into power." Their constant strategy was to promise this or that group that they will be given, in exchange for support, "a back seat somewhere near the trough, a little nearer than the other party would let you have."[2] By constantly dividing the electorate into competitive groups fighting for scraps, the large business interests are effectively able to retain power while championing the virtues of rugged individualism.

If the first thing that stood out in Dewey's address was his contempt for the American party apparatus, the second thing was his radicalism, for in emphasizing the importance of thinking to his political vision, he also emphasized the need for training in rhetorical expression and advocacy. For him, "this compulsion to think more fundamentally has also the advantage of bringing with it a greater freedom not merely of thought but of expression. In that way it gives the minority, the oppressed, groups of this country a better opportunity to express themselves, their needs, their wrongs, their demands for greater freedom, a larger opportunity and a wider field than they have done in the past." Furthermore, the stimulation to thinking as expressed in public discussion, argumentation, and persuasion made possible the organization of a new broad-based constituency, for "the depression has also disclosed a community of interest among all the minority, repressed and oppressed groups in the country." Lastly, and most radically, Dewey suggested there was only one possible platform that would satisfy the complex demands of this constituency—the demand for intelligent social planning.

For him, "in the degree in which all the minority groups cut loose completely from both of the old parties and join in some new party which will help bring about a social and economic reconstruction in the interest of a society which is cooperative and human, in that degree the day of economic slavery for the masses in this country will come to an end."[3] The politics of a new political party would thus be committed to a social organization that rejects the competition of all against all in favor of one that supports cooperation and the use of intelligent social planning to allow all people to have the resources to construct a flourishing individuality.

Dewey would come to call this new politics "renascent liberalism." This name represented an effort to fulfill the promise of the meaning of the term *liberal*. For him, "to be liberal is all one with being liberating, with effecting a release of human powers."[4] Unfortunately, this original meaning had been lost as it took on primarily an economic interpretation that celebrated the competitive and unrestricted pursuit of individual or corporate wealth. But Dewey believed that the "values of freed intelligence, of liberty, of opportunity for every individual to realize the potentialities of which he is possessed, are too precious to be sacrificed to a régime of despotism, especially when the régime is in such large measure merely the agent of a dominant economic class in its struggle to keep and extend the gains it has amassed at the expense of genuine social order, unity, and development." Although the racism suffered by African Americans in the 1930s was not entirely the product of economic motives, the ideology of liberalism inherited from the eighteenth century nonetheless provided the rationalization for their oppression while hindering their ability to organize among themselves and with other publics for the purpose of organizing a new social order. A new liberalism was needed that encouraged organized social planning that would be "put into effect for the creation of an order in which industry and finance are socially directed in behalf of institutions that provide the material basis for the cultural liberation and growth of individuals."[5] Dewey thus saw the values of renascent liberalism as the civic extension of the ideals of democratic humanism and the corrective to the outdated ideology of laissez-faire liberalism. And in doing so, it provides us today the political end-in-view by which an education in democratic humanism is guided.

Pedagogically, the civic emphasis of Dewey's renascent liberalism challenges romantic approaches that tend to retreat to the safety of an uncritical self-expression that leaves students at the end basically where they started. According to educational theorist Henry Giroux, such approaches continue to proliferate today, despite the fact that teaching in such classrooms collapses "into a banal notion of facilitation, and student experience becomes an unproblematic vehicle for self-affirmation and self-consciousness." The attraction of these types of expressivist classrooms is that they heed Paulo Freire's call for dialogue and exchange; to this extent, they have the merit of offering students the opportunity to have their voices heard. The drawback, however, is that they lack the political awareness and critical energy inherent in Freire's pedagogy. As Giroux points out, "In this version of critical pedagogy, there is a flight from authority in a narrow definition of politics that abandons the utopian project of educating students to both locate themselves in their particular histories and simultaneously confront the limits of their own perspectives as part of a broader engagement with democratic public life." As a corrective to this limited interpretation of humanism, Giroux advocates for what he called a "border pedagogy" that intentionally confronts and crosses the many forms of borders that define and maintain differences, hierarchies, and power. In border pedagogy, "students cross over into borders of meaning, maps of knowledge, social relations, and values that are increasingly being negotiated and rewritten as the codes and regulations which *organize* them become destabilized and reshaped."[6] In other words, border pedagogy stresses the *democratic* in the teaching of democratic humanism and in doing so helps bring out in Dewey's work a political commitment to educating engaged citizens.

The border pedagogy of Giroux provides a road map for teaching in a way consistent with Dewey's democratic values. At the basis of border pedagogy is the assumption that all cultures and societies regulate themselves by the enforcement of codes, both formal and informal, that divide a population into discrete groups, each with their own narratives, histories, rules, and disciplinary practices. These codes represent borders, both physical and cultural. These borders are "historically constructed and socially organized within maps of rules and regulations that limit and enable particular identities, individual capacities, and social forms." To teach a border pedagogy, therefore, is to help each student define himself as what Giroux calls a "border-crosser, as a person moving in and out of borders constructed around coordinates of difference and power."[7] In practical terms, this means intentionally finding those texts, individuals, and events in history in which borders are constituted, called into question, and overturned, thus revealing the essential conflict at the root of any human drama. Such teaching does not simply retrace events in chronological time or speak in terms of abstract forces, qualities, or tendencies; it is "directed more towards specificity and struggle, it resurrects the legacies of actions and happenings, it points to the multitude of voices that constitute the struggle over history and power."[8] For border pedagogy, it is therefore not only what is *within* these constituted borders that matters, as important as that subject matter might be; it is rather the *process* of border creation and transgression that matters.

Importantly, border pedagogy is not just a critical exercise in disrupting cultural codes; it crosses borders in order to give students the freedom to start building new and more expansive, sympathetic, and intelligent publics. Giroux calls this type of constructive practice an exercise in "counter-memory." If a culture's memory represents the inheritance of a traditional set of codes, a countermemory "represents a critical reading of not only how the past informs the present but how the present reads the past.... It represents an attempt to rewrite the language of resistance in terms that connect human beings within forms of remembrance that dignify public life while at the same time allowing people to speak from their own particular histories and voices."[9] Countermemory thus brings together a humanistic concern for student experience with a democratic emphasis on cultural narratives and their role in constituting collective public agency. Students are thus encouraged to find those points in their own experiences in which they have encountered these borders; to investigate their origin, structure, and effects; and finally, to "recover communities of memory and narratives of struggle that provide a sense of location, place, and identity to various dominant and subordinate groups."[10] The aim of these pedagogical practices is neither to celebrate nor to undermine existing borders; it is rather to cultivate a sense of curiosity, creativity, and collective possibility. When students are able to see themselves as agents in history, they begin the process of linking their own experiences to those of others and, out of that communication, to develop a more expansive intelligence. Democracy represents the political culture in which that intelligence can be put into practice.

If Dewey could point to a single event that relegated the old individualism to obsolescence and condemned the old political order to irrelevance, it was the detonation of the atomic bombs over the skies of Hiroshima and Nagasaki. Before the war, one could still revel in the fantasies of rugged individualism and wax nostalgic for the pioneer conditions of the American West as they were unfolded on movie screens and in paperback novels. Or, with a more sophisticated veneer of realpolitik, one might still talk about "oldtime diplomacy, power blocs and power politics" as if one was conspiring with a Machiavellian prince for control of the Romagna. But with the invention of a weapon that could destroy an entire city in a single event with a single order by a single individual, such concepts became "about as outworn and impotent as the oldtime muzzle-loading gun."[11] The clear fact was that after the splitting of the atom, "no intelligent person can henceforth fail to note that the physical science and the industrial technology of our time are out of gear with the heritage of moral values and aims by which we belatedly profess to live."[12] The splitting of the atom, in other words, called attention to the much more enduring split between the spiritual and material, the ideal and the actual, and the moral and the technological that makes for a politics that combines impractical idealism with amoral materialism. In sum, if anything became clear after the war for Dewey, it was "the fact that if the atomic splitting by science and its technological application in the bomb fail to teach us that we live in a world of change so that our ways of organization of human interrelationships must also change, the case is well-nigh hopeless."[13]

It was not only the sheer destructiveness of the weapon that Dewey found so tragic; it was what this destructiveness highlighted about our current politics. For him, "the tragedy of our time is that every person on earth actually belongs to a world unit without being a member of world-society." In other words, technology has bound us together into a network of causal relationships without developing corresponding political institutions to regulate them. Nothing brought that home with greater impact than the war and its aftermath. Although it affected every single person on earth, at the same time, it made every one of those people feel impotent to make any changes because of the lack of coherent political institutions through which to operate. For Dewey, this was the road to anarchy. As Dewey explained, "A world whose parts are intimately tied together, but which has no means of keeping those parts from clashing, is actually anarchy. This condition of world anarchy is displayed most strikingly in the perpetual threat of global war. But this threat is only one of the symptoms and evidences of a world-chaos due to lack of common rule of law and of the machinery necessary to bring about social adjustments in a peaceful way." What was clear to Dewey in the wake of the atomic bomb was that "the unutterable seriousness of the physical, industrial, cultural, moral destructiveness of war must be met and countered by equally serious constructive effort. The extensive range of combat must evoke, if civilization is not to go down in ruin, an even greater manifestation of cooperative goodwill."[14] This was the only way in which the human species would not find in its culmination of its idealism the seeds of its own destruction.

Yet the Second World War also demonstrated a further tragedy, which was that the political ideologies developed to confront the problem of modernity were directly responsible for bringing it to its suicidal conclusion. Exploiting the failure of laissez-faire conceptions of democracy to deal with the challenges of the modern age, "the military assaults of Japan, Italy, and Germany and their satellites was attended and supported by the ever repeated charge that the democratic ideal had outlived its usefulness, and that new and different order was urgently required."[15] This order came to be known as fascism. The establishment of this order was fairly straightforward—espouse the highest "humanistic" ideals while harnessing every technological means to manufacture a facile public opinion and discipline a mass populace to serve the ends of the machinery of an authoritarian state. Thus their method consisted of, in the first place, "filling the air with certain notions every minute of the day and suppressing the expression of every inquiry, opinion and belief that might in any way compete." And then in the second place, the method called for using this propaganda to spread the ideology of fascist antihumanism based on the assumption that allowing the masses freedom of mind would lead inevitably to conflict, division, and disintegration.[16] All this is made possible, in turn, by advances in scientific and technological power that have given oppressive governments far more, rather than less, instruments of domination than they have given ordinary citizens the means to freedom; they have "put at the disposal of dictators means of controlling opinion and sentiment of a potency which reduces to a mere shadow all previous agencies at the command of despotic rulers."[17] In other words, fascism responded to the problem of the growing interconnectedness of the global population by dreaming of total global domination by an elite cadre of authoritarian dictators wielding the latest technology in the name of achieving racial and ethnic superiority.

The detonation of the atomic bomb may have cemented the military victory over the totalitarian powers of the Axis, but it did not address the more fundamental question that still lingered after the war: "Namely, what is the centre and the foundation of the democratic idea and policies?"[18] One could not return to the status quo as existed before the war, which would be to "return to subjection to the alleged authority of representatives of the dogmas and institutions which embody and perpetuate the divisions from which we suffer." Rather, the atomic bomb demonstrated that first and foremost we must commit ourselves to making sure that the application of scientific and technological innovations "will operate within, not just outside of and against, the moral values and concerns of humanity." Reverting to a laissez-faire rugged individualism, which relegates morality to the private sphere while allowing private capital to accumulate and wield technological power for the sake of maximizing profit, would be to sow the seeds for a return of an even more suffocating totalitarianism that would only be a prelude to global collapse. Rather, "it is the business of modern man to use every effort to see to it that the immense technological resources now at our command are not limited in use to aims which are degraded in advance as merely material or utilitarian in some low sense, but are systematically employed in behalf of human—that is, common and widespread—security and well-being."[19] Dewey called the form of social life most capable of securing these good "democracy."

But what is the nature of democracy? To answer this question, Dewey often found himself returning to one of his heroes, Thomas Jefferson. In his 1946 essay "What Is Democracy?," he pointed out with some pride that in our "Bill of Rights inserted there by the efforts of our first great and typical Democrat, Thomas Jefferson, is a guarantee of freedom of speech, writing, publication, and assembly for discussion, with respect to all public issues." It was this fact that gave him historical ground to claim "freedom of intelligence in public communication by means of speech, publication in daily and weekly press, in books, in public assemblies, in scientific inquiry, as the centre and burning focus of democracy."[20] But Jefferson provided Dewey more than just a means to celebrate free speech as the core of the democratic way of life. In *Freedom and Culture*, Jefferson also provided the three fundamental principles that established democracy less as a system of government and more as an attitude toward history.[21] First, democratic governments must adapt to historical circumstances. Second, democratic power grows out of a sense of community. Third, democratic tradition is guided by the morality of individual happiness. For Dewey, these principles were most eloquently expressed by Jefferson and continue to define what it means to be democratic.

The first principle establishes democracy not as a fixed structure of government but as a changing pragmatic relationship between a public and the state. Dewey quotes Jefferson: "I know that laws and institutions must go hand in hand with the progress of the human mind. . . . As new discoveries are made, new truths disclosed, and manners and opinions change with the change of circumstances, institutions must change also and keep pace with the times."[22] Within this quote are three interconnected assumptions. First, it assumes that human nature is adaptive and potentially progressive rather than fixed and static. Second, it assumes that history itself is constantly in the state of becoming, creating new circumstances to which a changeable human nature must adapt. Lastly, it assumes that the role of laws and institutions is to mediate between human nature and an environment by creating new paths of more productive collective action. The practical consequences of these assumptions are both negative and positive. Negatively, democracy calls into question "the idolatry of the Constitution" as a document that has been set in stone and forever must remain a constraint on human action and innovation. Positively, it means that citizens have a right to criticize their structure of government and propose modifications and changes as circumstances and needs demand. Thus "as believers in democracy we have not only the right but the duty to question existing mechanisms of, say, suffrage and to inquire whether some functional organization might not serve to formulate and manifest public opinion better than the existing methods."[23] Democracy, in short, must be constantly remade by its citizens to adapt to changing historical conditions.

The second principle of democracy roots its practice in the overlapping coordination of local communities and larger publics. Dewey cites the precedent for this position in Jefferson's theoretical writings in which "chief importance is attached to local self-governing units on something like the New England town meeting plan." This includes Jefferson's unrealized project "for general political organization on the basis of small units, small enough so that all its members could have direct communication with one another and take care of all community affairs." Of course, Dewey was well aware that Jefferson's initial conception has long been rendered obsolete by the machine age. On the one hand, in *The Public and Its Problems*, Dewey had written that "democracy must begin at home, and its home is the neighborly community."[24] But on the other hand, he fully acknowledged in *Freedom and Culture* that "on account of the vast extension of the field of association, produced by elimination of distance and lengthening of temporal spans, it is obvious that social agencies, political and non-political, cannot be confined to localities." What was Dewey calling for? His call was for a new definition of locality that integrated the power of transportation and communication technology to create a sense of community on a more diffuse and broader scale. As people establish common interests in affairs outside of the locality (for instance, in environmental preservation, travel, social justice, athletics, tourism, and the like), communities and localities "having a functional basis will probably have to replace those based on physical contiguity." Through long-distance communication and periodic organized meetings, a sense of functional community can be created to replace the lost contiguous community. This effort "involves development of local agencies of communication and cooperation, creating stable loyal attachments, to militate against the centrifugal forces of present culture, while at the same time they are of a kind to respond flexibly to the demands of the larger unseen and indefinite public."[25] If this seemed an impossibly utopian project in 1939, it appears as a restatement of common sense after the development of interactive digital technologies at the turn of the twentieth century.

Lastly, the third principle of democracy rejects its subordination to the economic rationality of capitalism and instead ties it to a moral conception of individual development. Dewey thus emphasizes the radical nature of Jefferson's replacement of Locke's right to property in the Declaration of Independence with the right to the "pursuit of happiness." This statement was no mere celebration of hedonism; it was a recognition that "property rights are created by the 'social pact' instead of representing inherent individual moral claims which government is morally bound to maintain."[26] It was, in other words, a claim that property is but a means to a moral and social end that in itself cannot be held superior to other human rights and values. Furthermore, by "happiness," he did not simply mean physical pleasure; he meant the "liberation of the values of intellectual, esthetic and companionship life"—the development of a whole person.[27] As Dewey explains, "The right to pursue happiness stood with Jefferson for nothing less than the claim of every human being to choose his own career and to act upon his own choice and judgment free from restraints and constraints imposed by the arbitrary will of other human beings—whether these others are officials of government, of whom Jefferson was especially afraid, or are persons whose command of capital and control of the opportunities for engaging in useful work limits the ability of others to 'pursue happiness.'"[28] The key to interpreting the moral significance of Jefferson's appeal to "happiness," therefore, is not to revert to an economic interpretation that associates happiness with the uninhibited accumulation of property at the expense of the imposed misery and enforced labor of another. Jefferson's own practice as a slave owner, of course, flew in the face of this principle, yet despite his own personal hypocrisy, the universal validity of the principle—and the eloquence by which he expressed it—remains.

Yet if we are looking for a comprehensive definition of democracy, these three principles add up to a single commitment to one thing—communication. From Jefferson, Dewey articulated a vision of democracy that was pragmatic, local, and moral—pragmatic because it continually experimented with different forms of the state to adapt to changing circumstances and human nature, local because its values and policies grew out of the needs of interlocking community interests, and moral because it took as its overarching mission a development of individual capacities. From this perspective, democracy represents a commitment to "plural, partial, and experimental methods in securing and maintaining an ever-increasing release of the powers of human nature, in service of a freedom which is cooperative and a cooperation which is voluntary." But looked at more closely, all these elements are communicative. Developing shared interest in the community, being able to express one's sense of individuality within a society, and engaging in criticism and reform of the institutions of state are all communicative activities that go on *within*, not *outside* of, our institutions and attitudes. Consequently, Dewey concludes that democracy can never be achieved by merely mechanical adjustments to a system: "It can be won only by extending the application of democratic methods, methods of consultation, persuasion, negotiation, communication, cooperative intelligence, in the task of making our own politics, industry, education, our culture generally, a servant and an evolving manifestation of democratic ideas."[29] Democracy as a way of life may entail things like voting, serving on juries, or running for office, but all these things might also exist as empty formalities in a totalitarian state; only when all these activities occur within a free culture of communication does a democracy exist.

It is with this democratic commitment in mind that Dewey developed a political philosophy of renascent liberalism that might translate the values of democratic humanism more directly into the foundations of actual political practice. This is not to say that Dewey's renascent liberalism outlined any specific blueprint to be followed. Consistent with democratic ideals, he rejected the notion that any political philosophy—no matter the aims toward which it aspired—could design institutions that would be adapted for all circumstances and all times. But he did believe that certain methods, approaches, and attitudes had lasting value in guiding judgments concerning the structure of the state and its policies. Dewey chose to call his political philosophy "liberalism" in order to recover the original reformist spirit of eighteenth-century liberalism that found its highest expression in the writings of Thomas Jefferson. For Dewey, the many accomplishments of early liberalism proved that it "can be a power in bringing about radical social changes:—provided it combine capacity for bold and comprehensive social invention with detailed study of particulars and with courage in action."[30] However, he added the modifier "renascent" in recognition of the failure of old liberalism to adapt to changing circumstances and the need for a new, modified, and more thoroughgoing liberalism to give new meaning to its values consonant with the changes brought about by the machine age.

The transformation at the heart of renascent liberalism is a shift from a critical to a constructive philosophy. When it was originally conceived, for instance, liberalism was developed as a weapon of attack against the dying *ancien régime* with its suffocating hierarchy and traditionalism. With the rise of a new, mobile, educated middle class challenging the old propertied aristocracy, liberalism naturally developed an emancipatory philosophy that celebrated the rights of the individual, which are intrinsically opposed to state control. The Enlightenment individual, born with innate rights, reason, conscience, and powers, was thus not a result of some "impartial inquiry into human nature. It was rather a political weapon devised in the interest of breaking down the rigidity of dogmas and of institutions that had lost their relevancy." However, while "the doctrine was potent in exposure of abuses; it was weak for constructive purposes."[31] This weakness became readily apparent once the power of the old feudal state was replaced with the power of the new industrial order. The old liberals, including Jefferson, had "no glimpse of the fact that private control of the new forces of production, forces which affect the life of everyone, would operate in the same way as private unchecked control of political power."[32] The revolutionary individualism that had found its expression in the Declaration of Independence thus became an ideological rationalization for the inequalities of the emerging industrial capitalism.

A renascent liberalism would thus return to its original values but reinterpret them with the awareness that true emancipation requires constructive and positive policies that actively support the growth of authentic individuality. For Dewey, "these values are liberty, the development of the inherent capacities of individuals made possible through liberty, and the central role of free intelligence in inquiry, discussion and expression." In each case, Dewey takes a term originally designated as an innate right of an individual granted simply by being born and reinterprets it as a shared social value that we must actively seek to promote through every avenue of our culture. In renascent liberalism, the problem is not only to criticize oppressive state actions and give individuals the negative freedom that comes from their removal, although that remains a central component of liberalism; rather, "the problem of democracy becomes the problem of that form of social organization, extending to all the areas and ways of living, in which the powers of individuals shall not be merely released from mechanical external constraint but shall be fed, sustained and directed."[33] A renascent liberalism thus challenges the calcified tenets of the old liberalism (which over time became the laissez-faire ideology of the new economic conservatism) and encourages a new set of attitudes and methods by which to meet the challenges of our time.

In renascent liberalism, liberty is defined not only in terms of individual "rights" but also in terms of the expression of individual power. To be sure, the legal liberties in the form of the rights established by early liberalism must be preserved, for no liberty is possible under a totalitarian regime. However, merely legal liberty without what Dewey calls the "effective liberty of thought and action" is an empty shell. What Dewey means by "effective liberty" is the capacity to conceive, pursue, and accomplish individual aims within existing social conditions. In the first place, "liberty is not just an idea, an abstract principle. It is power, effective power to do specific things." Consequently, "the demand for liberty is a demand for power, either for possession of powers of action not already possessed or for retention and expansion of powers already possessed." But this power is not the possession of an *individual* either. Individuals may acquire an exceptional intelligence, a powerful physique, or extraordinary skills, but if they are prevented from expressing them in society—perhaps because of their gender, race, religion, or class—then they do not possess *effective* liberty. Therefore, "in the second place, the possession of the effective power is always a matter of the *distribution* of power that exists at the time." Power is therefore a *relational* concept, particularly as it relates to power in society. Just as there is "no such thing physically as manifestation of energy or effective power by one thing except in relation to the energy manifested by other things," so too "there is no such thing as the liberty or effective power of an individual, group, or class, except in relation to the liberties, the effective powers, of *other* individuals, groups, and classes."[34] Far from being an individual right, liberty is actually a product of a complex system of social relationships.

What this means is that under renascent liberalism, the achievement of effective liberty for more than just a tiny minority of the population requires the active and constructive modification of the distribution of power in society. The issue is not, as promoted by the various manifestations of the Liberty League, a zero-sum battle of "liberty versus restraint and regimentation." Such a framing ignores the fact that the "liberty" that exists currently is itself a product of a system of social control—namely, one in which liberty "is exercised by the few who have economic power, at the expense of the liberties of the many and at the cost of increasing disorder." Rather, the liberty of renascent liberalism represents a commitment to achieve "a more equal and equitable balance of powers that will enhance and multiply the effective liberties of the mass of individuals."[35] But Dewey is not only speaking of a new distribution of *economic* power, as in classical Marxism; he means a distribution of power throughout *culture*, by which he means "a state of interaction of many factors, the chief of which are law and politics, industry and commerce, science and technology, the arts of expression and communication, and of morals."[36] In renascent liberalism, effective liberty is not restricted to the power to accumulate wealth; it is also associated with the power to express oneself creatively, to live a moral life, to pursue science and innovation, and to argue and debate about a shared political future.

Reinterpreting "liberty" as the capacity to effectively develop and express power lies behind his critique of rugged individualism and his concept of individuality as a work of art. As we have already seen, early liberalism posited the existence of an autonomous "rugged" individual primarily as a rhetorical premise to undermine the collapsing feudal order that still thought in terms of fixed classes and estates; the idea of an individual who was born bearing not only rights but innate powers was their way of ensuring that order rather than chaos would follow from what amounted to bourgeois revolutions. Rather than admit that individuals still required support from the larger culture or society, "social arrangements were treated not as positive forces but as external limitations." Of course, the effect of this argument by the nineteenth century was to further empower a class already empowered—namely, the rising merchant and professional middle classes—while leaving the rest to trade the forced slavery of feudal serfdom for the voluntary slavery of factory labor. But this sort of "individualism" exists in name only when just a few can actually attain effective liberty while masses remain in the state of dependence. For Dewey, "liberalism that takes its profession of the importance of individuality with sincerity must be deeply concerned about the structure of human association."[37] But this is another way of saying that individuality develops through the same cultural and social nexus as effective liberty; it only stresses that democracy allows individuals to pursue their own definitions of effective liberty rather than adhere to a single, fixed notion determined by a class or nation.

Most important of the three values of renascent liberalism, however, is that of intelligence. That intelligence was one of the original values of liberalism is perhaps most evident in the characters of its original representatives, keen intellects such as John Locke, David Hume, Adam Smith, Jeremy Bentham, and John Stuart Mill. These were men, Dewey observes, who were "animated by a strikingly unselfish spirit, in contrast with their professed theories." Although their theories gained traction because they "coincided with the interests of the class that was constantly rising in prestige and power," their own personal detachment from the profit motive "enabled them to detect and make articulate the nascent movements of their time—a function that defines the genuine work of the intellectual class at any period."[38] For the early liberals, intelligence was particularly important in exposing abuses, criticizing dogmas, and disrupting the traditions that kept the mind and the body in chains. It was, in fact, their recognition of the emancipatory power of intelligence when given voice in a public sphere that accounted for "their valiant battle in behalf of freedom of thought, conscience, expression and communication."[39] The Enlightenment celebration of public reason was the culmination of the early liberal commitment to the role of critical intelligence in society.[40]

However, whereas earlier liberalism restricted intelligence to the operation of the entrepreneurial individual, renascent liberalism advances a specifically communicative and cooperative form of intelligence directed toward managing shared problems through social planning. This kind of intelligence would be both scientific and democratic. It would be scientific insofar as it would be committed to an empirical, experimental, and coordinated method of inquiry in which "thought would be connected with the possibility of action, and every mode of action would be reviewed to see its bearing upon the habits and ideas from which it sprang."[41] But it would also be democratic because these methods would not be employed only by professional scientists and their conclusions implemented by technocrats; these methods would be incarnate within public action itself as citizens work together to respond to problems in their own communities and develop solutions in cooperation with experts and activists. Renascent liberalism thus advances a "conception of intelligence integrated with social movements" as a central "factor in giving them direction."[42] In short, "the two things essential, then, to thoroughgoing social liberalism are, first, realistic study of existing conditions in their movement, and, secondly, leading ideas, in the form of policies, for dealing with these conditions in the interest of increased individuality and liberty."[43]

But what this means is that the work of renascent liberalism is first and foremost educational. In other words, if intelligence is to contribute to creating a society in which all people possess the effective liberty to grow as individuals, then the most important social movement of our time is to further the development of shared intelligence throughout all aspects of society and to direct that intelligence toward the implementation of progressive reforms. Nothing less than the fate of democracy depends on its success. As Dewey explains, "The *problem* of education and its relation to direction of social change is all one with the *problem* of finding out what democracy means in its total range of concrete applications; economic, domestic, international, religious, cultural, *and* political." Thus if we believe that democracy is merely the means by which a ruling class manufactures majority consent for its policies through the means of propaganda, then education means nothing more than the training in basic literacy that makes a manufactured public opinion possible; however, if we believe that democracy "means a way of living together in which mutual and free consultation rule instead of force, and in which cooperation instead of brutal competition is the law of life," then education means learning how to actively cooperate with others to develop intelligent policies in response to shared problems.[44] It also means that Dewey meant by "planning" something very different from the meaning given to it by totalitarian states and their "five-year plans" developed without any public input by authoritarians and their technocratic lackeys. For instance, "Russia and Italy both present us with patterns of planned societies. We believe profoundly that society requires planning; that planning is the alternative to chaos, disorder, and insecurity. But there is a difference between a society which is plann*ed* and a society which is continuously plann*ing*—namely, the difference between autocracy and democracy, between dogma and intelligence in operation, between suppression of individuality and that release and utilization of individuality which will bring it to full maturity."[45] Renascent liberalism advances a vision of social planning as a cooperative, experimental, and deliberative endeavor. It envisions a form of government whose primary aim is to provide the means by which citizens, publics, intellectuals, and scientists are able to identify common problems and intelligently propose solutions that can be enacted, tested, and modified through the technologies of the state. This is a daunting task, but it is one pursued with the recognition that the only other option is a society ruled by habit, force, or manipulation.

When Dewey spoke to the NAACP in 1932, it was still possible to imagine that somehow, the nations of the world would continue stumbling along their uneven paths without heeding the call for the kind of cooperative intelligence and social planning that he championed. The two parties of Tweedledee and Tweedledum would continue riding their rickety political bus, allowing this or that group to get a seat in the rear before being kicked off at the next stop. But when Dewey addressed the same problem more than a decade and a half later, after four years of global war and the detonation of the atomic bomb, such naïveté was at an end. At that point, it was possible to now imagine the human species consuming itself in a fire of its own invention. No rational being could look upon the atomic bomb and believe anymore in the fable of laissez-faire. To allow technology to develop unhinged from any social value in the name of intelligence, to allow social forces to spin out of control in the name of liberty, and to allow millions of people to suffer and die violent deaths in the name of individualism made such a bastardization out of old liberal ideals that it is a wonder that they survived. Yet with the passing of time comes the fading of memory and the resurgence of old romantic dreams. The atomic bomb had proved in the past—and global warming proves today—that we have reached a point at which we must collectively determine our fate by organizing social forces to serve the genuine needs of liberty, individualism, and intelligence, and yet still today, there is a concerted effort to stifle such a movement and to wax nostalgic for the old days of pioneer individualism. But Dewey's audience in 1932 already knew that the old days too were full of horrors. It is overdue to harness the resources of such public intelligence and put them to use to make the ideal of democracy a reality for all peoples of our interconnected world.

6

INTELLIGENCE AND SOCIAL MOVEMENTS

Another great American democrat, Abraham Lincoln, left as his heritage the statement that democracy is Government of, for, and *by* the people. I have italicized the preposition "by" because government cannot possibly be by the people save when and where the freedom of intelligence is publicly and actively supported.

—JOHN DEWEY, "WHAT IS DEMOCRACY?"

What does Dewey mean by italicizing the word *by* in Lincoln's famous defense of the democratic experiment? I believe we can construct a working idea of Dewey's communicative vision of free intelligence "by the people" by starting with what at first seems to be one of his more innocuous works—a minute-long radio address he delivered in 1934 over the WEVD radio program *University of the Air*. The title of his address was "Radio's Influence on the Mind." As was typical of Dewey, he began with a statement of a problematic situation that directly implicated what was then the latest media technology: "The radio is the most powerful instrument of social education the world has ever seen. The eye is superior to the ear with respect to the understanding of physical and technical matters. But in all social matters the mass of people are guided through hearing rather than by sight. The progress of democracy has been greatly hindered by the fact that modern means of exchange of physical things has advanced far beyond the means for exchange of knowledge and ideas." This observation, of course, was a restatement of what he had said in *The Public and Its Problems*, only now with the added optimism that "the radio brings us the possibility of redressing the balance." Yet this was a possibility only. Indeed, Dewey also recognized that the opposite outcome was also possible: "The radio lends itself to propaganda in behalf of special interests. It can be used to distort facts and mislead the public mind." Consequently, for Dewey, the question of how to use technologies like the radio to serve the public interest is one of the most crucial problems of the age: "Upon the way in which it is practically answered depends to a larger extent than we yet realize the formation of that enlightened and fair-minded public opinion and sentiment that are necessary for the success of democracy." His active support for stations like WEVD that attempted to give a "genuine education of the millions who daily listen" is perhaps the best concrete example of what Dewey's appeal meant in practice.[1]

This example becomes all the more provocative when one looks at the history of WEVD itself. One might think, for instance, that Dewey was making a rather conventional fund-raising appeal for a local public radio station. In fact, the call letters of WEVD stood for "Eugene V. Debs," the radical labor leader and four-time candidate for president on the Socialist Party ticket who had died in 1926. A product of efforts by socialist leaders like Upton Sinclair and Jane Addams to create a privately owned, independent voice for their reformist efforts, WEVD debuted in Manhattan on the day of Debs's death and was housed in space donated by the International Ladies Garment Workers Union. Because of its outspoken support of leftist causes and labor interests, WEVD was quickly put on a list of 162 stations ordered by the Federal Radio Commission to shut down. Testifying in its defense, the station shot back, "If WEVD is taken off the air and in fact if it is not treated on a parity with others who are richer and more influential with the government, the people of the nation can truly recognize that radio which might be a splendid force for the honest clash of ideas—creating a free market for thought—is nothing but a tool to be used by the powerful against any form of disagreement, or any species of protest." The station, surprisingly, was successful in its defense and in 1933 created the *University of the Air* series, which regularly featured Dewey and many other liberal intellectuals, including Albert Einstein. With this history in mind, Dewey's defense of the station takes on a much more rhetorical character. His promotion of the station was not just to raise money—although that was always an issue—but also to defend it against political enemies.[2]

From this example, one can see that Dewey envisioned a government by the people in which a flexible network of public and private institutions actively inquired into social conditions and disseminated their conclusions through publicly accessible media. This endeavor would involve multiple levels of cooperation, including from scientists and researchers, social activists and politicians, artists and publicists, and the members of the public whose problems formed the substance of these inquiries and whose feedback was essential to their verification. Public forms of broadcasting as well as publicly funded universities would be essential to its success, but even media "in private hands is affected with a profound public interest."[3] Certainly, none of these ideas was particularly unique to Dewey. However, when placed within a larger framework of his democratic humanism, these efforts at using all channels of communication to promote the development of public intelligence take on a new imperative. In particular, such efforts place the burden on social movements to be both the initiators and drivers of democratic reform. In sum, Dewey's conception of organized and cooperative intelligence forms the foundation of his entire understanding of democracy as a form of communication and an expression of public opinion. Consequently, it makes education in the history and nature of social movements essential to the teaching of democratic humanism.

An example of this type of education is described by Argentinian educator Adriana Hernández. She recalls how, in the extreme repression of the dictatorship that lasted from 1976 to 1983, her country's military regime tried to enforce a "political culture which stressed the values of machismo, female subordination, heroism, and patriotism." Even as the state was busy systematically undermining the public sector, reducing social and educational services, and destroying the internal market with neoliberal economic policy, it also expended a great deal of energy enforcing heteronormativity, which was "negativity displayed in terms of punishing homosexuality, long hair for males (beards and mustaches), pants for women, and unmarried men and women living together." It was, in other words, an attempt to annihilate the possibility of improving public intelligence and to impose on the mass population the will of a small sector by force. Yet one particular group found a way to make its voice heard: "women, through the organization of Madres de Plaza de Mayo," challenged the military in order to reclaim their disappeared children.[4] But what fascinated Hernández even more than their courage was the process by which they formed a movement: "The Mothers in Argentina came together as private individuals seeking their children, and they ended articulating a discourse that moved them beyond these immediate concerns, constructing them as political subjects that actively denounced authoritarian rule and reclaimed a democratic order."[5] For Hernández, the actions of these women not only represent the highest principles of democracy but also highlight the type of practices toward which any critical pedagogy should be directed; that is to say, pedagogy should aim to give citizens the ability to self-organize into publics capable of exerting political power and challenging the social order with the truth.

When Hernández turned from the women of the Madres de Plaza de Mayo to the concerns of classroom pedagogy, she took with her the commitment that the university has an important responsibility in providing intellectual resources for democratic social movements. For her, "the University represents an important public sphere in the sense that it constitutes a legitimate space for the analysis and discussion of those questions [raised by critical pedagogy] within the perspective of empowering counter-discourses, as well as acting as a site for negotiation and policymaking." This does not mean turning the classroom into a site of ideological indoctrination; as her appeal to "negotiation" implies, Hernández calls for a pedagogy focused on opening up possibilities and voices, not narrowing them down to those approved by the instructor. Thinking in terms of democracy means "pointing to the need for providing students with the opportunity to develop a sense of agency framed by ethical terms such as justice, solidarity, and community. This means to empower students not only in order to understand their positions, experiences, stories, and voices within the complexity of society but also to be able to produce alternate responses that escape binary oppositions and contribute to the development of communities of solidarity."[6] What matters, in other words, is that students acquire the attitudes of communication that allow solidarity to grow out of the sharing of experience, particularly when that shared experience acquires a political edge in situations marked by conflict, domination, or dissent.

An essential part of this type of pedagogy, for Hernández, is finding opportunities to give students agency in speaking back to course material from their own situated perspectives. This allows them to actually enact challenging authority—in this case, the authority of knowledge texts—by appealing to their own subject positions. To facilitate this activity, Hernández organized what she called a "critical reading practice," in which students engaged in a three-step process. First, students read and discussed the text material in a traditional manner to acquire what she called "basic understanding." Second, students then contextualized these artifacts by reading them in terms of their historical moment, their method of publication, and the perspective of the author—a step she called "interpretation." Finally, and most importantly, she invited students to reconstruct these texts in a way that modified their claims in conformity with the students' own perspectives—a step she called the "re-write." The point of this exercise was to help students "consider themselves situated subjects, subjects belonging to a particular social group in terms of class, gender, and race/ethnicity; subjects that were capable of critical appropriation and transformation." But even more important than this, "the challenge to the students was to situate themselves not merely as consumers but as subjects capable of producing new meanings."[7] It is this act of empowering intelligence—that is, of encouraging students to find their own voices and connect their interests to those of others in solidarity—that provides the energy for progressive change in a democracy consistent with Dewey's vision.

If one were to identify a single passage in Dewey's work that captured the spirit of his political philosophy, it would be the closing lines of *The Public and Its Problems*—perhaps to its own detriment. The book had been published in 1927 in part as a response to two books by the journalist Walter Lippmann—*Public Opinion* in 1922 and *The Phantom Public* in 1925—both of which attacked the traditional philosophical and moral foundations of democracy. In his review of *Public Opinion*, Dewey famously remarked that "one finishes the book almost without realizing that it is perhaps the most effective indictment of democracy as currently conceived ever penned."[8] At the heart of Lippmann's critique was skepticism about the possibility for publics to ever become educated or coherent enough to participate constructively in governmental affairs—a damning indictment coming from a celebrated journalist. Dewey took Lippmann's challenge as an opportunity to articulate a philosophical defense of democracy, but the meaning of his closing words was something less than clear. He wrote, "We lie, as Emerson said, in the lap of an immense intelligence. But that intelligence is dormant and its communications are broken, inarticulate and faint until it possesses the local community as its medium."[9] In the face of a hard-hitting journalistic critique by a democratic realist, Dewey chose to wax poetic about Emerson and express a Jeffersonian nostalgia for the local community. For democratic idealists looking to Dewey for a clear road map to follow through the turbulent 1920s, being reassured that we lie in the lap of an immense intelligence was hardly helpful and certainly even more difficult to believe after the rise of fascism in the 1930s.[10]

If Dewey can be faulted for a lack of rhetorical force or logical clarity, it is less clear that the principles that lay behind his defense of democracy were inadequate. In fact, Dewey would spend the next two decades trying to work out the practical implications of his opaque conclusion to *The Public and Its Problems*. We have already seen, for instance, how Dewey redefined the boundaries of the local community by seeing it as a functional rather than a continuous unit organized through communication and transportation media. But it was really his allusion to Emerson that was the most challenging and the most important. It is significant that Dewey chooses to cite the same passage he had quoted in his lecture on Emerson in 1903. It comes from the essay "Self-Reliance," in Emerson's discussion of the original ground of self-trust and independence. Emerson writes, "We first share the life by which things exist, and afterwards see them as appearances in nature, and forget that we have shared their cause. Here is the fountain of action and of thought. Here are the lungs of that inspiration which giveth man wisdom, and which cannot be denied without impiety and atheism. We lie in the lap of immense intelligence, which makes us receivers of its truth and organs of its activity. When we discern justice, when we discern truth, we do nothing of ourselves, but allow a passage to its beams."[11] In neither case did Dewey cite this passage to appeal to some "Oversoul," or what Emerson had referred to as a transcendent "great responsible Thinker and Actor working wherever a man works."[12] In his 1903 lecture, Dewey had used this passage to celebrate the fact that we found truth on the highway. Rejecting an idea of truth as something taught through books or enforced by authority, Dewey cited Emerson to insist that truth is a product of our experience in nature as it is enriched, reinforced, and expanded through history, science, conversation, and commerce. In *The Public and Its Problems*, Dewey expanded its meaning to refer to the collective social intelligence that was latent in the experiences of individuals and awaiting expression. In short, it was an appeal to develop the institutions, practices, and technologies that would allow local communities to work together to define common problems and articulate shared solutions based on their collective experiences. The appeal to Emerson was thus an eloquent reminder that we are never solitary actors; to recognize that we lie in the lap of an immense intelligence is to acknowledge, with gratitude, that the cause of our powers is grounded in our relations in society and our environment, just as our sense of justice is an expression of the values of our shared culture as enacted in concrete situations.

Dewey ended on this Emersonian note because it captured the central point of contention in what came to be known as the "Lippman-Dewey debate." This point was whether democratic publics could possess, in any *productive* fashion, a political intelligence that could be useful in making or directing public policy. Lippmann denied that they could. The root of his skepticism was not necessarily any disdain for individuals or classes of individuals; it was his realistic appraisal that public opinion could never accurately represent or account for the scope and complexity of political affairs that such intelligence requires. Because of the limitations on a person's time and effort, the public's reliance on stereotypes to make judgments, and most of all, the news industry's inability to do anything but turn the spotlight on passing events, public opinion is—as Dewey summarizes Lippmann—merely "casual, the product of limited contact with the environment of facts and forces where opinion manifests itself in action, and . . . it is shaped chiefly by tradition, by stereotyped pictures, and by emotions, by personal interests unintelligently conceived."[13] Instead of a Jeffersonian rugged individual making shrewd judgments in town-hall meetings, one had in most cases a lost individual in an industrial society bewildered by events across the globe and interested primarily in his or her private affairs. To believe that public opinion in such a circumstance was a real entity capable of intelligently contributing to public policy would be, in Lippmann's terms, to believe in a mere "phantom."

Given Dewey's own critique of rugged individualism, it is clear that he did not take issue with the diagnosis of the challenges to modern democracy; in fact, he agreed with almost all of it. After reading *Public Opinion*, he wrote that "it shivers most of our illusions, and this particular Humpty Dumpty can never be put together again for anyone who reads these chapters with an open mind." However, it was what Dewey called the "constructive portion" of Lippmann's books that formed the core of their debate.[14] In short, Lippmann made "a plea for recognition that actual government, whether or no we like it, must be carried on by nonpolitical agencies, by organs which we do not conventionally regard as having to do with government."[15] Specifically, Lippmann made two recommendations, one positive and one negative. Dewey summarized them thus: Positively, Lippmann recommended the creation of autonomous intelligence bureaus (such as our current Federal Department of Agriculture, Central Intelligence Agency, and Environmental Protection Agency) that would be charged with investigating and reporting on the "unseen environment" directly to those politicians or administrators charged with developing and implementing policy. Negatively, he recommended that "the real interest of the public lies in insisting that problems shall *not* come before it until they have passed through a definite procedure of analysis and record."[16] Only *after* a policy has been developed and proposed before the public does the public then enact its sole agency, which is to approve or disapprove of the policy in consideration of whether adequate and fair procedures have been followed. In Dewey's phrasing, Lippmann "points out that the mass does not really think about issues, but after having become habituated in childhood to authority, merely says Yes or No to the formulation of the issues made by a few persons—constituting the machine."[17] By this remedy, Lippmann encourages a minimalist interpretation of democracy that necessitates public approval of policies while requiring that the policies themselves will be crafted by experts.

Dewey's objection to these "constructive" proposals lies in neither Lippmann's recommendation of intelligence bureaus nor his assignment of a critical role to the public. In the first case, Dewey admits that "the expert organization for which Mr. Lippmann calls for is inherently desirable."[18] This is hardly surprising to hear from a philosopher who had spent his entire career stressing the need for a widespread education in intelligence if democracy is to be possible. As he would later stress in *The Public and Its Problems*, "Genuine public policy cannot be generated unless it be informed by knowledge, and this knowledge does not exist except when there is a systematic, thorough, and well-equipped search and record."[19] In the second case, he credits Lippmann with at least giving the public the responsibility to critically examine whether or not a policy was developed according to the rules of fairness, impartiality, and prudence. In Lippmann's model, writes Dewey, "the path of reason is the path of willingness to follow some regular rule; lacking insight into the substance of rationality in different proposals, the public may at least judge of its form, its method and spirit."[20] Moreover, to his considerable credit, Lippmann advocated for an education in media literacy as well as the ethics and rationality of logic and decision-making. Aware of the great potential that the machine age had given to the manufacture of consent, he called for a critical education to give people the tools to prevent themselves from being manipulated by special interests into supporting this or that policy. Both of these proposals Dewey supported as consistent with the democratic way of life.

Where Dewey parted ways with Lippmann was the latter's insistence that the conditions of modernity—namely, the scope and complexity of affairs combined with the limitations of the modern press—required abandoning the ideal of constituting intelligent public opinion as an active and constructive force in democratic life. Recognizing the very real challenges to this ideal, Lippmann had given it up as hopeless, in effect advocating a technocratic vision of democracy in which intelligence became the property of a new priestly class while modern publics were relegated to being peasants with the added benefit of saying yes or no. Dewey, by contrast, interpreted all of Lippmann's obstacles to democracy as challenges to be overcome. For him, "democracy demands a more thoroughgoing education than the education of officials, administrators and directors of industry. Because this fundamental general education is at once so necessary and so difficult of achievement, the enterprise of democracy is so challenging. To sidetrack it to the task of enlightenment of administrators and executives is to miss something of its range and its challenge."[21] In other words, the Lippman-Dewey debate came down to whether or not we could develop technologies of publicity and communication to educate publics much in the same way that intelligence bureaus might educate insiders.

The appearance of Emerson at the end of *The Public and Its Problems* expresses more than an affirmative to this question; it actually radically extends the proposition by suggesting that the public is not merely a passive audience for education but rather a *source* of intelligence itself. To realize that we lie in the lap of an immense intelligence is to become aware of the richness of experience that surrounds us in the varied lives of individuals, each with his or her own perspective and insights on the world. Reading Lippmann, one never gets a sense that individuals are anything but passive spectators in the movie theater of appearances; they create nothing and contribute nothing. But Dewey channels the spirit of the transcendentalists in his belief in the integrity, richness, and connectedness of individual experience. It is not surprising that Dewey would end the second-to-last chapter of *The Public and Its Problems* with perhaps an equally opaque reference to another nineteenth-century poet. He writes, "Democracy will come into its own, for democracy is a name for a life of free and enriching communion. It had its seer in Walt Whitman. It will have its consummation when free social inquiry is indissolubly wedded to the art of full and moving communication."[22] Just what Dewey means in practice by "the art of full and moving communication" will be explored later, but for now it is worth noting that Walt Whitman was not a publicist for an intelligence bureau; he was a national poet whose work threaded together the unique experiences of people from every walk of life into a complex fabric of the nation.

In many ways, Whitman is a better model then Emerson for understanding the form and function of organized and cooperative intelligence in democratic society.[23] Dewey had to work to demonstrate the social and public implications of Emerson's thinking, mainly because of the latter's well-earned reputation for radical individualism. Whitman required no such reconstruction. He was the self-proclaimed poet of democracy who wished to build a pluralistic unity out of the multiplicity of American experience. In an earlier essay, Dewey had praised Whitman for having "been able to discard the conventions of literature and build his poems around the common and elementary actions of every-day human beings."[24] For democracy to come into its own required an art of communication capable of building a public out of the common and elementary actions of its citizens. But Dewey expanded his idea of communication to include more than the works of the transcendentalist poet; his idea of communication would bridge the divide between art and science. This had been a long-standing aim in his work. Perhaps its most vigorous first expression was in 1890, when he argued that "this present separation of science and art, this division of life into prose and poetry, is an unnatural divorce of the spirit. . . . We must bridge this gap of poetry from science. We must heal this unnatural wound."[25] But this theme would continue throughout his work until it became the centerpiece of his agenda for radical democratic reform of the public.

At the heart of his reformist project was a commitment to help the public tackle what he called "its most urgent problem: to find and identify itself."[26] The way Dewey phrases this problem is important. First, for the public to *find* and *identify* itself means that it is not just a preexisting entity awaiting recognition; it must be actively created and constituted in time. In this way, Dewey rejects the animistic tendency to see the public as a latent "spirit" simply awaiting recognition. Second, for the public to find and identify *itself* means that it is created and constituted by its own individual members through collective and progressive acts of self-recognition that involve establishing relationships with others. In this way, Dewey rejects the fascist tendency to see the public as something manufactured from above through propaganda and technology. Instead, he highlights the need for forms of free and open communication between individuals that transform merely mechanical forms of association into relationships that are "emotionally, intellectually, consciously sustained."[27] That is why Dewey stresses that the only possible solution to the problem of the public is "the perfecting of the means and ways of communication of meanings so that genuinely shared interest in the consequences of interdependent activities may inform desire and effort and thereby direct action."[28] But this is another way of saying that it is only through communication that the public comes to realize that it lies in the lap of an immense intelligence.

What is the nature of this "public" that Dewey believes must find itself? And what is its relationship to a democratic state? Dewey answers that "the public consists of all those who are affected by the indirect consequences of transactions to such an extent that it is deemed necessary to have those consequences systematically cared for."[29] By this definition, Dewey means that a public is interdependent, multiple, imagined, communicative, and pragmatic. First, it is *interdependent* because the activities of any one member affect, directly or indirectly, the lives of other members. Second, it is *multiple* because there are an infinite number of "publics" within any single public, each of them formed in the self-conscious recognition of their interdependence. Third, it is *imagined* because each of its members must be able to visualize the character of his or her interdependence with enough clarity and significance as to make it a factor in political judgments. Fourth, it is *communicative* not only because these relationships are formed through communication but also because it expresses its judgment through a public opinion, which "is formed and entertained by those who constitute the public and is about public affairs."[30] Lastly, a public is *pragmatic* insofar as its constitution in the minds of its constituents has a bearing on regulating and directing collective action to bring about desired effects. The administrative arm of the public in the form of officials, institutions, and laws then stands for the "state," and a state is "democratic" to the extent that it genuinely represents the interests of a public in its legislation and actions. In sum, a public represents an imagined community of interdependent individuals and groups formed through communication and committed to collective pragmatic self-regulation. Therefore, democracy represents the capacity for a public to direct the actions of an administrative state through the agency of public opinion.

For critics of democracy, however, Dewey's very definition of a democratic public reveals its impossibility. For them, by making the formation of a genuine public contingent on continual and collective acts of self-recognition and self-understanding, Dewey reveals the fact that he dwells in the realm of fantasy. Dewey admits, for instance, that "the problem of a democratically organized public is primarily an essentially intellectual problem, in a degree to which the political affairs of prior ages offer no parallel." For fascist antihumanists, however, to define democracy as an intellectual problem is to admit that the problem is unsolvable. They would readily agree with Dewey's observation that "the machine age has so enormously expanded, multiplied, intensified and complicated the scope of the indirect consequences, has formed such immense and consolidated unions in action, on an impersonal rather than a community basis, that the resultant public cannot identify and distinguish itself."[31] But for them, that would show that the moral foundation of democracy has been so eroded that a new "totalitarian moral code" must be put in its place. Under this regime, we would accept the fact that "the truths which have the authority to direct social action are by right the possession of a small superior elite, and that the mass of human beings cannot be trusted to judge and to believe aright in moral matters; that if they are permitted to exercise freedom of mind their policies and decisions will be so swayed by personal and class interests that the final outcome will be division, conflict and disintegration."[32] In other words, without a fascist Leader to direct them, a public would be just a mere phantom in the way described by Walter Lippmann; it would become an aggregate of lost individuals whose actions must be regulated by the imperatives of technique and the dictates of a self-interested machinery of state.

Dewey admits the challenge of the task ahead but nonetheless calls for the courage and faith to admit that democracy is possible; to admit otherwise is to accept the totalitarian moral code. Writing in 1948, when democracy still remained under a cloud even after its victory over totalitarian states, Dewey admitted that "democracy is not an easy road to take and follow. On the contrary, it is, as far as its realization is concerned in the complex conditions of the contemporary world, a supremely difficult one." However, to admit that it is difficult is also to say that it is possible. Yet faith is empty if it is not accompanied by courage: "But to this courage we must add, if our courage is to be intelligent rather than blind, the fact that successful maintenance of democracy demands the utmost in use of the best available methods to procure a social knowledge that is reasonably commensurate with our physical knowledge."[33] If an individual has neither faith nor courage, then no amount of argument will make democracy seem anything more than a naïve fantasy. However, for those prepared to take a hard road, Dewey outlined a road map for producing the kind of social knowledge that could help the public find itself in a complex world and produce a democracy guided by intelligence and morality.

The first task in establishing the moral basis of democracy is to give support for the reestablishment of local communities adapted to the conditions of a global technological age. This does not mean, as we have already seen, reproducing the conditions of community life as existed in a romantic ideal of the eighteenth century. Communities would no longer be thought of as strictly territorial organizations whose community character derived from the fact that people lived and worked together within the same contiguous space; community would also grow out of functional or professional organizations and contribute to "ties formed by sharing in common work." At the same time, Dewey rejects the notion that anything like a purely "virtual" community, such as those formed today in online digital environments, can ever exist as an *actual* community either. Any theory of social life, he argued, that "relies upon associations which are remote and indirect, would if carried into effect soon be confronted by all the troubles and evils of the present situation in a transposed form." What is important about community is not only possessing and communicating about a shared interest, profession, or function; it is also having the opportunity to communicate about them with others within a face-to-face setting. For him, "there is no substitute for the vitality and depth of close and direct intercourse and attachment."[34] In short, Dewey makes oral communication about shared interests the foundation of community. The communities may connect people from across the globe and organize themselves using written or digital media, but the mortar of the community is nonetheless found in the moments of direct intercourse in which people develop the habits of sympathy, understanding, and care that are the building blocks of a humane civilization. Dewey writes,

> It is said, and said truly, that for the world's peace it is necessary that we understand the peoples of foreign lands. How well do we understand, I wonder, our next door neighbors? It has also been said that if a man love not his fellow man whom he has seen, he cannot love the God whom he has not seen. The chances of regard for distant peoples being effective as long as there is no close neighborhood experience to bring with it insight and understanding of neighbors do not seem better. A man who has not been seen in the daily relations of life may inspire admiration, emulation, servile subjection, fanatical partisanship, hero worship; but not love and understanding, save as they radiate from the attachments of a near-by union. Democracy must begin at home, and its home is the neighborly community.[35]

The reason for the importance of face-to-face communication is thus rooted deeply in our human nature, specifically the nature of our emotional lives. First, Dewey argues that "the connections of the ear with vital and out-going thought and emotion are immensely closer and more varied than those of the eye. Vision is a spectator; hearing is a participator." When we speak directly with others in a shared situation, we lack the detachment that we often feel when encountering merely visual symbols or even recorded images. We can even feel ourselves completely immersed in what another person says—namely, because "the winged words of conversation in immediate intercourse have a vital import lacking in the fixed and frozen words of written speech." This sensitivity of the ear is then complemented by the sense of connection brought about by having our bodies physically close to the bodies of others. We want the people that we care about close to us, even if that means occupying the same space in relative silence. There is thus "something deep within human nature itself which pulls toward settled relationships. Inertia and the tendency toward stability belong to emotions and desires as well as to masses and molecules. That happiness which is full of content and peace is found only in enduring ties with others, which reach to such depths that they go below the surface of conscious experience to form its undisturbed foundation."[36] Any social theory that denies this deep yearning for settled relationships with face-to-face communication as their foundation is destined to reproduce the conditions that make for the lost individual.

If encouraging local communities can be considered the reconstruction of democracy from the inside out, the second task is to empower the communities by making full utilization of the social sciences to provide them perspectives from the outside in. This is what Dewey meant by the term *organized* in his appeal for organized intelligence. For him, social science means something more than scientific methods applied to social phenomena, as we might think about contemporary psychology or sociology; it also represents a sustained and experimental inquiry into the direct and indirect consequences of policies and proposals on diverse publics across time. Under these conditions, the social sciences will "then be an apparatus for conducting investigation, and for recording and interpreting (organizing) its results."[37] This proposal was similar to that of Lippmann insofar as it stressed the need for scientific expertise to make sense of the unseen environment, but it differed insofar as it stressed the role of the social as well as the physical sciences, encouraged its dissemination to the public, and developed its conclusions by studying specific policies in action. For Dewey, it was not enough to call attention to the power of physical science to understand and control the natural world while moral and political judgment remained in the hands of dogmatic moral theory and abstract philosophical principles. The fact was that "the greatest scientific revolution is therefore still to come. It will ensue when men collectively organize their knowledge for social application, and when they systematically use scientific procedures for the objective control of social relations."[38] This does not mean subordinating political judgment to scientists; it recognizes that moral judgment requires not only moral principles but empirical knowledge of one's social environment and a pragmatic analysis of the consequences of political action.

This might seem like a platitude at first, but when put in an actual circumstance, one can appreciate the degree to which this call for free inquiry and dissemination of intelligence is resisted to this day. In 1932, Dewey published an essay in the *Nation* called "Education and Birth Control" in which he encouraged instituting sexual education in the schools in order to empower women to be able to manage their pregnancies and control the size of their families. What he recognized was that when faced with new empirical knowledge that has any bearing upon the conduct of social life, "there is always a rearguard of ignorance, prejudice, dogma, routine, tradition, which fights against the spread of new ideas that entail new practices." The increasing pace of scientific development does not lessen this reaction but increases it, which places all the more demand on education and communication to integrate these new methods into society in a moral and controlled manner. In the case of birth control, meaning here any techniques for family planning, Dewey notes that "as long as multitudes of families have too many children and those children badly spaced, it is not possible for each child to have proper individual attention—physical, intellectual, moral."[39] Moreover, the resulting poverty, stress, and neglect stem largely from the fact that "present ideas of love, marriage, and the family are almost exclusively masculine constructions."[40] Yet when women are educated and then given the rights and the means to control their own bodies, a new freedom results that carries with it a more realistic and moral sensibility. As Dewey explains, "There is always wholesome sanitation wherever there is free circulation of intelligence. We need light and circulation of air in intellectual and moral matters as in physical. Suppression and secrecy breed unfairness, mental and moral disorder. Our plea, from the side of education, is that there be removed arbitrary restrictions to that movement of knowledge and understanding which brings the action of the blind forces of nature under the control of intelligence."[41] It is approaching a century since Dewey wrote those words, and yet still policies of abstinence-only education in the schools and restrictions on the dissemination of information about methods of birth control in hospitals continue. To believe that the free circulation of intelligence is something we can today take for granted is to enable the rearguard of ignorance that will exist "as long as man lives with the past behind him and a future ahead of him."[42]

Given the imperative to disseminate the resources of intelligence to the public, the third task is to develop the art of publicity that makes scientific knowledge accessible and engaging for public audiences through popular media. In *The Public and Its Problems*, Dewey appealed to art as a solution to the problem of bridging the gap between the complex and technical nature of science and the public's desire for easily consumable news, a gap that Walter Lippmann thought was too daunting for the modern news media. For Dewey, "the objection is well taken save as the potency of art is taken into account. A technical high-brow presentation would appeal only to those technically high-brow; it would not be news to the masses. Presentation is fundamentally important, and presentation is a question of art." What Dewey called for was a greater attention to the power of art to condense complex material into a form that was contemporary, quotidian, and provocative. It is for this reason that Dewey made the bold assertion that "artists have always been the real purveyors of news, for it is not the outward happening in itself which is new, but the kindling by it of emotion, perception and appreciation." For him, artists solved the problem of presentation and therefore of democratic intelligence itself. He concludes, "The highest and most difficult kind of inquiry and a subtle, delicate, vivid and responsive art of communication must take possession of the physical machinery of transmission and circulation and breathe life into it."[43] Scientists are responsible for organizing the results of inquiry, but artists provide the delicate, vivid, and responsive art that brings about full and moving communication of the type he associated with Walt Whitman.

It should be stressed, however, that Dewey was not content with a "popularization" of science that had no aim other than making obscure facts interesting; he was calling for an art that related developments in scientific intelligence to practical situations that had a bearing on human beliefs, habits, and well-being. He complained that "the trouble with much of what is called popularization of knowledge is that it is content with diffusion of information, in diluted form, merely as information. It needs to be organized and presented in its bearing upon action. Here is a most significant phase of the obligation incumbent upon the scientifically trained men and women of our age."[44] Dewey was calling for something more than the production of popular science for the sake of entertainment, the type of which developed rapidly after the innovation of cable television. He also wanted an art specifically committed to creating what he called "informed publicity" of the type he heard on WEVD that could weaken the influence of propaganda by constituting intelligent public opinion.[45] Consider, for instance, the role of art in the environmental movement, which has now made it common sense to support policies that encourage recycling, renewable energy, and sustainable development. Despite the continued resistance of a rearguard of ignorance, it is undeniable that the art of informed publicity has had an enormous role in informing public opinion and altering everyday habits in accordance with new discoveries in science and developments in technology.

To help empower the public to make full use of the resources of intelligence also required a fourth task, which was the cultivation of a scientific mind through education in the methods of experimental inquiry and intelligent skepticism. Part of Dewey's lifelong complaint against the educational system was that it resulted in the sorry fact that "many young people leave school with the attitude of wanting and expecting to be *told*, rather than with the attitude of realizing that they must look into things, must inquire and examine."[46] A good deal of this outcome was due to the reliance on methods of education that employ rigid instruction in subject matter mandated on standardized tests and include science as a body of particularly difficult and obscure subject matter. But for Dewey, science was primarily an attitude and a method "manifested in any walk of life" that had both a constructive and a critical side. Critically, it represents "freedom from control by routine, prejudice, dogma, unexamined tradition, sheer self-interest." Constructively, it stands for "the will to inquire, to examine, to discriminate, to draw conclusions only on the basis of evidence after taking pains to gather all available evidence."[47] Science certainly produces a body of highly technical and complex subject matter that should be taught as a part of any curriculum, but for Dewey, the most important part of a scientific education is the creation of a scientific attitude that develops habits of thought and action that endure for the rest of a person's life.

Perhaps the most important of these habits in a democratic society is an active critical mind with the skills to judge conclusions and interrogate the basis of arguments. People constantly complain, Dewey observes, that the population is too amenable to the influence of propaganda: "But why is it? Why are so many people so ready to swallow what is persistently told them, or told them with an air of authority? Why is there so much gullibility?" The answer comes back to education: "It is because they have acquired the habit of listening and of accepting, instead of that of inquiry, and, if you please, of intelligent skepticism." The consequence of this failure to cultivate the scientific attitude is more than a lack of knowledge about this or that fact, knowledge that today is readily available for recall in the digital environment. Rather, the consequence is the failure to know the difference between what facts are warranted and what are erroneous, between what sources are legitimate and what are propaganda, and between what reasoning is logical and what is fallacious. Sadly, when the ways school subjects are taught "aid in establishing the mental habit of passive acceptance, while docility at the expense of an inquiring disposition is too generally cultivated, the evil culminates in the attitudes that are formed in political, social and economic matters."[48] In short, "democracy will be a farce unless individuals are trained to think for themselves, to judge independently, to be critical, to be able to detect subtle propaganda and the motives which inspire it."[49] Only when, as a society, we become committed to cultivating the scientific attitude not only in school but throughout all culture will democratic citizenry become an active rather than a passive calling.

The final task is then to create the networks of communication and practice that make intelligence a genuinely cooperative endeavor. For democracy to be a reality, intelligence must be created through the interaction between local communities, scientists, artists, and activists, all working together to define common problems and develop experimental policies for their resolution. Dewey famously used a folksy analogy to stress the necessity for public participation as well as expert counsel in the development of policies, observing that "the man who wears the shoe knows best that it pinches and where it pinches, even if the expert shoemaker is the best judge of how the trouble is to be remedied." However, the problem with this analogy is that it restricts the public to the role of a beta tester. But Dewey's ideal of cooperative intelligence carried with it a much stronger vision of participation and interaction. Although it acknowledged the obvious fact that "what we call intelligence be distributed in unequal amounts," the democratic faith committed one to the belief that "each individual has something to contribute whose value can be assessed only as it enters into the final pooled intelligence constituted by the contributions of all." The important corrective of this comment is that the type of intelligence is not restricted to any category of knowledge or type of response; it might concern the nature of a problem, the desirability of an aim, the evaluation of a policy, or the fairness of a law. His comment about shoes was designed to make the easiest case for public participation—namely, by stressing that of all forms of intelligence possessed by any individual, "there is one thing they are wiser about than anybody else can be, and that is where the shoe pinches, the troubles they suffer from."[50] The comment was meant not to place limits on citizen wisdom or the nature of public involvement but to establish its baseline.

Although Dewey often frustrated even his supporters by remaining vague on what this commitment meant in practice, I believe his work makes it clear that he encouraged the development of social movements at all levels of society to influence public opinion and leverage control over political policy. In other words, Dewey did not place his faith in top-down administrative reforms of the type that Lippmann recommended; his faith was in public participation. Consequently, the only genuine and sustainable form of cooperative intelligence in a democracy had to occur outside of the restrictions and imperatives of the administrative state. It had to arise from largely voluntary movements in which individuals from multiple communities and with a diverse set of skills and knowledge could work together for a common end. And it is important to point out that this cooperation occurs not only out of desire but out of necessity: "Changing conditions have brought men much closer together. Individuals are now more dependent upon other individuals whom they never see or know; all alike are much more dependent upon social movements that are beyond the control of individuals as such—movements that can now be directed only by organized collective effort."[51] It was thus the task of education, in particular, to cultivate what Dewey called "the social spirit and the power to act socially" if individuals were to be prepared to accept their role as democratic citizens. He writes, "Competitive motives and methods must be abandoned for cooperative. Desire to work with others, for mutual advantage, must be made the controlling force in school administration and instruction. Instead of imbuing individuals with the idea that the goal is to sharpen their powers so they can get on personally, they must be trained in capacity for intelligent organization so that they can unite with others in a common struggle against poverty, disease, ignorance, credulity, low standards of appreciation and enjoyment."[52]

Negatively, nothing proved this point more than the enthusiasm Dewey saw for fascist movements in Europe. When a society suppresses these capacities for intelligent organization and thwarts the impulses for progressive reform, the natural result is an outburst of totalitarian force. In this way, "the experience of the Old World, notably Italy and Germany, shows that 'youth movements' when they move in isolation from basic changes in the structure of society may be directed toward reaction even more readily than toward desirable ends. Youth, made desperate by finding that society makes no provision for it, may grasp at straws if the straws float on a current that supplies some immediate outlet for pent up energies." As long as the United States imitated their models, "we may expect in this country more and more appeals addressed to youth from American congeners of European Fascism." Conversely, if democratic nations wish to avert reproducing the culture of their enemies, they had to adopt a different path that placed faith in democratic humanist ideals rather than fearing them. According to Dewey, "For the youth problem in this country I see no solution (which also will be a solution of the problem of the future of society) save one that enlists their minds and hearts in behalf of intelligent plans for social change based upon understanding of existing conditions."[53] But this is nothing less than preparing the youth of the country to become active participants in social movements that grow out of their own community interests and then cooperate with larger publics for common ends.

But perhaps nothing reveals Dewey's commitment to cultivating cooperative intelligence in social movements more than his own participation in them. For instance, when Dewey participated in the *University of the Air* for WEVD, he did so to support the station and the reformist goals connected with its namesake, Eugene Debs. The station functioned to form community, disseminate informed publicity, and organize a social movement that had as its aim the reform of the economic and industrial order to ensure a more just distribution of resources for all. These same goals motivated Dewey's 1930 lecture to the New History Society in support of the League for Independent Action, a league of which he was a member and that he said was "formed because of a realization that our existing political parties in the conduct of government are more concerned to serve the selfish and financial interests of the few than the human needs of the many."[54] In the closing paragraph of his lecture, he not only asked for support from his audience but also laid out a rationale for social movements as the primary agents of reform in democratic life. Dewey concludes,

> Just as the Republican party was born in the irrepressible conflict against extension of chattel slavery, so the next party will be born to liberate men, women and children from the enslavement of governmental agencies to selfish and predatory economic interests. That is an issue which people can understand. But it takes organization, sacrifice, cooperation of all persons of good will, to get it presented to the people and to create in them the will to put into effect their vision of a new society and a new history. We ask your help; we have a right to ask it because we are not working for ourselves, not to gain something selfish by means of deluding voters, but as forerunners in helping usher in that new day which you too see about to dawn.[55]

When this lecture was reprinted in the league's bulletin, Dewey titled it "The Irrepressible Conflict." For him, this pointed to the task of organized and cooperative intelligence in society—namely, to identify and meet the challenge of the irrepressible conflicts that tear at the fabric of society and lead to the suffering of the many for the selfish interests of the few. This challenge would never be met or perhaps even recognized by experts in intelligent bureaus, insider politicians, or distracted and hurried members of a phantom public. It could only be met by sustained and intelligent social movements organized by those eager to usher in a new dawn.

PART 3
THE PEDAGOGY OF
DEMOCRATIC HUMANISM

7

LOGIC

Genuine freedom, in short, is intellectual; it rests in the trained power of thought, in ability to "turn things over," to look at matters deliberately, to judge whether the amount and kind of evidence requisite for decision is at hand, and if not, to tell where and how to seek such evidence.

—JOHN DEWEY, *HOW WE THINK*

To teach logic as part of the pedagogy of democratic humanism is to teach students a method of inquiry by which they order the world of experience through the power of inferences. In sharp contrast with the old medieval system that used logic to systematically defend every point of established doctrine about a static universe, logic in the pragmatic sense is concerned with promoting experimental attitudes to meet changing conditions. Its aim is "to cultivate deep-seated and effective habits of discriminating tested beliefs from mere assertions, guesses, and opinions; to develop a lively, sincere, and open-minded preference for conclusions that are properly grounded, and to engrain into the individual's working habits methods of inquiry and reasoning appropriate to the various problems that present themselves."[1] Logic is absolutely central to the humanistic project, for it involves the training of the mind, both in the *individual* sense of one's way of reflecting on private experience as well as in the social sense of learning how to think *together* about common problems. It is only through logic, through the ability to craft a common, ordered account, that democratic freedom is made real—and only when people have the power to define a shared aim and establish the means to its actualization. Dewey provides the methodological foundations to the teaching of logic in a way that cultivates the powers of the mind and guides them toward the aims of democratic humanism.

It was to Defoe's *Robinson Crusoe* that Dewey turned to find the perfect literary example to visualize the methods of logical judgment in practice. The reason for Dewey's affection for the book was that it offered an ideal thought experiment. Written in 1719, it dramatized the adventures of a "man who has achieved civilization, who has attained a certain maturity of thought; who has developed ideals and means of action, but is suddenly thrown back upon his own resources, having to cope with a raw and often hostile nature, and to regain success by sheer intelligence, energy, and persistence of character."[2] Defoe created the model, imitated innumerable times over the centuries, for the survivor story. For popular audiences of the time, this story provided a romantic escape from modern existence while at the same time celebrating the superiority of modern techniques to conquer nature. But for philosophers such as Dewey, the story also provided an opportunity to observe, in the imagination, the modern individual in isolation—particularly with respect to the socializing effect of language on the castaway's behavior and thought.

The particular episode that caught Dewey's attention is one of the most famous in literature. For years, Crusoe had been alone on an island with only animals as social companions and a Bible for intellectual company. But then everything changed:

> It happened, one day about noon going towards my boat, I was exceedingly surprised, with the print of a man's naked foot on the shore, which was very plain to be seen in the sand. I stood like one thunderstruck, or as if I had seen an apparition; I listened, I looked round me, I could hear nothing, nor see anything; I went up to a rising ground to look farther; I went up the shore and down the shore, but it was all one, I could see no other impression but that one. I went to it again to see if there were any more, and to observe if it might not be my fancy; but there was no room for that, for there was exactly the very print of a foot, toes, heel, and every part of a foot; how it came thither I knew not, nor could in the least imagine. But after innumerable fluttering thoughts, like a man perfectly confused and out of myself, I came home to my fortification, not feeling, as we say, the ground I went on, but terrified to the last degree, looking behind me at every two or three steps, mistaking every bush and tree, and fancying every stump at a distance to be a man; nor is it possible to describe how many various shapes affrighted imagination represented things to me in, how many wild ideas were found every moment in my fancy, and what strange unaccountable whimsies came into my thoughts by the way.[3]

Striking about these passages is the flurry of activity initiated by the encounter with such a simple phenomenon, which was no more than a shaped depression in the sand. As Dewey describes the scene, "At the moment when he identified the marks as a footprint, his set in action, his attitude, his mode of response to the environment changed. He was set, like a trigger, to react to a man as a potential and menacing factor in his environment. Not a single thing which he did remained quite what it would have been otherwise—not even to his lying down to sleep."[4] Crusoe stood thunderstruck, looked around, went up to a rising and back to the shore, searched for more prints, went home terrified, reacted to every sound in fear, and sent his imagination running wild, all because he encountered a single footprint of an unknown man.

But that is precisely the logical point at issue. Crusoe did not respond to a *present shape* in the sand; he responded to the sudden awareness of an *absent man*. This act represents *inference*, which is the practical foundation of all logical thought. At its most basic level, inference represents the "use of things as evidence of other things."[5] For example, Crusoe uses the footprint as evidence of another man on the island. Another way of expressing its function is as an act of pointing, such that to make an inference is to take "some given physical existence as a sign of some other existences not given in the same way."[6] The footprint as a physical phenomenon thus points toward the existence of a man not immediately present but somewhere hidden in the trees and bushes. Lastly, inference connects the seen with the unseen not only in *space* but in *time*. That Crusoe immediately feels confusion and terror at the prospect of an *imminent* encounter with a dangerous stranger is indicative of "the fact that inference takes absent things as being in a certain real continuum with present things, so that our attitude toward the latter is bound up with our reaction to the former as part of the same situation."[7] All inferences thus highlight the "temporal development of experience," such as when Crusoe infers not only that the footprint is the result of the past event of a man walking on the beach but also that his continued existence will culminate in a possibly violent encounter in the future.[8] Both of these elements of inference we take for granted when we read the story; they are common sense. The function of logic is to reveal the processes that underlie our judgments of common sense so they can become more self-conscious and intelligent.

Notably, the importance of logic already is a central theme that runs through the discourse of critical pedagogy, even if it may not always be called by that name. Most critical pedagogues prefer the language of criticism, dialogue, or inquiry, but in actuality, they share a concern for logic despite their reluctance to use the word. The case of Ira Shor is representative. In his *Empowering Education*, he describes a form of intervention in which he suggests "literary exercises to help students become strong users of language—through composing, editing, revising, analyzing, and listening, individually and in groups."[9] To establish a contrast, he then turns to logic, explaining that its "standard usage is not learned here in isolation from a thematic study; critical thinking is not a set of abstract logic skills or problem-solving techniques; they are activities in a meaningful inquiry."[10] The irony in the passage is that the activity of meaningful inquiry is *precisely* Dewey's definition of logic, just as the mastery of precise language use is a thoroughly logical process. Indeed, Shor's passionate advocacy for Paulo Freire–style "problem-posing" education is thoroughly consistent with Dewey's conception of logic as a process of inquiry. Shor argues that "the problem-posing approach views human beings, knowledge, and society as unfinished products in history, where various forces are still contending," and its goal is "critical thinking and action, which starts from perceiving the social, historical, or cultural causes of problems in one's life."[11] But this is to return logic to its classical Greek roots, in which logic came from *logos*, "the ordered account" in which "the power to interpret and explain was connected with the ability to set forth a consecutive story."[12] In sum, logic in Dewey is an extension of the power of logos to create order and freedom out of chaos and constraint.

One of the great virtues of Shor's classroom is his commitment to developing the attitudes of logical inquiry in his students. Specifically, his "problem-posing" approach to education captures the absolute centrality of the first step in the process of inquiry, which is doubt; Shor always begins with something to be interrogated and investigated rather than something to merely be absorbed and memorized. Reminiscent of the sophistical method of *dissoi logoi*, the intentional placing together of opposing arguments, Shor recommends even "presenting science as debates and controversies and competing interpretations [in which] the critical teacher would pose the subject matter as a problem for students to think through rather than a bland official consensus for them to memorize."[13] In this way, the teacher ensures that "knowledge will be offered in a context that is functional to student life and work that reveals critical problems in society."[14] These are precisely the methods and aims of logic.

Moreover, Shor successfully integrates an experimental method into his teaching by encouraging the crossing of disciplines to develop hypotheses and the integration of active testing outside the classroom. Rejecting the banking model, Shor suggests a classroom in which multiple disciplines inform a common problem and where students are actively engaged in the process of inquiry. He gives the following example related to the teaching of science:

> For an activist science curriculum, students can do research outside the classroom. An interdisciplinary science class studying sound and light might send students supervised by a teacher and equipped with cameras, tape recorders, and measuring devices, to different neighborhoods to see if wealthier areas have different sounds and different illumination than poor ones. They could write up reports on their findings to integrate language arts into science education and could chart the differences they find to integrate math into the study. They could compare the housing, police presence, garbage, and printed messages on the streets. The comparative study of neighborhoods would be an activist introduction to social inequality, expressed here through living conditions.[15]

Consistent with Dewey's experimental model is the image of students physically engaged in the activity of testing in order to address a problem situation that not only implicates multiple forms of knowledge but also has clear consequences for an environment, social or natural. Notable about this example is that although it originated within a science curriculum, it involved problems of art and composition, of mathematics and technology, and of sociology and economy. Any discipline can integrate the practices of logical inquiry. Nor should the complexity and labor-intensive aspect of this example imply that all logical inquiry must be so involved; inquiry can happen at any level, and indeed, the smaller and more contained problems are often the most effective because they are most focused. What matters in logic is less the subject matter than the fact that students learn to discover through a method of inquiry, for then they take with them the kind of empowerment that will make them capable of confronting the new challenges of the future.

When we take a moment to reflect upon the human capacity for inference, it takes on a wondrous and even spiritual dimension—at least when not stripped of its significance by reinterpreting it through technical jargon. For instance, instead of describing this episode of Crusoe's life in terms of his emotions, imaginings, and actions, one might rely on the language of dualistic psychology that talks of external objects, inner consciousness, sensory stimulus, data processing, and mental states. By stripping away the tangible and temporal elements of experience and translating the rest into a programming language, Crusoe's reaction can be explained the same way as one might talk about a computer. But for Dewey, this denies the existential and experiential character of inference that makes it a distinctly *human* activity. Indeed, it is our capacity to draw inferences that makes us *transcendent* beings rather than stones:

> We have not got very far with our question of distinctive, unique traits called into existence by inference, but we have got far enough to have light upon what is called the "transcendence" of knowledge. All inference is a *going beyond* the assuredly present to an absent. Hence it is a more or less precarious journey. It is transcending limits of security of immediate response. The stone which reacts only to stimuli of the present, not of the future, cannot make the mistakes which a being reacting to a future taken to be connected with the present is sure to make. But it is important to note just what this transcendence consists in. It has nothing to do with transcending mental states to arrive at an external object. *It is behaving to the given situation as involving something not given.* It is Robinson Crusoe going from a seen foot to an unseen man, not from a mental state to something unmental.[16]

A further way to draw this distinction between human beings and stones is that whereas a stone is merely *reactive*, a human being *acts* upon inferences by altering subsequent behavior to account for these *unseen* (but *for that individual* very *real*) existences. Neither we nor Crusoe needs access to his inner mental states to be able to witness the activity of inference; rather, "that inference is describable as the specific change induced in his behavior by what he saw."[17] And it is precisely this *behavior* that arises from inference—and not the technical process of inference itself—that human beings take such enduring fascination in witnessing. *Robinson Crusoe* has remained a classic not because it lays bare the mental states of its hero's consciousness; it has remained a classic because it is a portrait of the transcendence of knowledge in action.

Yet as any logician would point out, just because Crusoe experiences such transcendence does not mean that his inference is warranted or even logically coherent. For instance, Crusoe not only questions the validity of his inference about the footprint but also allows his "affrighted" imagination to give way to wild ideas and strange, unaccountable whimsies once back in his camp. If inference allowed him to transcend his immediate environment and project himself into a future time and space, it also allowed him to mistake dreams for realities and fill his imagination with fantasies and deceptions: "Inference brings, in short, truth and falsity into the world, just as definitely as the circulation of blood brings its distinctive consequences, both advantages and liabilities into the world." And it hardly needs to be argued that Crusoe at this moment is in many ways representative of the state of human nature in general: "The barest glance at human history shows that mistakes have been the rule, and that truth lies at the bottom of a well.... If the classic definition of man as a rational animal means simply an inferring or guessing animal, it applies to the natural man, for it allows for the guesses being mostly wrong." To identify the origins of logic in our instinctive and spontaneous inferences is not to romantically celebrate human beings in the state of nature; it is simply to acknowledge that we carry that nature with us even as we "transition from natural spontaneous performance to a technique or deliberate art of inference."[18] The goal of logic is not to suppress or supplant human nature; it is to develop the capacities of that nature into a conscious and deliberate power.

The example of Robinson Crusoe appealed to Dewey because it so perfectly exemplified the conception of "cultural naturalism" that underlies his logical theory. Reminiscent of his earlier notion of naturalistic humanism, cultural naturalism posits the "continuity of the lower (less complex) and the higher (more complex) activities and forms."[19] By "naturalism," Dewey means that the "higher" acts of logical inference—or the more "complex" forms of syllogistic deduction—are not imported into human nature from outside or above; they rather grow out of and remain connected to the innate impulses, capacities, responses, and behaviors that make up the native equipment of our biological natures. By "cultural," Dewey means to emphasize that the products of our shared and social relationships, most notably language, are as influential, real, and lasting as any natural environment. Adapting the language of St. Paul to make his point, Dewey stresses that "neither inquiry nor the most abstractly formal set of symbols can escape from the cultural matrix in which they live, move and have their being."[20] The religious imagery he employs at this point is telling and reminiscent of his definition of God that he used in his address to the students at the University of Michigan. For Dewey, neither logical inquiry nor religious faith is a way to escape from the world into a realm of abstract relations; they are ways of using the power of reflective thought to immerse oneself even deeper within the cultural and natural world to discover deeper meanings and truths.

Crusoe provides a literary case study by which to exemplify the two matrices in and through which logic can develop as a deliberate art. The first matrix is biological and has for its starting point the fact that human beings are not disembodied minds; rather, "they employ their eyes and ears, their hands and their brains."[21] This obvious fact entails, as a necessary precondition, an outside world in which our sensory organs operate and to which our senses are adapted. When Crusoe lands on the island, he reports in great detail what he sees, feels, tastes, smells, and hears. But even more than that, our biological natures lead us to treat this outside world as an "environment," as a source of nourishment and deprivation, of opportunity and resistance, and of support and threat. As organic beings, a *human* being thus "does not live *in* an environment; it lives *by means* of an environment."[22] Crusoe thus perceives the island primarily as a resource to survive, and he uses all his sensory and mental apparatus to adapt to and control his environment. The plot of the story thus revolves around a series of tensions that occur when Crusoe finds himself out of balance with his environment, whether because he is hungry or cold or alone or terrified. For Dewey, a tension represents "an actual state (not mere feeling) of organic uneasiness and restlessness" that defines not only a need but "passes into search for material that will restore the condition of balance."[23] In short, Crusoe hunts, builds a fire, writes in his journal, and searches for evidence of a threat. The satisfaction of these tensions then represents the temporary consummation of coordinated activity until the next need arises.

The biological matrix of inquiry locates the origin of all logical inquiry in the outgoing energy we exert when seeking to restore balance to an imbalanced situation. The activities and forms through which this energy is expressed vary widely from person to person and situation to situation. Crusoe's inquiry into the significance of the footprint follows a different path than his later inquiry into the ethics of killing the man to which it belonged. But both share the same biological origin in a feeling of *doubt* and the same determinate end, which is the establishment of *belief*. Neither of these terms should be interpreted in regards to a purely cognitive relationship to some hypothetical fact; doubt and belief are existential conditions that arise in response to a situation. In the first case, doubt manifests itself as a *feeling*: "Doubt is uneasy; it is tension that finds expression and outlet in the processes of inquiry." Doubt thus arises in situations that might be characterized as "disturbed, troubled, ambiguous, confused, full of conflicting tendencies, obscure, etc. It is the situation that has these traits. We are doubtful because the situation is inherently doubtful." In the second case, belief is embodied in a *habit*.

What this means is that belief signifies both *what* is believed and *how* one behaves toward something in a given situation: "*Belief* here names the settled condition of objective subject-matter, together with readiness to act in a given way when, if, and as, that subject-matter is present in existence."[24] For instance, when Crusoe encounters the footprint, he experiences doubt because of its potential meanings that disrupts his entire existence and throws him into turmoil; his ultimate determination is that it represents a possible enemy that he must prepare, if necessary, to kill. This readiness represents a belief insofar as he begins actively preparing for that encounter. Inquiry represents all the conscious activities of searching that occur between the stimulus to doubt and its consummation in belief.

Another way to talk about the cultural matrix of inquiry is through the more quotidian notion of "common sense." We often think of common sense as a combination of good *sense* or good *judgment*—namely, about the everyday affairs that have a bearing upon our uses and enjoyment of things and events. Common *sense* thus represents a "power of discernment; in a proverbial phrase, ability to tell a hawk from a hernshaw, chalk from cheese, and to bring the discriminations made to bear upon what is to be done and what is to be abstained from, in the 'ordinary affairs of life.'" But common sense also represents the *common* sense, which is to say the collective and shared body of settled truths and accepted meanings of any language community; in this way, it is "commonplace that every cultural group possesses a set of meanings which are so deeply embedded in its customs, occupations, traditions and ways of interpreting its physical environment and group-life, that they form the basic categories of the language-system by which details are interpreted. Hence they are regulative and 'normative' of specific beliefs and judgments."[25] It is through our cultural matrix that we absorb this common sense through shared experiences in which a taken-for-granted background language is used to evaluate and direct behavior in familiar, traditional, and practical situations.[26]

The importance of common sense to the development of logic is that it provides a starting point for inquiry. Namely, it is through the *language* of common sense that our instinctive capacity for inference, based on the interpretation of natural signs, becomes transformed into a more deliberate art of inquiry mediated by cultural symbols. For instance, it does not require common sense for Crusoe to be able to see a footprint and infer the *real* presence of an *absent* man; in this case, he still operates within the largely animalistic realm of spontaneous inference. The footprint performs the function of a natural sign that acquires its representative capacity because of its existential connection with another thing in proximate space and time. For instance, "when it is said that smoke as an actual existence points to, is evidence of, an existential fire, smoke is said to be a *natural* sign of fire." Natural signs are ubiquitous in the animal world, either because animals are born with the instinct to interpret them or because they have the capacity to learn their significance through direct, nonlinguistic experience. A symbol, by contrast, acquires its meaning as determined by social usage. For instance, whereas smoke *itself* is a natural sign, "the *word* 'smoke' stands in the English language for an object of certain qualities." And perhaps even more important with respect to logic, the symbol "smoke" also stands in a relationship to *other* symbols in a language system, each connected within an infinite and flexible web of possible implications. "Smoke" thus relates not only to the meaning "of fire but to such apparently unrelated meanings as friction, changes of temperature, oxygen, molecular constitution, and, by intervening meaning-symbols, to the laws of thermodynamics"—and these are only the *scientific* implications of the word.[27] Through common sense, smoke might also be connected with cooking, smoking a pipe, burning a field, or war. With respect to Crusoe, the natural sign of the footprint takes on a far wider meaning because the common sense of his time associated it with the symbol "cannibal" and all its implications, thus provoking his imagination to spin out all the catastrophic consequences of their presence on the island.

In the movement of spontaneous inference from natural signs to that of deliberate inquiry through symbols, Crusoe shifted from the realm of the temporal to the nontemporal. This does not mean that Crusoe suddenly transcended to a realm of pure mind outside of time; of course the activity of his thought and consciousness remained as temporal as his breathing. Rather, Dewey means that the relations of the language system in which his thinking operates at any point in time are not *themselves* temporal. Thus "it was a temporal event when someone landed on Robinson Crusoe's island. It was a temporal event when Crusoe found the footprint on the sands. It was a temporal event when Crusoe inferred the presence of a possibly dangerous stranger. But while the proposition was about something temporal, the relation of the observed fact as evidential to the inference drawn from it is nontemporal. The same holds of every logical relation in and of propositions." Crusoe's encounter with the footprint and his act of inference are temporal and, as such, perfect material for dramatic fiction, but the logical propositions that (1) "a human footprint in the sand is indicative of the presence of a human being" and (2) "many native populations on Pacific islands practice cannibalism" are not. Like mathematical propositions, they exist out of time as part of the storehouse of possible relations and functions.

Teaching logic in the pedagogy of democratic humanism requires attention to these nuances of inference in order to develop the critical attitudes necessary for inquiry to become a *deliberate* art guided by conscious method rather than intuition or impulse. Consequently, the first and most necessary attitude to cultivate is that of *detachment*. In the case of Crusoe's initial reaction, we see the problem of the failure to develop this attitude. As indicated by his own subsequent self-criticism, he accepted immediately, emotionally, and uncritically the real and actual presence of a man that he perceived to be a direct and imminent threat. Of course, Crusoe had only seen a *natural sign* of that man, but with his naïve realism, that just made the threat all the worse. As Dewey explains, his absence just meant that the man was "farther off, or more concealed, and hence (probably) more mysterious, more powerful and awesome, on that account. The man indicated to Crusoe by the footprints was like a man of menacing powers seen at a distance through a telescope. Things naturally inferred are accepted, in other words, by the natural man on altogether too realistic a basis for adequate control; they impose themselves too directly and irretrievably. There are no alternatives save either acceptance or rejection in toto."[28] That Crusoe further inspected the sign to see if it really was a footprint, to learn how fresh it was, or to check whether it matched his own footprint does not alter Dewey's judgment on this matter; such actions are no different in kind than a dog sniffing more thoroughly around an environment to confirm whether a scent is strong and identifiable enough to act upon. What Crusoe needed was a method by which he could step outside of the imperatives of his immediate situation and reflect more thoroughly and freely on its *meaning* as an *idea*. This is the essential nature of detachment. Dewey explains,

> We need some method of freely examining and handling the object in its status as an inferred object. This means some way of detaching it, as it were, from the particular act of inference in which it presents itself. Without some such detachment, Crusoe can never get into a free and effective relation with the man indicated by the footprint. He can only, so to speak, go on repeating, with continuously increasing fright, "There's a man about, there's a man about." The "man" needs to be treated, not as man, but as something having a merely inferred and hence potential status; as a meaning or thought, or "idea."[29]

This capacity to detach oneself from the immediate and spontaneous meaning of an inference and turn it into an idea makes possible the cultivation of a second attitude that contributes to the process of inquiry—that of *playfulness*. Crusoe cannot play around with the footprint insofar as he believes it to actually signify an imminent threat just around the corner; the only thing he can do is *act*. However, detachment allows him to transform the footprint from something that *has* meaning into *a* meaning itself, which is to say an idea that obtains possible relationships to any number of other ideas. It is this detachment that allows him to *think* before he acts and to think in such a way that he allows himself the space and freedom to experiment with different combinations of ideas and possibilities. It is once again language that brings about the possibility of this kind of imaginative playfulness. For him, words and terms of discourse are "the solution of the requirement for greater flexibility and liberation. Let me repeat: Crusoe's inquiry can *play freely around* and about the man inferred from the footprint only as he can, so to say, get away from the immediate suggestive force of the footprint."[30] This sense of playfulness for Dewey represents the liberating spirit of logic. The spirit is often concealed, even denied, when the meanings developed within an active inquiry process become frozen by calling them "notions, forms, essences, terms, subsistences, ideas, meanings, etc." But for Dewey, a meaning should be thought of as a surrogate for the objects of inference for the purpose of imaginative manipulation, reconstruction, and recombination. Unlike actual objects, surrogates "can be brought into relation with one another, quite irrespective of the things which originally suggested them. Without such free play reflective inquiry is mockery, and control of inference an impossibility."[31] But when playfulness is embraced, the available paths and possible outcomes of logical inference are literally infinite.

But it is precisely this unbounded nature of symbolic relations that necessitates the development of the third attitude to bring inquiry to its conclusion—that of *experimentalism*. At the heart of the experimental attitude is the eagerness to reveal the truth and value of our ideas by using them to direct the course of future experience. Experimentalism is thus *active*; after *detaching* oneself from a situation and *playfully* developing a hypothesis, experimentalism directs our attention back toward a situation with an eye toward predicting and controlling its development. Experimentalism thus "signifies *directed activity*, doing something which varies the conditions under which objects are observed and directly had and by instituting new arrangements among them."[32] Experimentalism is therefore not simply any activity, undirected, impulsive, or random; it must be *directed* activity that takes its direction from ideas formed within a particular situation. For instance, immediately after Crusoe saw the footprint, he engaged in all manner of activity, including imagining strange, unaccountable whimsies. But this was not experimental action; only after he was able to detach himself from the situation and develop a working hypothesis did he return to his environment with conscious intent—mostly searching the island for other evidence and building a fortifying wall. These types of directed activities exemplify the *active* nature of experimentalism. It "recognizes that experience, the actual experience of men, is one of doing acts, performing operations, cutting, marking off, dividing up, extending, piecing together, joining, assembling and mixing, hoarding and dealing out; in general, selecting and adjusting things as means for reaching consequences."[33] And this sort of activity is not restricted to the kind of practical acts of self-preservation such as those of Crusoe; it also implies the activities of the laboratory scientist, the business entrepreneur, the political legislator, the caring parent, and the curious child. Any activity that involves the conscious development of ideas to direct actions intended to produce consequences or anticipate effects is experimental.

The way in which experimentalism can cover the activities of all these individuals is by expanding our idea of what counts as a "consequence." One of the reasons that Dewey preferred the term *experimentalism* to *pragmatism* was that the latter tended to be taken to "signify some quite definite utilities of a material or bread-and-butter type."[34] It thus became associated with an idea of truth as crass expediency, where truth was defined only in terms of producing immediate consequences that could provide material and personal benefit. Experimentalism, by contrast, expanded the notion of consequences both in terms of quality and time. Qualitatively, it placed absolutely no restrictions on "the nature of the consequences; they may be aesthetic, or moral, or political, or religious in quality—anything you please. All that the theory requires is that they be in some way consequences of thinking; not, indeed, of it alone, but of it acted upon in connection with other things."[35] Temporally, it acknowledges that many forms of inference consist of highly technical and abstract symbol systems whose consequences (outside of the purely aesthetic pleasure of symbolic problem solving, that is) may be realized only indirectly in an experience far in the future. Even mathematical ideas developed in complete detachment from practical application have born unexpected fruit, as "the history of science is full of illustrations of cases in which mathematical ideas for which no physical application was known suggested in time new existential relations."[36] Experimentalism thus does not define beforehand what counts as a consequence; quite the opposite, it insists that what counts as a consequence is precisely determined by the nature of the idea itself. Experimentalism judges the worth of an idea by its own lights and calls "true" that which guides accurately and "valuable" that which guides well. What is important for an experimental idea is that it *guides*.

We have already seen the core attitudes of logic—*detachment, playfulness,* and *experimentalism*; it now remains to explicate the method of inquiry that forms the basis of its pedagogy across the curriculum. This method follows the six steps of reflective thought that Dewey defined in his 1910 pedagogical treatise *How We Think*. These include (1) *doubt*, the realization of a felt difficulty; (2) *definition*, the identification of a problem and its location; (3) *hypothesis*, the inductive inference to a possible explanation; (4) *reasoning*, the deductive relations that reveal its implications; (5) *observation*, the experimental verification of those implications; and (6) *judgment*, the rendering of a decision of value with a bearing on future action and belief. This method of thought applies to any and all situations in which reflection on experience is necessary to bring a situation to some unity or consummation, whether one is a scientist, poet, philosopher, politician, parent, child, or citizen. Consequently, the aim of teaching this method is wholly general; that is, "it is its business to cultivate deep-seated and effective habits of discriminating tested beliefs from mere assertions, guesses, and opinions; to develop a lively, sincere, and open-minded preference for conclusions that are properly grounded, and to engrain into the individual's working habits methods of inquiry and reasoning appropriate to the various problems that present themselves."[37] When teaching the arts of democratic humanism, there is no such thing as certain situations or problems that count as logical while others do not; wherever there is thinking, there is logic. The goal of the teacher is to accept the diversity of experience and to find those situations that stimulate the wonder and curiosity of students.

The first step in the process of inquiry is to encounter a situation that produces genuine and not merely feigned doubt. In other words, this is not the kind of Cartesian doubt in which a person plays pretend because she has been ordered to doubt something that she really does not. Doubt arises not in response to an order or obligation but because an individual finds herself within a situation that *actually* possesses these traits. If we call a situation "*confused,* then it is meant that its outcome cannot be anticipated. It is called *obscure* when its course of movement permits of final consequences that cannot be clearly made out. It is called *conflicting* when it tends to evoke discordant responses."[38] These are qualities that do not just occur within a person's mind but are qualities evoked by a problematic situation in which she finds herself. Thus in extreme "cases of striking novelty or unusual perplexity, the difficulty . . . is likely to present itself at first as a shock, as emotional disturbance, as a more or less vague feeling of the unexpected, of something queer, strange, funny, or disconcerting."[39] But these qualities are as much properties of the events and objects themselves as they are of the person experiencing them; they are in this sense as "real" as any physical substance. For instance, when Crusoe encounters the horrific scene on the beach, he did not attribute his reaction to his internal mental states; he described the entire qualitative feeling that pervaded the situation itself.

However, it is important not to restrict our interpretation of "situation" to such dramatic events that engage our instinctual fight-or-flight mechanism. As human beings, we live not only in a biological matrix but also within a cultural matrix. Biologically, we can all relate to animals who are suddenly roused by an unexpected scene, scent, or sound and focus all their conscious energies on determining its nature, but rarely do we encounter such disturbances in the raw. The objects and the events that surround us are already invested with cultural meanings to the extent that a mere word or symbol might throw us into a state of anxiety and perplexity. For instance, Crusoe's immediate response to seeing the bones on the beach was a ready conviction to murder the next cannibal he saw; he did not experience *doubt* but rather *confidence*. It was only after he dwelt upon the nature of God and his supreme authority that doubt crept into his mind. The "word" of God was the stimulus to doubt because it disrupted his established habits. It is in this way that the act of communication itself, in writing, word, image, gesture, or thought, can be one of the most powerful sources of stimuli that can throw into doubt our most cherished beliefs.

The second step of inquiry is to locate the cause of the feeling of doubt and thereby transform a *problematic* situation into a *problem*. When faced with instances that are unexpected, strange, or disconcerting, we engage in "necessary observations deliberately calculated to bring to light just what is the trouble, or to make clear the specific character of the problem."[40] In the animal world, this amounts to the difference between being startled awake by some disturbance and realizing that a disturbance comes from a particular rustling and growling behind a nearby bush. In the case of Crusoe's initial encounter on the beach, he defines his problem by focusing less on the multiple signs of the presence of other human beings—the circle dug in the earth, footprints, and evidence of boat landings—and more on the specific threat of *cannibals* indicated by the presence of human skulls, hands, and feet. By being so identified and named as significant objects and events within a total field of experience, they become thereby transformed into "data" that function to direct the course of inquiry and determine its project subject. Narratively speaking, data are what we select as important within a complex environment to set the scene, as it were, and to focus the attention of our audience on what is to come, much as the facts that are admissible in court establish the ground for prosecution. Data can come in the form of either immediately observable facts or "data derived from recollections of earlier observations."[41] They can be the various visible symptoms we describe to our doctor as well as our past medical history that is relevant for diagnosis. They are the product of careful observation and selective judgment concerning what is significant and what is not within a particular problematic situation in order to give it clarity and definition.

From a communication standpoint, it is important to emphasize that the activity of determining the data is very much an active rather than passive affair. Data are not simply "there," as if objects existed as discrete entities with labels already attached that needed only to be noted and recorded. The act of naming something, as we have already seen, is a *transformative* act. Outside of language, the world is in a state of constant flux and change characterized by a stream of events and qualities. Naming transforms the pushing and pulling of these events into discrete *objects*, or "things with a meaning," that endure beyond the flux of becoming. Events "once they are named lead an independent and double life. In addition to their original existence, they are subject to ideal experimentation: their meanings may be infinitely combined and re-arranged in imagination."[42] In other words, the colors and shapes Crusoe might see from a distance coalesce into recognizable qualities, which he then names first "bones," then "humans," and finally "victims." With each name, Crusoe bestows upon the raw events and qualities a meaning that endures beyond their physical existence—and indeed, that still endures today. But for the cannibals, such data might be called "enemies" or "sacrifices" or "dinner." By naming them differently, they are transformed into different objects of meaning. This contrast in perspective thus demonstrates the degree to which all "thinking is specific, in that different things suggest their own appropriate meanings, tell their own unique stories, and in that they do this in very different ways with different persons."[43] To use one of Dewey's favorite examples, the choice to label something "water" instead of "H_2O" is to actively designate something useful for "drink and cleansing and the extinguishing of fire" as opposed to something that has a particular molecular structure of hydrogen and oxygen atoms.[44] Consequently, it is not enough to point to something and call it "data"; one must actively *name* the data so that it can tell its own unique story and thereby play its own particular role within a situation under inquiry.

And it is important to stress that naming data is an entirely *realistic* process. Despite the idealistic-sounding tenor of Dewey's language, he does not mean that naming a phenomenon *directly* transforms one physical substance into another by some sort of word magic. What he means is that it transforms the flux of events and qualities into a stable *object of thought* that can be manipulated and rearranged in the imagination in relationship to other objects. Idealism would only arise if the process of inquiry had as its only end the production of an *idea valid for its own sake as a representative truth*, a notion often conveniently forgotten by those who call themselves "realists" and yet hold to a notion that truth represents a mystical correspondence between ideas and things. For Dewey, realism means that thinking arises in response to a genuine problem and finds its confirmation by directly contributing to its resolution. The realism of the experimental attitude, in short, means that "thinking ends in experiment and experiment is an *actual* alteration of a physically antecedent situation in those details or respects which called for thought in order to do away with some evil."[45] To name data is therefore to define data's role and function in the process of experimentation and to make a promise that its name has been well chosen. Dewey remarks that a lot of confusion would have been avoided in the history of philosophy if "instead of the word 'data' or 'givens,' it had happened to start with calling the qualities in question 'takens.'" To name data "takens" would better indicate how data are actively "*selected* from this total original subject-matter which gives the impetus to knowing; they are discriminated for a purpose."[46] Part of the joy of the discovery of logic, in fact, comes precisely from allowing students themselves to participate in *taking* data and *naming* them in a way that establishes the "facts of the case" such that they reflect their own unique perspectives and aims within a particular situation.[47]

The creative heart of inquiry, however, is located in the third step of developing a hypothesis. This is the activity Dewey described as having a "transcendent" quality insofar as transcendence represents an act of "going beyond." In logic, what an act of hypothesis "goes beyond" is not only the data but also the immediate situation itself; it makes a suggestion about the nature and origin of the situation as well as pointing to its future development and consequences. As Dewey explains, "Suggestion is the very heart of inference; it involves going from what is present to something absent. Hence, it is more or less speculative, adventurous." There is no way to "mechanically" safeguard inference, to make it something purely necessary and deterministic: "Since inference goes beyond what is actually present, it involves a leap, a jump, the propriety of which cannot be absolutely warranted in advance, no matter what precautions be taken."[48] For example, Crusoe's hypothesis that the bones he saw on the beach were the result of a ritualistic cannibal feast, despite being warranted by the data, is by no means a necessary conclusion. It is a speculative leap from the sheer presence of bones to the reconstruction of an entire course of events in the imagination of Crusoe. All hypotheses have this character; they move from what is observed to what is not observed in order to bring some order, coherence, and control to some situation by going beyond what is "given."

At the same time, the plausibility of his conjecture—and the fact that it was confirmed by future events—also shows that a hypothesis is no mere random guessing; it is an idea that springs out of the data, is guided by habit, and is constrained by the context of the situation. Of the three characteristics, the *habitual* nature of hypothesis is often the most neglected. Crusoe betrays his cultural habits by drawing on the clear eighteenth-century stereotype of "cannibal," but in most of our own daily lives, we hardly notice the influence of our cultural matrix. We act on hypotheses that are largely guided by the habits we have acquired through common sense. For instance, Dewey describes possible reactions to an imminent rainstorm. When we look to the biological world, "an animal without thought may go into its hole when rain threatens, because of some immediate stimulus to its organism." The habits that guide their hypotheses are hardwired into their biological beings. In contradistinction, "a thinking agent will perceive that certain given facts are probable signs of a future rain, and will take steps in the light of this anticipated future. To plant seeds, to cultivate the soil, to harvest grain, are intentional acts, possible only to a being who has learned to subordinate the immediately felt elements of an experience to those values which these hint at and prophesy."[49] For the farmer, these reactions to the prospect of rain, while acquired from culture, become a "second nature" of habit. But culture also provides a stock of habits that go well beyond the cultivation of crops; they make ordinary what were once the most complex and controversial scientific conjectures. Dewey notes that "the child today soon regards as constituent parts of objects qualities that once it required the intelligence of a Copernicus or a Newton to apprehend."[50] A child looks up at the sky today and see stars and galaxies and planets and takes for granted that she lives within an infinite universe, yet these are all inductive inferences by which a mere pinpoint of light offers a hint and prophesy about the nature of the world beyond experience.

Once a hypothesis is accepted as a possibility, the fourth step is to engage in reasoning that reveals the implications of the presence of that object or event. Thus just "as an idea is inferred from given *facts*, so reasoning sets out from an *idea*."[51] It is with the stage of reasoning that detachment fully sets in and the play of ideas begins in earnest. The activity of reasoning is a movement from one symbolic implication to the next, meaning that "if such and such a relation of meanings is accepted, then we are committed to such and such other relations of meanings because of their membership in the same system. Through a series of intermediate meanings, a meaning is finally reached which is more clearly *relevant* to the problem in hand than the originally suggested idea."[52] The object of the hypothesis, as a symbolic idea, thus becomes removed from the temporal flux of events and establishes itself as a *starting point* for moving through a series of logical relationships—namely, by drawing on warrants based on analogies, generic categories, or causal consequences. For instance, after Crusoe has time to think after his initial reaction to hypothesizing the existence of cannibals, he compares their acts to the atrocities committed by the Spanish (analogy), places cannibals within the larger category of human beings and thus deduces who should be respected as children of God (principle), and sees that as long as he remains hidden, they will not represent a threat to his life (causation). In each case, Crusoe starts from the initial idea and uses reasoning, made possible through the creative activity of the imagination, to expand his consciousness beyond his initial animalistic reaction to dwell upon the larger significance of their presence on or near his island.

Of all the capacities that human beings possess, it is the capacity for reasoning through symbols that Dewey consistently praises as the most spectacular achievement in history that deserves an almost religious reverence, for it is only through symbols that we can, as it were, "act without acting." That is to say, rather than acting directly on our physical environment, symbols allow us to act within the sphere of thought, particularly as it is stimulated by communication with others and with ourselves. Dewey explains,

> By means of symbols, whether gestures, words or more elaborate constructions, we act without acting. That is, we perform experiments by means of symbols which have results which are themselves only symbolized, and which do not therefore commit us to actual or existential

consequences. If a man starts a fire or insults a rival, effects follow; the die is cast. But if he rehearses the act in symbols in privacy, he can anticipate and appreciate its result. Then he can act or not act overtly on the basis of what is anticipated and is not there in fact. The invention or discovery of symbols is doubtless by far the single greatest event in the history of man. Without them, no intellectual advance is possible; with them, there is no limit set to intellectual development except inherent stupidity.[53]

And what is even more remarkable than the fact that, as individuals, we can rehearse and act symbolically in privacy is the fact that, as a society, we can learn from each other's experiences and thereby *reason together*. As has been already said, even Crusoe on his island benefits from the common possessions he inherited from his English education and culture; it is only because he was able to "act without acting" that he survived for so many years on his own.

From a communication perspective, moving from hypothesis to reasoning also entails a shift in emphasis from individual creativity to cooperative discussion. The inductive process of generating hypotheses is often associated with the word *discovery* for a reason; it is a transcendent leap into the unknown stimulated by the imagination based on a reading of signs and qualities.[54] As a result, hypothesis generation should be considered a creative activity of the individual mind. In contradistinction, the deductive character of reasoning begins with the ideas of induction and pursues "their elaboration into fullness and completeness of meaning."[55] It "involves running over various ideas, sorting them out, comparing one with another, trying to get one which will unite in itself the strength of two, searching for new points of view, developing new suggestions, guessing, suggesting, selecting and rejecting."[56] Whereas induction represents a single act that ends with positing a possibility in the form of an idea, deduction represents a sustained and comprehensive process that traces out, potentially into infinity, the implications of that idea. As a part of this activity, discussion with others is an invaluable resource. Associated in Dewey's mind with the origin of logical theory in Greece, discussion involves "bringing various beliefs together; shaking one against another and tearing down their rigidity. It is conversation of thoughts; it is dialogue—the mother of dialectic in more than the etymological sense."[57] Whether one calls it discussion, dialogue, or dialectic, communication within the process of reasoning is a collaborative endeavor to reveal all the possible implications of an idea, regardless of whether it is an idea about bones on a beach, the structure of a poem, the existence of the afterlife, another person's motives, or a text from history.

The outcome of such rational discussion, whether it goes on between individuals or within one's own mind, is the tracing out of multiple possible *implications* of hypothetical inference. In Dewey's logical theory, implication differs from inference. An inference always goes from that which is present to that which is absent; it involves a reading of signs and qualities to infer the existence of some object or event. An implication, by contrast, is a characteristic of symbols and propositions; it deals with the potentially observable effects or consequences that follow from some meaning. Crusoe *infers* the existence of cannibals, but his inference that his life is in danger is an *implication*. Importantly, whereas inferences can be made by all conscious organisms, implications can only exist for a being capable of using symbols. Dewey explains that once named and given symbolic significance, "natural events become messages to be enjoyed and administered, precisely as are song, fiction, oratory, the giving of advice and instruction. Thus events come to possess characters; they are demarcated, and noted. . . . They are more than mere occurrences; they have implications. Hence inference and reasoning are possible; these operations are reading the message of things, which things utter because they are involved in human associations."[58] The metaphor Dewey uses is illuminating. When we engage in reasoning, we quite literally read the messages that things utter to us, whether that thing is a bone or a book, a beach or a song; in reasoning, we translate all events into symbols that speak our language and tell us where they are leading. It is the job of reasoning to listen carefully to things and to identify those situations in which we can interact with those consequences, regardless of their quality. To feel joy at hearing a song is as much a consequence as touching marks on a stone or seeing words on a manuscript.

Within the pedagogy of democratic humanism, all logical reasoning then returns to the world of experience; it is not enough to dwell in the realm of the symbolic or the possible. The fifth step of logic thus demands a return to active observation to close the circle of inquiry and engage the *realism* of the experimental method. In this way, "observation exists at the beginning and again at the end of the process: at the beginning, to determine more definitely and precisely the nature of the difficulty to be dealt with; at the end, to test the value of some hypothetically entertained conclusion."[59] The nature of observation can be understood by comparing it to its counterpart—recognition. An act of recognition is "relatively automatic and passive" as it "refers to the already mastered." We recognize something when it comes to us as a familiar object or event, already categorized and conceptualized within our common sense. By contrast, "observation is exploration, inquiry for the sake of discovering something previously hidden and unknown, this something being needed in order to reach some end, practical or theoretical."[60] Consequently, we might experience the very same object differently when we move from recognition to observation. When Crusoe first encounters evidence of cannibalism in the form of cooked and cut bones around a fire pit, he merely *recognizes* it and reacts according to his preconceived cultural biases; it is only after he goes through a process of inference and reasoning that he returns to the same phenomena and actively observes the degree to which the activity had the same qualities—except the *content* of the meal—as any traditional feast on the shores of England. By experiencing the same situation with a different perspective, Crusoe is able to *observe* features previously concealed from him that confirm his hypothesis that despite the violence of their rituals, their actions are for the most part consistent with any human culture.

The final step of inquiry, which represents its consummation, is *judgment*. If to doubt means to disrupt one's settled habits and to confront an indeterminate situation marked by perplexity, disorder, and confusion, then "to judge is to render determinate; to determine is to order and organize, to relate in definite fashion."[61] Judgment, that is to say, culminates in belief. But it is a belief expressed in a particularly logical fashion. A judgment in its most elementary form consists of three elements: a *subject*, a *predicate*, and a *copula*. The *subject* of a judgment is always singular and stands for some element of the situation and the observed data, such as "this footprint." The *predicate* represents the more general properties, conceptual contents, generic categories, or causal effects that the process of inquiry has revealed to be associated with the subject, such as "human." The *copula* is then the operation that joins the subject and predicate together into a relationship, thus making "this footprint is human." By rendering this particular judgment, Crusoe thus brings order to a disordered situation. He is able to give meaning to a certain set of qualities and events and label them as a specific object, a footprint, to which is attached certain characteristics consistent with the category of being human. By doing so, Crusoe can then make further judgments concerning this human ("this human is a cannibal"), how to feel about this situation ("this cannibal is threatening"), and what do ("murdering this cannibal is not justified"). In each case, a judgment is arrived at after a process of thinking, however instantaneous it might be, that passes through the stages of logical inquiry.

The active, temporal, and singular nature of logical judgment is best captured by thinking of the conclusion of inquiry much as the conclusion of a court trial. An individual pursuing an inquiry should think of herself as a "judge on the bench" presiding over a trial with three features: "(1) a controversy, consisting of opposite claims regarding the same objective situation; (2) a process of defining and elaborating these claims and of sifting the facts adduced to support them; (3) a final decision, or sentence, closing the particular matter in dispute and also serving as a rule or principle for deciding future cases."[62] In the case of a trial, of course, all these issues are around the actions of a single individual whose fate is decided by the actions of the prosecution and defense. In logical inquiry, the judge also plays prosecutor and defense attorney, at each point shifting roles and looking at elements of the situation in different ways. But they have in common the fact that the end result is a decision that "closes (or concludes) the question at issue." Furthermore, similar to the tradition of common law, "this determination not only settles that particular case, but it helps fix a rule or method for deciding similar matters in the future; as the sentence of the judge on the bench both terminates that dispute and also forms a precedent for future decisions."[63] In this we find the source of our warrants from generalization, leading to the conclusion that we can judge all such subjects as we treated this particular case. Crusoe, after all, need not learn his lessons a second time. In the course of several judgments, he develops habits of recognition and action that become a part of his own common sense. In this way, learning can be seen as the development of the common law within the tribunal of an individual's mind.

But the important qualification here is that in a democracy, actual trials are determined by the collaborative judgments of a jury, not the authoritarian pronouncements of a single individual. Consequently, logic stresses the importance of cooperative judgments that bring together multiple perspectives and experiences in order to render judgments more subtle, sophisticated, practical, and humane. Developing the attitudes of detachment, playfulness, and experimentalism is the foundation of creating these kinds of deliberative forums that stimulate collective inquiry. Stimulating detachment requires making use of the diagrammatic nature of creative thought. Often this requires little more than providing students with whiteboards, flip charts, markers, magnets, stickers, or any other tangible material that can "stand in" for objects, texts, ideas, or relations. Manipulating symbolic objects in a free space naturally produces detachment and its counterpart—playfulness. The second attitude is stifled, however, if a diagram is meant to reproduce what is already given, as if it were to be graded as an accurate representation. Playfulness requires the ability to continually manipulate materials on the diagram, to add or subtract objects and establish possible new relationships. It is the experimental attitude that brings the consummation to these playful ideas as students are encouraged to return to some original material with a fresh perspective. This original material might be a natural artifact or event, but it might also be a poem, a historical text, a painting, or a work of philosophy. What matters is that they return to some*thing* with a sense of having a new discovery.

In order to then show how the six stages in inquiry could function in the humanities curriculum, we can visualize how a teacher might apply them to the study of texts rather than events. One method by which to arouse a feeling of doubt is finding those places in history that still embody struggle, tension, ambiguity, and controversy. Teachers must find those specific events, texts, biographies, and testimonies that unsettle what were assumed to be settled accounts, not necessarily to overturn them but to stimulate student interest by challenging preconceived notions. Students then engage in definition when they identify the specific data in these texts that draw their attention and evoke their feelings of doubt. These might be specific quotations, unexpected happenings, or a conflict between intention and outcome. Once gathered together, students should thus be pressed to offer a hypothesis by actively *naming* the whole context of the data as a certain *type* of thing that strikes them to be true. This active labeling is an intervention, a way of summing up a nexus of events and predicting future qualities. But these hypotheses are not ends in themselves; they must then engage in the process of reasoning in order to determine implications. That is to say, students must speculate on where they might find those places that confirm or disconfirm their hypotheses, perhaps in other contemporaneous texts or within the same text. Finding this material by carefully reading with specific intent is thus a form of observation. These observations then provide the new data that allow a student to sum up their inquiry in a specific logical judgment, typically in the form of a thesis statement. Thus rather than beginning with the thesis, as so many paper assignments do, it ends with one.

The overarching aim and value of teaching logic is the same one that inspired Greek democracy—that of freedom. And what this meant was not a negative freedom but a positive one, for "freedom in its true sense" is a power—namely, "the habitual power of effective mental attack." This sounds overly aggressive until one contrasts it with a merely passive and negative freedom to be left alone, which in actual life means to be thrown back upon the whims of impulse and unreflective habit. Freedom for Dewey was thus acquainted with the freedom of mind, which in turn meant the "mental power capable of independent exercise, emancipated from the leading strings of others, not mere unhindered external operation."[64] It meant to engage in a constructive and positive discipline. For Dewey, those who talk about freedom as if it was something that we were born with, something that did not need to be earned, to be worked for, and to be developed in cooperation with others, actually produced something very different from freedom. As Dewey explains, "If a man's actions are not guided by thoughtful conclusions, then they are guided by inconsiderate impulse, unbalanced appetite, caprice, or the circumstances of the moment. To cultivate unhindered, unreflective external activity is to foster enslavement, for it leaves the person at the mercy of appetite, sense, and circumstance."[65] Robinson Crusoe presented Dewey with a case study of an individual who survived on an island precisely because he had arrived equipped with the greatest tool—the power of an inquiring mind. But the example is misleading if we forget the circumstances in which that mind was developed. Crusoe developed his mind in an active social life working, learning, and communicating with others. It is the task of the modern educator to do the same for the individual in a democratic society, for no longer must we be prepared to live stranded on a lonely island to struggle violently against those of a different culture. Quite the opposite. Our whole planet has effectively shrunk to the size of an island in which its populations are increasingly huddled together in anxiety and hope. We must be prepared to think alongside others within a diverse global community, engaged in ongoing processes of inquiry into our common problems in the awareness that each of our own freedoms now relies on the freedom of all.

8

AESTHETICS

Creation, not acquisition, is the measure of a nation's rank; it is the only road to an enduring place in the admiring memory of mankind.

—JOHN DEWEY, "ART AS OUR HERITAGE"

On April 25, 1940, Dewey delivered another radio address, this time over station WMAL in Washington, DC, to highlight the importance of the arts for civilization. The same month that Nazi forces continued their invasion of Norway in the opening salvo of a war that would cost millions of lives and destroy countless artistic treasures across the world, Dewey attempted to preserve and promote the arts in his own country. He told the story of a "gracious white-haired woman" he had once met while crossing the Atlantic during the early years of the Depression. Like so many others during that time, she had lost almost all her money because of the bank failures and bad stock investments, yet unlike most people, she had decided that she was "now going to buy herself something nobody could take away from her. She was going to Athens to see the Acropolis and the Parthenon." The encounter had left a lasting impression on Dewey. It was one thing for a person to have the luxury to see the sights of the world as a way of passing the time on vacation and escaping for a while from the routine of work and daily life; it was another to use one's last dollars to make "an investment in something that is imperishable, because it enriches personal life and becomes a part of one's very self."[1] And when juxtaposed with the rising tide of violence that was then sweeping across the world in an acquisitive frenzy, it was a reminder that what endures of once great civilizations are not their material conquests but their artistic creations that continue to speak with the universal language to all who are willing to listen.

As with his earlier praise of WEVD's *University of the Air*, however, Dewey's WMAL encomium to the power of art acquired even greater significance when looking closely at the context of its broadcast. Dewey had delivered "Art as Our Heritage" at the invitation of Edward Bruce, who in 1933 had been named by Franklin Delano Roosevelt to be the national director of his Public Works of Art Project. By 1940, he had become the national director of the Section of Fine Arts, an agency of the treasury department tasked with selecting high-quality muralists to decorate public buildings, thus making fine art accessible to all people. Dewey's story about the Parthenon was thus carefully chosen to highlight the importance not just of art but of publicly funded, publicly accessible art designed such that "our public buildings may become the outward and visible sign of the inward grace which is the democratic spirit." To bring this point home, Dewey tells another story of a letter received by Director Bruce from a postmaster whose building displayed one of those murals. At the end of his letter, the postmaster "included a sentence which might also be a motto of the whole project: 'How can a finished citizen be made in an artless town?' How indeed can an all-around and complete citizenry be developed without that development of creation and enjoyment of works of art to which the government, itself, must contribute?"[2] This story expressed the belief that Dewey would affirm with ever greater vigor in his later works—that a political democracy is barren if individuals are denied the exposure to works of art that allow them to feel more deeply, to think more broadly, and to imagine themselves in universes different from their own.

And it is important to point out that Dewey did not restrict his praise only to self-consciously civic art such as that supported by the New Deal; artworks of all genres and tenors had a crucial role to play in the development of the human personality. Art was important not merely in the conventional sense of praising community values, as if the only good art was the morality play; art was also important as a provocation to our established sensibilities, a disruption of our accepted habits, and an invitation to imagine possibilities. Offering his own interpretation of Matthew Arnold's dictum that "poetry is criticism of life," Dewey suggests that poetry criticizes life by forcing us to contrast our actual lives with some imaginative experience offered to us by a work of art, for "it is by a sense of possibilities opening before us that we become aware of constrictions that hem us in and of burdens that oppress."[3] Dewey tends to speak of these possibilities as *ideal* possibilities, as when we catch a glimpse of a better world only to return to our lived experience with an eagerness to make a change, but the same logic also applies to art that would force us to confront those possibilities we had previously denied. As John McDermott notes, in 1937, "the Paris World Exhibition unveiled Picasso's mural *Guernica* as the Spanish Civil War raged," thus disclosing the true nature of fascist violence and forcing the world to confront its horrific possibilities.[4] For Dewey, what is important is less the *substance* of the work of art but its *effect*—to expand our horizons of experience so that we can view the world from perspectives not our own.

Dewey called the study of our qualitative experience "aesthetics." The second part of the pedagogy of democratic humanism takes this name in order to emphasize that it is the *experience* of art that matters more than the objective character of the art itself. As Dewey points out, art "denotes a process of doing or making," akin to the Greek word *poiesis*, but the word *aesthetic* refers to "experience as appreciative, perceiving, and enjoying. It denotes the consumer's rather than the producer's standpoint."[5] To teach the method of producing art is, of course, central to the humanistic project of creating a meaningful world; without artists, only raw nature itself could be appreciated. However, the specific task of the democratic humanist is to cultivate the *capacity* for this appreciation, perception, and enjoyment in all people no matter their chosen calling. He named this capacity for enriched aesthetic appreciation "taste." As Dewey forcefully argued, "The formation of a cultivated and effectively operative good judgment or taste with respect to what is esthetically admirable, intellectually acceptable and morally approvable is the supreme task set to human beings by the incidents of experience."[6] In this passage, Dewey makes the establishment of taste the foundation of not only aesthetic enjoyment but also intellectual insight and moral conscience. To acquire "taste" is thus to expand the range of our sensibilities, allowing us to make qualitative distinctions in experience that enrich our lives and the lives of those around us.

One of the genres of art most central to this pedagogical project is that of literature, and one gets a sense of how to develop this critical sense of taste in the classroom through using literature in the work of Rosa Eberly. In the opening pages of her book *Citizen Critics: Literary Public Spheres*, Eberly recalls an experience in which a literary scholar came to campus to speak on the topic "Joyce and the Common Reader." To her disappointment, however, the lecturer failed to deliver on his promise; in fact, he "neglected to mention the oral or written words of even one actual reader of the novel, other than himself." What the scholar meant by James Joyce and the "common" reader was how Joyce integrated common words, phrases, and speech patterns into his novel *Ulysses*, not how actual common *readers* of the novel interpreted the texts. The only interpretation that mattered was that of the scholar himself. For Eberly, by contrast, the voices that make a difference in democracy are those of *actual* common readers who participate in public discourse about the value of popular works of art and literature. She calls this type of individual a *citizen critic*, who is "a person who produces discourses about issues of common concern from an ethos of citizen first and foremost—not as expert or spokesperson for a workplace or as member of a club or organization." Her book thus examines the voices of citizen critics through four historical case studies in which citizen critics argued, in popular media, over actual interpretations of major literary works and their social and political value. For her, each citizen critic might have started out speaking as a separate individual, but in the act of deliberation, "these people came together because, in John Dewey's terms, they recognized—through the work of literature—that they had common interests." Eberly thus captured precisely the function of aesthetics within democratic humanism—to create publics of shared interest and common taste that have a bearing not only on aesthetic preferences but on the values of political culture.[7]

Resonant with Dewey's emphasis on the importance of cultivating aesthetic judgment in the form of taste that has a bearing on shared experience, Eberly emphasizes the centrality of keeping alive a vibrant literary public sphere in democratic social life. For her, "literary public spheres are discursive spaces in which private people can come together in public, bracket some of their differences, and invent common interests by arguing or writing about literary or cultural texts. They are able to do so because, by moving from reader to rhetor, they have begun to manifest a public-oriented subjectivity, that is, a self that is more or less able to turn private reactions about literary or cultural texts into discourses that address some shared concerns." In other words, these are *public* spheres in that they are forms by which citizens deliberate about common affairs through publicly accessible media, but they are *literary* to the extent that they focus primarily on the evaluation of literary texts rather than the prudence of political policy. Ironically, "literary public spheres have nothing de facto to do with aesthetics; historically and temporarily, literary public figures reflect various publics' common concern about the consequences of the news of literary and cultural texts for their collective lives."[8] But Eberly uses the word *aesthetics* here in a restricted way, referring to an elite discourse; from the perspective of democratic humanism, aesthetics is precisely what these deliberations are about, for they are deliberations about taste.

Pedagogically, Eberly emphasizes the importance of creating a classroom environment that becomes what she calls a "proto-public space." For her, the ideal classroom is "a proto-public space that can foster literary public spheres and through which students may choose to form and enter publics and public speakers and to become citizen critics."[9] The classroom thus becomes a miniature forum that mirrors public discourse and invites students to deliberate about matters of taste concerning the value of literary works. In such a space, students "study and practice the discourses of literary public spheres as well as write arguments that they may choose to send out for publication, thus engaging with and possibly even forming publics." These literary texts thereby become "inventional prompts for discussion about various publics and their possible reaction to the texts in question."[10] This kind of assignment demonstrates how aesthetics takes advantage of the unique power of art to bring people together to discuss what might seem, at first, to be merely idiosyncratic preference. But aesthetic judgment is never merely superficial; it is a reflection of a complex life experience. In the humanist classroom, this experience becomes a resource that, in communication and reflection, can become a broad and penetrating critique of individual value and cultural practice.

In 1819, the twenty-three-year-old aspiring British poet John Keats composed a verse that in many ways came to embody the aestheticism of nineteenth-century romanticism. The verse appeared in his "Ode on a Grecian Urn," inspired by sculptures he had seen in the British Museum in London, including the then newly installed Elgin Marbles, which had been taken from the Parthenon. In the poem, Keats imagines himself speaking to the marble urn on whose surface is carved characters from two scenes, one portraying a lover eternally pursuing a beloved, another of priests and villagers preparing for a sacrifice. The opening lines call attention to the universal expressiveness of the object whose communicative power has only increased over time. Keats writes, "Thou still unravish'd bride of quietness, / Thou foster-child of silence and slow time, / Sylvan historian, who canst thus express / A flowery tale more sweetly than our rhyme." Having humbled his own poetic art before the Greek sculpture, Keats uses his verses to try to call forth in the imagination the eternal beauty of its action, which is forever fixed in marble. Of the lover, for instance, he says, "Though winning near the goal yet, do not grieve; / She cannot fade, though thou hast not thy bliss, / For ever wilt thou love, and she be fair!" But as the poem closes, Keats dares to make an even stronger claim about the significance of the urn and of art itself. Recognizing his own mortality and the fate of all things that live to pass away, he sees in the work of art something that will endure forever. He closes the poem:

> When old age shall this generation waste,
>   Thou shalt remain, in midst of other woe
> Than ours, a friend to man, to whom thou say'st,
>   *"Beauty is truth, truth beauty,—that is all*
>   *Ye know on earth, and all ye need to know."*[11]

Interpreted as an expression of stereotypical nineteenth-century romanticism, the concluding verses at first glance seem to stand in direct opposition to Dewey's philosophy. In *A Common Faith*, Dewey had written that "there is but one sure road of access to truth—the road of patient, cooperative inquiry operating by means of observation, experiment, record and controlled reflection."[12] But with Keats, we seem to have not only collapsed truth into beauty but also asserted that anything outside the bounds of the beautiful is not worth knowing. In *Art as Experience*, Dewey complained that "the elevation of the ideal above and beyond immediate sense has operated not only to make it pallid and bloodless, but it has acted, like a conspirator with the sensual mind, to impoverish and degrade all things of direct experience." But with Keats, we seem to encounter a notion of beauty that is wholly idealistic and transcendental, a type of Platonic Form that exists separate from lived experience and the temporal flux of becoming. Furthermore, Dewey borrowed from Keats the word *ethereal* in the chapter of *Art as Experience* that he titled "The Live Creature and 'Ethereal Things,'" a word chosen in part "to designate the meanings and values that many philosophers and some critics suppose are inaccessible to sense, because of their spiritual, eternal and universal characters—thus exemplifying the common dualism of nature and spirit."[13] One would therefore anticipate that Dewey would use Keats to exemplify the problems with a dualistic aesthetic philosophy that places the poetic in opposition to the scientific and posits a realm of values that exists in a transcendent realm of being that remains inaccessible to reason.

Yet Dewey does nothing of the kind. Instead, he quotes these verses to *challenge* philosophical dualism and to advance a competing philosophy that embraces the experimental and naturalistic attitudes of democratic humanism. In fact, Dewey spends four pages in *Art as Experience* discussing Keats's perspective on art in order to praise it against his detractors. In Dewey's hands, Keats emerges from the shadow of romanticism to become a prophetic voice for a modern, naturalistic view of art rooted less in ethereal things than in what he called the attitude of the "live creature"—that is to say, the biological organism that exists as a purposeful, sentient being in space and time. Far from rejecting the radical assertion that "beauty is truth, truth, beauty," Dewey accepts it and makes it the basis of his own aesthetic theory. It is therefore in Dewey's encounter with Keats that we find a key to understanding the radical implications of his aesthetics for the pedagogy of democratic humanism.

Notably, *Art as Experience* was not the first time that the poetry of Keats appeared in Dewey's work. In 1886, Dewey published a textbook called *Psychology*. Written at the time when Dewey was still influenced by his Christian humanist interpretation of Hegelian absolute idealism, *Psychology* integrated all the latest insights of psychological science into a larger idealistic world view in which "all psychical life may be indifferently described as the progressive realization by the will of its ideal self, or as the progressive idealization of the actual through the ultimate, absolute reality."[14] From this perspective, Keats seemed a natural fit to describe the workings of the "creative imagination." For Dewey in 1886, the "creative imagination is not to be considered as the production of unreal or fantastic forms, nor as the idle play of capricious mind working in an arbitrary way. It is a universalizing activity; that is to say, it sets the idea of memory or perception free from its particular accidental accompaniments, and reveals it in its universal nature." In other words, the creative imagination is the way we make a leap from the particular to the universal, the way we overstep the limits of our finite selves to catch a glimpse of that ultimate, absolute reality of which we are all a part. It is for this reason, the younger Dewey tells us, that Aristotle claimed that poetry is truer than history: "The latter only tells us that certain things happened; poetry presents to us the permanent passions, aspirations, and deeds of men which are behind all history, and which make it." It is at this point that Dewey quotes a lengthy passage from book 2 of Keats's poem "Endymion" (which had opened with the famous line "A thing of beauty is a joy for ever"). The specific passage he quotes diminishes the importance of learning about the battles of classical history, such as the triumphs of Alexander the Great, when compared to such moments as "Juliet leaning / Amid her window flowers, sighing, weaning." For Dewey at the time, Keats shows how the universalizing activity of the creative imagination has no fixed boundaries and ranks no experience as more or less universal; its function everywhere is "to seize upon the permanent meaning of facts, and embody them in such congruous, sensuous forms as shall enkindle feeling, and awaken a like organ of penetration in whoever may come upon the embodiment."[15] In short, the creative imagination is both receptive and productive. As a receptive power, it is able to seize upon phenomena to discern their universal meanings; as a productive power, it is able to isolate those universal meanings and reembody them as congruous, sensuous forms that enkindle feelings in others. In Dewey's early idealistic theory, the creative imagination plays an absolutely central role in the progressive movement of the self toward a union with the ideal personality by glimpsing and then objectifying its spirit in art.

This wholly romantic reading of Keats appealed to the younger Dewey because it supported the Christian humanism of his early work. As we have already seen, Dewey's writing while at the University of Michigan in the 1880s and early 1890s often had an overtly religious character about it. His social theory of democracy was intimately tied up with the idea of God as a living spirit who interpenetrates the social organism and reveals his spirit not only through art and science but through our ordinary relations with one another. A truly religious life was therefore not confined to a specific holy day or institution. As he made clear in his address to the Students' Christian Association, "God is in history, is in the social state of life, reconciling men unto Him. He who finds in every true and pure relationship in life a bond of union with God, has his religious life built upon a rock which cannot be shaken by the storms of life, nor undermined by the subtleties of temptation."[16] Dewey writing at the time of *Psychology* therefore found in the creative imagination a great ally in helping others achieve this revelation of the universal being—an ever-presence of God. Through the creative imagination, one could look upon the everyday scenes of life with new eyes, penetrating those congruous, sensuous forms to perceive the beauty of that rock that could not be shaken by the storms of life. In this way, for Dewey in 1886, the beauty we perceive through the creative imagination is one with the truth of God's love, which is really the only thing we need to know.

By the time Keats reappeared in Dewey's writings, after almost five decades of absence, this background of religious and philosophical idealism had long been replaced by a naturalistic humanism. This shift from idealism to naturalism is punctuated in *Art as Experience* when Dewey puts Keats's phrase "ethereal things" in quotation marks in order to immediately undermine its romantic interpretation. The phrase comes from a letter Keats wrote to his friend Benjamin Robert Haydon. After Keats confesses his feelings of turmoil and anxiety, he takes consolation in the fact that, as Dewey quotes him, "the artist may look 'upon the Sun, the Moon, the Stars, and the Earth and its contents as material to form greater things, that is ethereal things—greater things than the Creator himself made.'" When Dewey had read Keats, while still under the influence of absolute idealism, he would have interpreted "ethereal things" as did most philosophers and critics, which was as meanings and values "inaccessible to sense, because of their spiritual, eternal and universal characters—thus exemplifying the common dualism of nature and spirit."[17] But as a naturalist, Dewey was motivated to make a more critical examination of Keats's writings, particularly his private letters. What he found was another side of Keats. Although sharing with other artists of the romantic period an emphasis on the role of feeling and imagination, Keats did not view these faculties as means of leaping *out* of oneself into the realm of the supernatural in which one communed with ethereal things, as one might leap *into* the Grecian urn to be one with the eternal lover. Rather, he viewed ethereal things as amplifications of our animal senses and extensions of our native powers, as a kind of *reaching* that propels us into future experiences with greater expectation, awareness, creativity, and receptivity. Whether we are creating or bearing witness to a work of art, therefore, we are experiencing an outgoing flow of our powers that carries in its wake a quality that we may associate with the divine but that is, in reality, a product of the relationship between our organic being and our environment.

Two points emerge from his encounter with Keats that provide a basis for understanding the rest of Dewey's aesthetic theory. The first is Keats's "conviction that 'reasonings' have an origin like that of the movements of a wild creature toward its goal, and they may become spontaneous, 'instinctive,' and when they become instinctive are sensuous and immediate, poetic." Keats interprets ideas instrumentally as tools for directing thought, feeling, and action within a particular situation. Dewey finds evidence of this attitude in a letter Keats wrote to his brother comparing human action to that of a hawk, a stoat, and a field mouse. In Keats's words, "The greater part of Men make their way with the same instinctiveness, the same unwandering eye from their purposes as the Hawk." Whether the action is finding a mate, building a nest, acquiring food, or seeking pleasure, both hawk and man expend the energies of their bodies and conscious minds to achieve their purposes. And so too with the smaller animals. Keats writes, "I go out among the Fields and catch a glimpse of a Stoat or a fieldmouse hurrying along—to what? The creature has a purpose and his eyes are bright with it. I go amongst the buildings of a city and see a man hurrying along—to what? The creature has a purpose and his eyes are bright with it." But Keats goes further even than this, noting that the animals too have their own sense of the poetic; it belongs not only to the race of Adam and Eve. Taking a God's-eye view, Keats looked down at human activity from above and saw it with the same perspective with which we might look upon the field mouse. This is what he saw: "Though a quarrel in the streets is to be hated, the energies displayed in it are fine; the commonest Man has a grace in his quarrel. Seen by a supernatural Being our reasonings may take the same tone—though erroneous, they may be fine. *This is the very thing in which consists Poetry.*" In Dewey's later reading of Keats, the essence of poetry is not the embodiment of ethereal things understood as supernatural essences. As Dewey concludes, "There may be reasonings, but when they take an instinctive form, like that of animal forms and movements, they are poetry, they are fine; they have grace."[18] Poetry is thus found in the instinctive embodiment of reasoned action in graceful animal forms and movements, as expressed in a common quarrel as much as figures carved in a Grecian urn.

Having transformed Keats from a nineteenth-century romantic into a twentieth-century naturalist, Dewey's second takeaway lays the foundations for a reinterpretation of Keats's subordination of truth to beauty. In Dewey's words, Keats advances the notion that "no 'reasoning' as reasoning, that is, as excluding imagination and sense, can reach truth." In Keats's view, according to Dewey, this is because reason without aesthetic imagination lacks concreteness and substance: "'Reason' at its height cannot attain complete grasp and a self-contained assurance. It must fall back upon imagination—upon the embodiment of ideas in emotionally charged sense." Dewey thus rejects the notion that Keats meant to establish a binary between beauty and truth, between reasoning and sense, or between ideas and imagination. Rather, Keats wished to show how truth, reasoning, and ideas are only *made possible* by our possession of a sensible imagination capable of the intuitive grasp of something beautiful. Again, Dewey derives this conclusion from two of Keats's letters, one to his brothers George and Tom and the other to Benjamin Bailey. In the letter to his brothers, Keats praises Shakespeare for what he calls his "Negative Capability," which in Keats's words represented a person who was "capable of being in uncertainties, mysteries, doubts, without any irritable reaching after fact and reason." Unlike a writer like Coleridge, who refused to admit any poetic insight unless it could be completely justified and rationalized, Shakespeare was content with *"half-knowledge,"* or knowledge that had an imaginative basis while it might have lacked a sufficiently logical justification. Keats's letter to Bailey then provides further evidence for Dewey's reading, in which Keats observes that "never yet has been able to perceive how anything can be known for truth by consecutive reasoning.... Can it be that even the greatest Philosopher ever arrived at his Goal without putting aside numerous objections?" Thus Keats writes, "The simple imaginative Mind may have its rewards in the repetitions of its own silent Workings coming continually on the Spirit with a fine Suddenness."[19] Particularly significant for Dewey in these latter remarks is how Keats collapses the distinction between philosopher and poet. For Keats, the workings of the imaginative mind are central even to the greatest philosopher who seeks truth by consecutive reasoning. To possess "Negative Capability" thus means to possess a willingness to trust one's own imaginative intuitions and to have the courage to follow a line of thought and a creative impulse even when one lacks sufficient data and justification.[20]

These two interpretations in hand, Dewey then moves to the conclusion of his chapter, his humanistic reading of Keats's famous verses: "*Beauty is truth, truth beauty,—that is all / Ye know on earth, and all ye need to know.*" For Dewey, there are three lessons to be learned here. First, the "truth" of which Keats speaks is not the truth of experimental logic. Dewey stresses that in the intellectual tradition in which Keats wrote, "'truth' never signifies correctness of intellectual statements about things, or truth as its meaning is now influenced by science. It denotes the wisdom by which men live, especially 'the lore of good and evil.'" For Keats, the truth of the Grecian urn does not concern the historical accuracy of its portrayal of sacrificial rituals or romantic seduction; it rather discloses something about the quality of goodness that pervades these actions and escapes the language of fact. Second, the "beauty" of which he speaks is not a property of attractive works of art housed in museums. Beauty is a quality associated with those "imaginative intuitions" that come to consciousness with suddenness and are accompanied by a sense of revelation, excitement, harmony, and form. According to Dewey, this concept of beauty "solves for man the baffling problem of destruction and death—which weighed so constantly on Keats—in the very realm where life strives to assert supremacy."[21] His encounter with the Grecian urn was beautiful less because the urn itself was sculpted to perfection and more because his experience with it evoked imaginative intuitions that made life worth living and that gave it a sense of immortality that lasted beyond mere bodily existence.

But this leads to Dewey's third and most central point to understanding aesthetics within the context of democratic humanism. Although Keats is consoled by the enduring spirit of beauty captured in the frozen figures of the carved marble, he resists the temptation to slide into the solace of supernaturalism. For Keats, the experience of the encounter with beauty itself has to suffice. Dewey's concluding words of the chapter both represent a strong case to define Keats (as well as Shakespeare) as a forerunner of his own naturalistic humanism. He writes,

> Man lives in a world of surmise, of mystery, of uncertainties. "Reasoning" must fail man—this of course is a doctrine long taught by those who have held to the necessity of a divine revelation. Keats did not accept this supplement and substitute for reason. The insight of imagination must suffice. "This is all ye know on earth and all ye need to know." The critical words are "on earth"—that is amid a scene in which "irritable reaching after fact and reason" confuses and distorts instead of bringing us to the light. It was in moments of most intense esthetic perception that Keats found his utmost solace and his deepest convictions. This is the fact recorded at the close of his Ode. Ultimately there are but two philosophies. One of them accepts life and experience in all its uncertainty, mystery, doubt, and half-knowledge and turns that experience upon itself to deepen and intensify its own qualities—to imagination and art. This is the philosophy of Shakespeare and Keats.[22]

Although Dewey is silent on the character of the "other" philosophy, it is clearly one that remains trapped within the hierarchical dualisms of idealistic philosophy. In such a philosophy, rather than accepting the contingency of our mortal lives on earth, we seek to escape from them by positing another realm of pure form to which art or revelation might transport our disembodied spirits. In Keats and Shakespeare, Dewey finds allies against this "other" philosophy. For them, the only world we have is the one "on earth." This is a world in which uncertainty constantly outpaces our capacity for reason, but it is also a world in which imaginative insight provides moments of deep meaning. Neither Keats nor Shakespeare nor Dewey would ever say that these moments compensate for the limitations of reason or supplant the necessity for judgment, but what they would say is that a life without beauty would be not only irrational but also not worth living.

The takeaway from this extended detour through John Keats is that the motto for teaching aesthetics could very well be taken from the concluding verses to "Ode on a Grecian Urn." In so many school curriculums, art often is viewed as an "elective," a kind of leisure class to learn basic techniques of composition and to rest the mind in between more "serious" courses.

Underlying this assumption is the familiar dichotomy of truth and beauty, with beauty representing a superficial effort to please the senses rather than to enlighten the mind. Keats challenges these assumptions at every point. For him, there is no truth without beauty. Not only would truth without beauty be ugly, barren, and useless; it would not even be truth. For Keats, as for Dewey, all truth springs first from imaginative intuition. That includes not only moral truths of good and evil but all truths whatsoever. To be able to accept something as a fact is first to be able to imagine it as a potentially real thing in the mind. Beauty underlies our conceptions of mathematical harmony, of gravitational laws, of sacrificial love, of international peace, and of atomic structure. Moreover, our encounters with beauty are what justify our lives in the face of destruction, death, suffering, and failure. We endure these trials because of the rewards that beauty promises, even if it appears only for a moment as a light in the darkness. To classify these functions under the elitist category of "elective" is to deny the universal creative and spiritual character of the human being. In the pedagogy of democratic humanism, aesthetics as a discipline not only becomes a *part* of a core curriculum; it becomes its *foundation*.

To embrace the role of art is to open oneself to encountering the quality of the aesthetic "in the raw." What this means is to forget our cultural distinctions, hierarchies, and biases that tell us that only a certain category of objects is worthy of an aesthetic response; instead, we should attend to our instinctive response to phenomena of *any* type "in the events and scenes that hold the attentive eye and ear of man, arousing his interest and affording him enjoyment as he looks and listens." Dewey offers some vivid examples of aesthetic experience in the raw that also tell something about his own background as a man writing in 1930s America:

> The sources of art in human experience will be learned by him who sees how the tense grace of the ball-player infects the onlooking crowd; who notes the delight of the housewife in tending her plants, and the intent interest of her goodman in tending the patch of green in front of the house; the zest of the spectator in poking the wood burning on the hearth and in watching the darting flames and crumbling coals. These people, if questioned as to the reason for their actions, would doubtless return reasonable answers. The man who poked the sticks of burning wood would say he did it to make the fire burn better; but he is none the less fascinated by the colorful drama of change enacted

before his eyes and imaginatively partakes in it. He does not remain a cold spectator.[23]

Of these examples, the man watching the fire gives us perhaps the best example of the method by which we encounter the nature of the aesthetic in the raw. Dewey carefully observes that the man's rationalization of his interest in the fire might appeal to some practical interest, just as a blacksmith or a cook might need to maintain a consistent heat. One might also imagine a scientific or intellectual explanation by which the fire serves a function in experimental logic to determine the validity of some hypothesis. But for Dewey, encountering the aesthetic in the raw means stripping away these purposes and isolating the sheer fascination of the phenomena itself *as* phenomena. The man may love the colorful drama of the shifting light and the waves of heat and might stand watching it even when practical imperatives or intellectual curiosity would call for some other action. Similarly, the purely aesthetic interest in the woman gardening would be the plants' present texture and color rather than their future growth, just as the child watching the game might revel in the sheer qualities of tension exhibited on the field, quite apart from the score or the consequences of victory or loss.

These raw qualities of aesthetic experience as *actual* existences in nature are as real as any table or rock. This is often the most difficult step of all for those acculturated to the antihumanist legacy of dualistic thinking. From this antihumanist approach, the experiences of the child watching baseball, the woman tending her garden, and the man stoking a fire are not properties of nature but merely subjective feelings that go on within the confines of that person's brain; this culminates in the absurd conclusion that the request to encounter aesthetic experience in the "raw" means not to go *outward* to objects but *inward* to one's own mental states. But for Dewey, these conclusions are not true to our experiences but foisted upon them by an intellectual tradition. In our everyday experience, we simply encounter *qualities*; in the immediate present, we feel these qualities belong to the things themselves. As Dewey explains, "When it is said that I have a feeling, or impression, or 'hunch,' that things are thus and so, what is actually designated is primarily the presence of a dominating quality in a situation as a whole, not just the existence of a feeling as a psychical or psychological fact."[24] For instance, the child does not say that the quality of "tenseness" belongs to her; she says it belongs to the players on the field. The gardener does not take pleasure in the mental state of "greenness" but in the actual appreciation of green leaves and stems. The man tending the fire is not burned by the quality of "hotness" that exists in his mind; the heat belongs to the fire that he tends.

Importantly, Dewey includes within the sphere of "quality" those feelings often relegated even by so-called empiricists to the subjective realm of morality or the emotions. In the contortions of dualistic epistemological thinking, for instance, only certain *types* of qualities are admitted as referring to realities, while others are deemed mere appearances. We are told that "hardness" belongs to a marble urn, but its "beauty" exists only in the eye of the beholder. Dewey rejects all these metaphysical categorizations as distinctions made after the fact. For him, *every* quality that is disclosed within a situation is *actually* a part of that situation *at that moment*. Dewey explains that "empirically, things are poignant, tragic, beautiful, humorous, settled, disturbed, comfortable, annoying, barren, harsh, consoling, splendid, fearful; are such immediately and in their own right and behalf." Regardless of whether we later categorize such qualities as moral, aesthetic, or emotional, they all "stand in themselves on precisely the same level as colors, sounds, qualities of contact, taste and smell."[25] To witness a play on the baseball field that was "brave," to say that the flowers of the plants were "gorgeous," or to encounter a roaring fire as "majestic" is to point out actual qualities of eventful situations as much as the words *tense* or *green* or *hot*. They form the substance of our stories and the reports of real happenings *as they were experienced in a temporal event*. One should thus not conflate the *qualities* of aesthetic experience with the *judgments* of experimental logic. To say that qualities *exist* in situations is not to say that those qualities are reliable, enduring, or significant; it does not deny that a subsequent experience might produce a contradictory quality. It says that those qualities pervaded a situation in which an individual had some transaction with an environment at a specific place and time.

When trying to cultivate an appreciation for the reality of qualitative thought, therefore, one can distinguish between the *reality of a quality* and the *truth of a proposition*. For a quality to be real means that it exists as a quality *in* some situation *for* some sentient being. The quality of fear, for instance, *really* belongs to an actual encounter with a ferocious animal in waking life no more than it does to the same encounter in a dream, a hallucination, a movie, or a poem. Understood as a logical assertion, however, to say "my life was in danger" is not *true* as a nonironic description of any encounter but the first. Dewey offers an example that speaks to almost every child's experience waking in a dark room:

> I start and am flustered by a noise heard. Empirically, that noise *is* fearsome; it *really* is, not merely phenomenally or subjectively so. That is what it is experienced as being. But, when I experience the noise as a *known* thing, I find it to be innocent of harm. It is the tapping of a shade against the window, owing to the movements of the wind. The experience has changed; that is, the thing experienced has changed.... This is a change of experienced existence effected through the medium of cognition. The content of the latter experience cognitively regarded is doubtless *truer* than the content of the earlier, but it is in no sense more real.... It is only in regard to contrasted content in a subsequent experience that the determination "truer" has force.[26]

"Truth," in this passage, refers to the pragmatic efficiency of a descriptive representation produced after a period of abstract reflection and experimentation; it thus stands for the worth of an idea for future practice. In contradistinction, "real" refers to qualities of experience that are felt to be *really there* in the moment of experiencing. *Truth* is cognitive and instrumental, while *real* is affective and aesthetic. Thus a child who awakes to a noise and believes it to be a monster often remains frightened even after the worried parents turn on the lights and reveal that monster to be a window shade. For the child, the cognitive truth that the noise was a window shade does not dispel the very real memory of fright. In this way, the child can simultaneously feel the *real* qualities of fear in a situation while cognitively appreciating the *truth* that there is nothing at all to fear. Indeed, that ability to exist simultaneously in two different realms—one primarily qualitative, eventful, and temporal and the other primarily cognitive, symbolic, and nontemporal—is the very precondition for distinguishing between the aesthetic and logical aspects of human experience.

The pedagogical significance of this attention to experience in the raw can be summarized in the cultivation of the first attitude fundamental to artistic process—that of *perceptivity*. Perceptivity is not simply a native capacity to receive sense impressions; it is a habit cultivated only after the removal of cultural prejudices that prevent individuals from being genuinely open to qualitative experience. To emphasize this tension, Dewey turns once again to a critique of "recognition." For Dewey, recognition in the sphere of aesthetics means to arrest qualitative thought before it has a chance to develop freely. A quality is no sooner perceived than it is harnessed by some stereotype and made to "serve some *other* purpose, as we recognize a man on the street in order to greet or to avoid him, not so as to see him for the sake of seeing what is there." Replace the sight of this man with a work of literature, a scene from nature, or the shape of another human body and the restrictive nature of recognition in art becomes clear. However, whereas in his logical theory, he had contrasted recognition with *observation*, in his aesthetic theory, its positive counterpart is *perception*. Like observation, perception is not passive but active such that we "begin to study and to 'take in'" in the vigorous sense of *taking*. As he explains, "Perception is an act of the going-out of energy in order to receive, not a withholding of energy. To steep ourselves in a subject-matter we have first to plunge into it."[27] Providing students the freedom and the confidence to plunge into an experience, to really be open to its qualities, and to be willing to experience those qualities without prejudgment, apathy, or fear is the most essential task in the teaching of aesthetics. Without perceptivity, art reproduces what we already recognize.

It must be stressed, however, that the cultivation of perceptivity in aesthetics is not simply about the identifying of qualities as "objective" phenomena; that actually is closer to the nature of observation in logic. Perceptivity in aesthetics is a wholly *emotional* affair. To perceive qualities in a work of art is also to be struck and aroused by them, to be *moved* in some way. For Dewey, an emotion is qualitative and has the same objective status; it exists in a relationship between an individual and an environment or specific objects within that environment. What distinguishes an emotion from a bare quality like "red" or "hard" is that we feel ourselves dramatically connected to these qualities within an ongoing story. Thus "all emotions are qualifications of a drama and they change as the drama develops."[28] For instance, a red stoplight seen from a distance might be observed and registered, but the red light of a fire alarm is perceived as a warning that arouses fear and urgency. Consequently, the "more anything, whether an object, scene, idea, fact, or study, cuts into and across our experience, the more it stirs and arouses. An emotion is the register of the extent and way in which we are personally implicated, involved, in anything, no matter how external it is to us physically."[29] As a form of emotional experience, "there is, therefore, no such thing in perception as seeing or hearing *plus* emotion. The perceived object or scene is emotionally pervaded throughout."[30] To cultivate perceptivity is therefore to encourage individuals to literally *plunge into* an experience, meaning to see oneself in a relationship with one's surroundings that takes on the character of a drama.

The dramatic aspect of perceptivity is captured by Dewey's notion of the rhythmic experience of a living creature. Rhythm, he says, is the "ordered variation of changes."[31] Our attunement to rhythm grows out of the fact that "life itself consists of phases in which the organism falls out of step with the march of surrounding things and then recovers unison with it—either through effort or by some happy chance."[32] By rhythm, Dewey means the quality of experience that relates explicitly to the consciousness of continuous changes through time. In nature, there is a kind of rhythm in the hunt, the beating of a heart, the sun rising and setting, the seasons changing, the wind blowing a leaf across the water, the storm clouds approaching over the horizon, the process of building a shelter, the rituals of mating, the cycle of birth, and the movement toward death. In short, "whenever each step forward is at the same time a summing up and fulfillment of what precedes, and every consummation carries expectation tensely forward, there is rhythm."[33] There is rhythm, for instance, whenever "human energy gathers, is released, dammed up, frustrated and victorious. There are rhythmic beats of want and fulfillment, pulses of doing and being withheld from doing. All interactions that effect stability and order in the whirling flux of change are rhythms. There is ebb and flow, systole and diastole: ordered change."[34] To highlight the importance of rhythm is thus to locate both the constructive and receptive aspects of art within the lived experience of a live creature and by doing so to connect even our most transcendent experiences to the rhythms of our organic being.

The importance of highlighting rhythm is to emphasize how every aspect of aesthetic experience is structured by time and therefore influenced by the sequences of our thoughts, emotions, and actions within specific interactions. In many arts, the importance of rhythm is obvious. The productive acts of constructing a building, rehearsing a dance, and composing a song are clearly rhythmic activities that have analogues in the natural world; similarly, walking through that building, witnessing that dance, or listening to a song also rely on some temporal development. Yet we often think of plastic arts like sculpture or painting as somehow existing out of time, as if the encounters with them happened in an instant and their qualities were readily apparent at first glance. This view of art is reinforced by idealistic notions of aesthetics by which the transcendent meaning of a thing is suddenly "revealed" all at once from on high, without the need for active and outgoing perception. Dewey's attention to rhythm challenges this view. He writes,

> What about the play of light on a building with the constant change of shadows, intensities, and colors, and shifting reflections? If the building or statue were as "stationary" in perception as it is in physical

existence, they would be so dead that the eye would not rest on it, but glance by. For an object is perceived by a cumulative series of interactions. The eye as the master organ of the whole being produces an undergoing, a return effect; this calls out another act of seeing with new allied supplementations with another increment of meaning and value, and so on, in a continuous building-up of the esthetic object. What is called the inexhaustibility of a work of art is a function of this continuity of the total act of perceiving.[35]

If one were looking for a natural analog, our rhythmic perception of a building or statue equates to the way an animal might investigate an abandoned den by approaching it from a distance, seeing it from all angles, and smelling and touching it, all in order to get a sense of its practical implications—namely, whether it is a threat or a resource. In the realm of aesthetics, however, human beings use their perceptivity to understand a thing's meaning and significance, to identify certain qualities that give rise to new insights and new perceptions. Even though the object might be static and fixed in stone, our experiences with it are rhythmic and active and continuous. At every point that we experience art, we do so as organic, temporal beings.

Our active perception of the rhythms of experience then helps develop the second attitude of aesthetics—that of *consciousness*. By consciousness, Dewey does not mean what goes on inside one's head in contrast to what happens outside; he means the foreground rather than the background of our conscious experience. To be conscious of something is to be attentive to "the place where the formed disposition and the immediate situation touch and interact. It is the continuous readjustment of the self and the world in experience."[36] Understood as an attitude, consciousness means to reflect on the actions and reactions of our conscious mind as we are undergoing experience; it means not to react instinctively like other animals but to be aware of the movements of our thoughts and feelings in order that they might be changed and influenced. It is the function of art, in particular, to bring about this awareness. For Dewey, "art is the living and concrete proof that man is capable of restoring consciously, and thus on the plane of meaning, the union of sense, need, impulse and action characteristic of the live creature. The intervention of consciousness adds regulation, power of selection, and redisposition."[37] Whereas perceptivity allows us to plunge into qualities without constraint, stereotype, or bias, consciousness makes us aware of our own power to select and direct the nature of those qualities through our own active effort.

To be conscious of rhythm thus means to attend not only to our biological relation to the natural world but also to our cultural relation to the symbolic world. A musician, for instance, might develop a heightened awareness of the rhythms of the songs of birds, the beat of machinery, or the flow of water over rocks; she may also become conscious of her own capacity to create rhythms out of instruments and lyrics that tap into the depth of human experience accumulated over time. In doing so, she becomes aware of the symbolic meanings we invest into phenomena and take to be their intrinsic qualities. Dewey gives an example, for instance, of a man who sees a "picture and says at first sight that it is by Goya."[38] Being "Goya-esque" thus becomes as much a quality of the painting as its color and shape and thereby influences its rhythm. Elsewhere, Dewey quotes lines from Wordsworth's "Prelude" as an example of rhythm: "the wind and sleety rain, / And all the business of the elements, / The single sheep, and the one blasted tree, / And the bleak music from that old stone wall, / The noise of wood and water, and the mist / That on the line of each of these two roads / Advanced in such indisputable shapes." The rhythm in this poem does not derive purely from the sound of its words spoken out loud, as one might tap out a rhythm on the table; it comes from the play of images that occur in succession that come to mind immediately on encountering the sequence of words. For Dewey, rhythm is found in the "variation in objects, some relatively motionless set over against those in motion; things seen and things heard, rain and wind; wall and music; tree and noise. Then there is the relatively slow pace as long as *objects* dominate, changing to an accelerated pace with *events*, with 'the noise of wood and water,' culminating in the push of the relentlessly advancing mist."[39] But of course these objects and events are only images in the mind called forth by our immediate reaction to symbols. To cultivate a consciousness of rhythm is thus to erase the distinction between the biological and the cultural; it is to accept that the rhythms of the qualities we experience are for the most part already suffused with symbolic meanings that we have in our power to call forth, to challenge, or to transform.

Consciousness also makes us aware of how our transactions with art in time contribute to the experience of form. From a naturalistic perspective, form represents the meaningful closure of rhythm. Living creatures, for instance, experience form at the conclusion of the hunt, the return to the nest, the giving of birth, the successful defense of their territory, and the attraction of a mate. All of these activities represent *consummations*, a word that Dewey used to signify "the carrying forward of an experience to fulfillment." In more ordinary language, form is present whenever we feel confident in labeling an entire sequence of events as "*an* experience," meaning a single unified experience that carries with it a dominant quality despite its different parts. For instance, Dewey imagines a person recollecting "that storm one went through in crossing the Atlantic—the storm that seemed in its fury, as it was experienced, to sum up in itself all that a storm can be, complete in itself, standing out because marked out from what went before and what came after." Whether or not that experience was productive or receptive doesn't matter; both types of experience still require an active perception of the rhythmic development of qualities that produces more integrated, unified qualities at its close. Other experiences might be that "a piece of work is finished in a way that is satisfactory; a problem receives its solution; a game is played through; a situation, whether that of eating a meal, playing a game of chess, carrying on a conversation, writing a book, or taking part in a political campaign, is so rounded out that its close is a consummation and not a cessation. Such an experience is a whole and carries with it its own individualizing quality and self-sufficiency. It is *an* experience."[40] It is also a manifestation of form.

As with his definition of emotion, Dewey emphasizes the *dramatic* nature of form. Form is not some Platonic "Idea," a fixed essence, shape, or mold that exists above or behind phenomena and belongs primarily to an object; form is rather the heightened emotional quality that discloses itself through a sequence of dramatic events that culminates in *an* experience. But this means, in turn, that to be dramatic, an experience must pass through and overcome tensions and resistances on its way to some greater fulfillment. Without tension, there may be sound, shape, color, and texture, but there is no "form" because there is no drama. For Dewey, the contrasts "of lack and fullness, of struggle and achievement, of adjustment after consummated irregularity, form the drama in which action, feeling, and meaning are one. The outcome is balance and counterbalance. These are not static nor mechanical. They express power that is intense because measured through overcoming resistance."[41] Once again, however, it must be stressed that these dramatic qualities are neither *in* an art object nor *in* an individual's consciousness; they are produced in the *transaction* between an individual and an environment. Consequently, when Dewey talks about a "work of art," he does not mean an external object; he means the work *done* or *performed* within that transaction over time. Thus the "real work of art is the building up of an integral experience out of the interaction of organic and environmental conditions and energies."[42] The "work" of the Parthenon is thus different for every individual experiencing it because the dramatic form that it discloses is unique within the drama of every person's life within a specific transaction. Consciousness thus emphasizes how each of us contributes something different to the production of form.

The recognition of our active involvement in the production of aesthetic form thus calls attention to the third attitude associated with the teaching of aesthetics—that of *imagination*. Of course, the cultivation of the imagination is an aim embraced by most aesthetic theories, no matter their philosophical presuppositions. The matter concerns the way in which imagination is defined. We have already seen, for instance, that Dewey in his *Psychology* had praised the function of the imagination but only insofar as he identified it as the capacity to grasp transcendent universal meanings that were latent within objects of beauty. In his later work, Dewey rejected such idealistic accounts that treat the imagination as a "self-contained faculty, differing from others in possession of mysterious potencies." Writing as a naturalist, Dewey redefined the imagination as the conscious adjustment of the old and the new in time. To be imaginative was not to possess some innate capacity to *leap over* experience in a rare moment; it was a trained capacity to *work through* experience in every process of making and observation. Imagination is therefore "a *way* of seeing and feeling things as they compose an integral whole. It is the large and generous blending of interests at the point where the mind comes in contact with the world. When old and familiar things are made new in experience, there is imagination."[43] Whenever we experience form, for instance, we freely allow the work of our prior experiences (the "old") to be reworked and integrated into the rhythms of a present experience (the "new") in order to produce a new qualitative unity that carries with it its own unique meaning and significance. Imagination is neither the revelry of the past nor the mere fantasy of the future; it is the active interplay among our past, present, and future within a continuous and moving present.

Teaching these attitudes reinforces the ethics of democratic humanism by making individuals aware of the methods by which they make their own unique contributions to the production of art and aesthetic experience. These attitudes therefore reinforce the humanistic understanding that art and aesthetics are fundamentally *communicative* activities. Just as one who produces art uses it as a medium of communication to touch the emotions and thoughts of others, aesthetic experience is the outcome of an encounter with expressive objects that we feel have disclosed some deep meaning. Dewey was emphatic about this point, arguing in fact that "art is the most effective mode of communication that exists."[44] The key to interpreting this passage is in his use of the words *effective* and *communication*. Clearly, he does not mean that art is more effective at developing hypotheses, proving claims, or constructing complex causal accounts of phenomena, all of which are functions of logic. He means "effective" in the sense of *affecting* change in others by creating some bond of commonality in thought and feeling. Thus "every art communicates because it expresses. It enables us to share vividly and deeply in meanings to which we had been dumb." And by "communication" he does not mean the announcing of an idea so that it might pass from one mind to another, as one might hand off a physical object. This is because, for Dewey, "communication is not announcing things, even if they are said with the emphasis of great sonority. Communication is the process of creating participation, of making common what had been isolated and singular."[45] The communicative character of art holds true even when the expressive object has no clear communicative intent. Works produced by nature, by artists who are long dead, or by individuals who had no specific purpose in mind still communicate insofar as they are experienced as such by one receptive to their qualities. As Dewey explains, the expressive nature of any object "lives only in communication that operates in the experience of others."[46]

Once the teaching of aesthetics is understood as a form of communication that is both enabled and constrained by our cultural matrix, the significance of the two attitudes it seeks to cultivate becomes readily apparent—those being intuitiveness and courage. For Dewey, *intuitiveness* represents the openness to embrace and act upon the sudden illuminations of the imagination. It thus represents a sensitivity to "that meeting of the old and new in which the readjustment involved in every form of consciousness is effected suddenly by means of a quick and unexpected harmony which in its bright abruptness is like a flash of revelation; although in fact it is prepared for by long and slow incubation."[47] What Dewey means by the closing phrase is that intuitiveness is not a native capacity with which we are born; it is something developed over time through experience and education. To exemplify the nature of intuitiveness, Dewey turns again to Ralph Waldo Emerson, quoting his essay "Self-Reliance," in which Emerson declares, "'A man should learn to detect and watch that gleam of light which flashes across his mind from within.'" But this is precisely the educational problem. As Dewey observes, "It is not easy to detect and watch the gleams of light that flash from within. Education and social surroundings are in a conspiracy to dim these flashes and to attract our watching to other things."[48] As we have already seen in the legacy of antihumanism, nothing is more feared by those who wish to defend the prevailing order than one with the intuitiveness to grasp a heretofore unknown possibility that springs up like a revelation in her consciousness. Consequently, encouraging that capacity is precisely an aim of the humanistic educator.

Courage is then required to act on these intuitions and express them publicly through works of art. For Dewey, "the primary requisite of critical ability is courage; its great enemy is cowardice." Courage is especially required of acts of critical imagination because they initiate new births into the world that come without defenses or justifications; we expose those possibilities—and ourselves—to censure and abuse. Yet the history of art can instill in us the courage to persevere. Again, Dewey turns to Emerson, who wrote, "Great works of art have no more affecting lesson for us than this. They teach us to abide by our spontaneous impression with good-humored inflexibility then most when the whole cry of voices is on the other side. Else to-morrow a stranger will say with masterly good sense precisely what we have thought and felt all the time, and we shall be forced to take with shame our own opinion from another."[49] Dewey takes from this passage the lesson of courage that Emerson had associated with the nonconformity of self-reliance. For Emerson, without the courage to follow our intuitions, we subordinate our individuality to the demands of others. By contrast, "the beginning of all development of individuality with adults usually comes when one learns to throw off an outer slavery to second-hand and ready-made opinions and begins to detect, watch, and trust one's own intuitions, that is, one's own spontaneous, unforced reactions."[50] Nothing in this statement says that our intuitions are always right or valuable; what it does say is that we can never know their value if they are not first detected and trusted enough to be given expression. It is to generate in others a capacity for self-trust in their own intuitions that is the most radical endeavor of aesthetic education.

Dewey's name for this capacity is *taste*, a term whose meaning he emancipates from its aristocratic legacy. At its most general level, Dewey defines taste as consisting in "habitual modes of preference and esteem, an effective sense of excellence."[51] Yet this definition only gets us so far. For instance, in the antihumanist tradition, what is "esteemed" are only those things that are understood to stand atop a hierarchy of values. For the antihumanist, to acquire taste is to develop a capacity to rank order all objects, people, and actions according to their "innate" worth, regardless of one's personal views or experiences. Consequently, only those individuals deemed worthy enough are given an education in so-called taste, while the masses whose opinions are thought irrelevant are only trained to labor rather than to experience. For Dewey, however, terms like *preference* or *esteem* refer primarily to experiences of valuation that are the products of the active imagination. Taste therefore does not refer to the capacity to affix the right label to some object; it refers to the capacity for "an enlarged, an intensified prizing" and the "enhancement of the qualities which make any ordinary experience appealing."[52] Taste is therefore to be understood as the power to discover within *any* situation those qualities that make experience worthwhile, whether for the individual experiencing them or for society as a whole. In sum, "taste, if we use the word in its best sense, is the outcome of experience brought cumulatively to bear on the intelligent appreciation of the real worth of likings and enjoyments."[53] Taste is the capacity by which we find value in our present experience.

Rather than deliberating about the future or reflecting about the past, taste concentrates its energies on the immediate qualities of our temporal existence, which is the only *existence* we have at any time. For antihumanists, dwelling on the present becomes a kind of idleness or selfishness, a distraction from the "ultimate" aims of life, whether they are religious, political, or economic. But for the democratic humanist, the goods of our everyday experience are things to cultivate and appreciate. When Dewey looked to education, for instance, he often found the emphasis on training for the future to have deadened a student's ability to appreciate what was immediately before her. It made him ask, "What avail is it to win prescribed amounts of information about geography and history, to win ability to read and write, if in the process the individual loses his own soul: loses his appreciation of things worth while, of the values to which these things are relative; if he loses desire to apply what he has learned and, above all, loses the ability to extract meaning from his future experiences as they occur?" For the antihumanist, these questions are irrelevant; the meanings that are important are those that transcend human experience and exist in some other realm. But from the perspective of the democratic humanist, "we always live at the time we live and not at some other time, and only by extracting at each present time the full meaning of each present experience are we prepared for doing the same thing in the future. This is the only preparation which in the long run amounts to anything."[54] Dewey does not name it here, but that is precisely the function of taste—to extract from each present time the full meaning of each present experience of every unique individual.

Developing the remaining three attitudes often requires turning away from the context of dialogue to the more reflective and productive outlet of writing. It is the solitude of the thinking mind, stimulated by the written word, that allows the imagination to freely move back and forth across space and time. An assignment that provokes the imagination is one that invites a student to make a connection between the old and the new, the distant and the proximate, and the absent and the present. The common basis of such assignments is the request to bring two things together in a relationship such that one thing illuminates a quality in another. Students might draw analogies in history, find metaphorical resonance in a shared quality, or find some commonality in the process of invention. The nature of the relation matters less than the fact that students have the freedom to make those relations on their own. Moreover, these relations are selected in reference to the students' intuitiveness of their significance. Rather than seeing the making of relations as an end in itself, one views it as establishing a new perspective that brings out different qualities in future experience. An interpretation of Keats's poem in relation to British imperialism, for instance, casts a new and darker light on the Elgin Marbles and the imperialist history of the great European museums, while an interpretation that relates it to the philosophical discourse on aesthetics encourages an openness to transcendent experience. Finally, teachers must recognize the risk involves in aesthetic judgments; they are not trivial acts. Students develop the attitude of courage when they are encouraged to take these judgments seriously, provided the freedom to think and create, and finally, constructively challenged on their conclusions with the aim of improving their tastes alongside the tastes of others.

The cultivation of taste has a central importance for democracy. Taste, that is to say, is not an ability to enhance idle pleasures, which of course would be the accusation of the antihumanist. Taste involves the capacity to detect and appreciate *any* quality present in experience, including those qualities that have a bearing on intellectual or moral affairs. Indeed, Dewey makes a radical claim that "most of the important crises of life are cases where tastes are the only things worth discussing, and where, if the light of reason is to exist and prevail, judgment must be performed with regard for its logical implications." What Dewey means is that we not only have a "taste" for jazz or Beethoven and for cubism or imagism; we also have a taste for pacifism or war, for chaos or order, for honesty or deception, for monotheism or paganism, for public authority or private ambition, and for universal laws or specific observations. In each of these objects, we develop a taste for their qualities and intuitions about their worth. We fail to notice this relationship because we often call taste by another name when outside the sphere of aesthetic, but the function is the same. For Dewey, developing an "educated interest or taste is, ultimately, supreme, the *unum necessarium*, in morals (where it is called conscience), in matters intellectual (where it is called insight), as well as in esthetics where it is more usually called taste."[55] Whatever name it is given—conscience, insight, or taste—the words all signify a power to intuit the underlying quality of experience, regardless of whether or not that quality is deemed good, true, or beautiful. This perception is only a starting point, of course; any crisis over taste must eventually pass into logical inquiry. Yet without a capacity to identify the qualities of one's own experience and communicate them effectively to another, the only possible outcomes of a crisis in taste are either silence or violence.

Hence we return to the significance of Dewey's interpretation of the closing verses of Keats's poem. Scientifically understood, truth of course cannot be reduced to beauty any more than the laws of quantum mechanics can be reduced to our feelings about Schrödinger's cat. However, our sense of that truth nonetheless relies on our intuitive grasp of natural qualities on which that truth is built. Thus even "'scientific' thinking, that expressed in physical science, never gets away from qualitative existence. Directly, it always has its own qualitative background; indirectly, it has that of the world in which the ordinary experience of the common man is lived." Similarly, our moral obligations need not always be beautiful, particularly when following the good requires sacrifice and punishment. However, our general sense of right and wrong grows out of our taste for the harmony that underlies our moral codes. As Dewey explains, regardless of the sphere of thought, "the gist of the matter is that the immediate existence of quality, and of dominant and pervasive quality, is the background, the point of departure, and the regulative principle of all thinking. Thought which denies the existential reality of qualitative things is therefore bound to end in self-contradiction and in denying itself."[56] This is what he took Keats to mean when he said that the only thing we need to know on earth was that truth was beauty and beauty was truth; it meant that without the development of a sense of taste that can discern the qualitative background of immediate existence, truth is both empty and blind.

Consequently, if democracy is to be a reality as a communicative form of voluntary association that allows for experimental growth over time, it has to commit itself to the development of taste through the promotion of education in the arts, for we acquire taste by actively *tasting* works of art—that is, by encountering their diversity in rhythm and quality and meaning by means of the attitudes of perceptivity, consciousness, imagination, intuitiveness, and courage. Developing this expanded sense of taste "constitutes the prime function of literature, music, drawing, painting, etc., in education. They are not the exclusive agencies of appreciation in the most general sense of that word; but they are the chief agencies of an intensified, enhanced appreciation." And as Dewey makes clear, they are "not only intrinsically and directly enjoyable, but they serve a purpose beyond themselves." Here lies their explicitly democratic function of the arts:

> They have the office, in increased degree, of all appreciation in fixing taste, in forming standards for the worth of later experiences. They arouse discontent with conditions which fall below their measure; they create a demand for surroundings coming up to their own level. They reveal a depth and range of meaning in experiences which otherwise might be mediocre and trivial. They supply, that is, organs of vision. Moreover, in their fullness they represent the concentration and consummation of elements of good which are otherwise scattered and incomplete. They select and focus the elements of enjoyable worth which make any experience directly enjoyable. They are not luxuries of education, but emphatic expressions of that which makes any education worth while.[57]

This is a weighty list of accomplishments. Encounters with works of art develop standards of taste, arouse discontent, reveal depths of meaning, and supply organs of vision. And these effects, it must be said, are not restricted to reading works of great literature in the school or encountering classical paintings in the museum. As Dewey stressed in his support of the Section on Fine Arts, we develop taste by being constantly surrounded by works of art that stimulate our imagination and encourage us to attend to their qualities because of our natural interest in their rhythms and forms. Tragically, the yearning for cheap profit continually leads us to construct an environment that deadens our senses rather than stimulates them. For Dewey, "the congestion of cities, the hideous surroundings of the ordinary workingman's home which is near a factory or a railroad, the almost universal practice under the profit motive of covering the ground in cities with multiple dwellings, leaving no space for the play of children or for the recreation of adults, except in so far as the city itself has stepped in to provide parks and playgrounds—these show the profit motive nearly at its worst." In other words, no matter what happens in the schools, "a civilization, in which the average man spends his day in a factory and his evening at a movie, has still a long way to go."[58] In short, education in art should attend more than what goes on inside the classroom; the cultivation of aesthetic taste is an imperative for culture as a whole no matter one's wealth or status.

The teaching of aesthetics in the pedagogy of democratic humanism thus takes as its task something more than just the training of artistic techniques or methods of literary interpretation; its task is nothing less than the capacity to imagine a better world. At the same time, it recognizes that imagining a better world occurs one possibility at a time. A better world is not to be equated with a utopian vision of a reconstructed society; it means rather a world in which every experience, no matter how seemingly small or insignificant, can be a source of rich meaning. Because of aristocratic overtones that still suffocate aesthetic freedom, we often think only of the great works of art, such as the Parthenon, as those worthy of our admiration, but imaginative possibilities are equally disclosed to the young child looking up at a mural while mailing a letter at the post office or leaping on the chalk outline of a flower she drew on a playground. The aim of the educator is not to put boundaries around experience, to limit its possibility, or to define ahead of time what quality it discloses; it is to develop the attitudes and capacities to discern the infinite depth of any experience and to discover what is new in every individual's life. That is because, for the democratic humanist, we do not exist to carry on the past; rather, "each individual that comes into the world is a new beginning; the universe itself is, as it were, taking a fresh start in him and trying to do something, even if on a small scale, that it has never done before."[59] There is nothing more potentially radical to say in this world than "a child is born." The calling of the aesthetic educator is to make that child a prophet.

9
RHETORIC

> The essential need, in other words, is the improvement of the methods and conditions of debate, discussion, and persuasion. That is *the* problem of the public.
> —JOHN DEWEY, *THE PUBLIC AND ITS PROBLEMS*

In 1945, King's Crown Press published a timely reprint of *Peace and Bread in Time of War* by Jane Addams with a new introduction by John Dewey. Coinciding with the final surrender of the Axis powers and the birth of a new international organization, the United Nations, the situation in 1945 mirrored the circumstances that preceded its original publication in 1922. Addams had written the book as a history of the pacifist advocacy of the Women's International League for Peace and Freedom, a movement formed in 1915 of which Addams was the first president. Spanning the years from 1915 to 1921, *Peace and Bread* tells a story that begins with the formation of the movement in response to the outbreak of war, passes through the hardships faced by the pacifist movement when confronted with the rise of militarism and nationalism, and closes after the founding of the League of Nations, which she believed might preserve peace. The words of its hopeful conclusion were written after the movement held a congress in Vienna two years after the conclusion of the war. Addams writes,

> And although we were so near to the great war with its millions of dead and its starved survivors, we had ventured at the very opening of the Congress to assert that war is not a natural activity for mankind, that large masses of men should fight against other large masses is abnormal, both from the biological and ethical point of view. We stated that it is a natural tendency of men to come into friendly relationships with ever larger and larger groups, and to live constantly a more extended

life. It required no courage to predict that the endless desire of men would at last assert itself, that desire which torments them almost like an unappeased thirst, not to be kept apart but to come to terms with one another. It is the very spring of life which underlies all social organizations and political associations.[1]

These hopes had been dashed with the rise of fascism and the mass slaughter it initiated in the decades to come, and yet with the close of the war, this tentative hope sprang forth anew. For Dewey, nothing was more important than to listen to her counsel at that crucial point in history, for "were Jane Addams with us today her voice and pen would tell us how the events of the years which have intervened between two World Wars have intensified the evils which will surely follow if leaders betray the trust committed to them—events which have deepened the need for those humane processes and organs which alone can bring hope of enduring peace to a tragically torn and bleeding world."[2] It had been a decade since her death, and yet the power of her words to rationally direct the course of events lived on.

But for Dewey, the relevance of her work was due not only to the similarities between the two situations but even more to their differences. Just a few years after the events of 1914, Addams had already come to reflect that "it is impossible now to reproduce that basic sense of desolation, of suicide, of anachronism, which the first news of war brought to thousands of men and women who had come to consider war as a throwback in the scientific sense," for by 1922, the optimism that wars of such magnitude were a thing of the past, relegated to ages of barbarity, had long been eclipsed by the despairing belief that modernity meant accepting "a world of widespread war with its inevitable consequences of divisions and animosities."[3] The publication of *Peace and Bread* thus highlighted a time in which ordinary citizens genuinely struggled for a cooperative peace between nations and "hoped and worked for a world free from the curse of war."[4] Dewey summed up its impact this way:

> There is, I believe, nothing paradoxical in saying that such differences as these, great as they are, increase, instead of lessen, the warning and the instruction, the timeliness, of the book Miss Addams wrote almost a quarter of a century ago. The *warning* is against adoption and use of methods which are so traditional that we are only too likely to adopt them:—methods which are called "Terms of Peace," but which in fact are but terms of a precarious interim between wars. The *instruction*

concerns the need for adoption of methods which break with political tradition, which courageously adventure in lines that are new in diplomacy and in the political relations of governments, and which are consonant with the vast social changes going on everywhere else.[5]

Dewey's introduction to *Peace and Bread* thus did not treat it merely as a historical artifact, something that preserved voices of the past but that had no direct relevance to the present. In Dewey's reading, it becomes an explicitly *rhetorical* artifact that functioned in the immediate present as a timely warning and instruction for contemporary actors tasked with the burden of political judgment. Her book is "timely because it points to the source of the failure of the hopes so ardently entertained a generation ago."[6] But these failed hopes did not belong to Addams; they belonged to those who believed "they could attain peace through an international organization of the traditional political kind, which relied more upon coercive force than upon constructive meeting of human needs."[7] Here we find her warning against seeking peace by relying on leaders of the representative powers to negotiate treaties and then enforce them from the top down by the same coercive forces that fought the war. This was the method of the Treaty of Versailles. But there is another hope—the hope of Addams—that serves as an instruction. This hope is in genuinely *political* action, which for her was not restricted to the governmental, legal, or economic actions of elites; it meant, in her words, "to replace coercion by the full consent of the governed, to educate and strengthen the free will of the people through the use of democratic institutions." As Dewey interpreted her message, "Miss Addams repeatedly called attention to the fact that all social movements *outside* of traditional diplomacy and 'international law' had been drawing the peoples of different countries together in ever closer bonds, while war, under modern conditions, was affecting civilian populations as it had never done before."[8] For her, the reliance on coercive international organizations to build peace was a means that could only produce further war; her rhetorical message for those encountering it in 1945 was that only by speaking directly to and through social movements that cut across class, national, and religious lines could a lasting peace be accomplished.[9]

For many critics of pacifism, this rhetoric was nothing more than idealism, but Dewey flipped this accusation on its head. For him, Addams is the exact opposite of an idealist, a point he thought important enough to emphasize in the title he gave to his introduction: "Democratic Versus Coercive International Organization: The Realism of Jane Addams." For critics of pacifism, Addams was an idealist because the nature of her aims was too hopeful, placed too much faith in human capacities, and seemed to deny the selfishness of human beings. Consequently, her critics put their faith not in cooperation but in coercion, believing that only through the threat of force, backed by the state, could the "Terms of Peace" be enforced. But for Dewey, the situation was in fact the opposite. It was those who relied on coercive force who were the idealists because they did not dwell in the realm of empirical fact or causal agency; they believed instead in the magic of state power. As Dewey explains, "To trust to traditional political 'organization' to create peaceful relations between nations involves reliance upon just that exaggerated nationalistic and power politics that has brought the world to its present pass." By contrast, the pacifism of Addams dwelt not in the realm of an airy ideal but in the complex relationships of the modern machine age. In this age, organization does not flow from the top down but moved horizontally within a complex network. Any lasting organization would thus have to cut both "*across* nationalistic lines" as well as "*under* those lines," thus putting "faith in extension of the democratic process to the still wider world of peoples."[10] Leaders had a role to play in this process, but their role was as "trustees for the interests of the common people. Theirs was the duty and the task of giving articulate and effective form to the common impulses she summed up in the word 'Fellowship.'"[11] Her realism was thus not judged by the optimism of her goal; it was judged by the degree to which her rhetoric advocated realistic means by which to achieve that goal through the hard work of persuasive effort over time.

As the third art of democratic humanism, rhetoric helps fulfill the task of creative democracy by teaching citizens not only the art of persuasion, by which different perspectives are given the power of expression, but also the civic virtues that allow these differences to negotiate their conflicts and arrive at more rational collective judgments, for rhetoric is neither the Platonic caricature of crass manipulation nor the medieval inheritance catalog of tropes and figures; rhetoric is an art of constituting and expressing one's own thought through logos in such a way that it moves an audience to voluntary action to achieve some reasonable public good. This does not mean that all rhetoric is good any more than all logic is true or all art is beautiful. What it does mean is that a genuinely rhetorical culture holds to the faith that a rhetoric that is truly free—which is to say, when all *individuals* are given not only the opportunity to speak but also the power of persuasive self-expression and access to a mediated public sphere—will produce over the long term a more intelligent discourse than one based on censorship, restriction, and paternalism.

For rhetorician Susan Jarratt, the task of creative democracy defined by Dewey had its origins in the thought and practices of the first great teachers in the Western civilization, the Greek sophists. These were itinerant teachers of rhetoric and the arts who appeared in the fifth century to give power to the citizens of the new democracies. For her, sophistic education "promoted the democratic process of group decision-making on which our own democracy still rests." In fact, Jarratt makes a strong claim that practitioners of contemporary critical pedagogy owe a great deal to the sophists and can still learn from listening to their voices. As she explains, "In their attempts to reinstate the public intellectual, conceiving of schools in Deweyan terms as laboratories for democracy, and empowering of students by giving them a voice, critical pedagogues revive the goals of the first sophists."[12] She thus imagines a classroom in which "students argue about the ethical implications of discourse on a wide range of subjects and, in doing so, come to identify their personal interests with others, understand those interests as implicated in a larger social setting, and advance them in a public voice."[13] Logic and aesthetics also have a vital role to play in this practice, but it falls to rhetoric to confront the contingency and urgency of events in a condition of human plurality, and in meeting that challenge, teachers channel the spirit of the sophists, the original humanists.

The great value that Jarratt sees in rereading the sophists is their capacity to challenge the dominant Aristotelian orientation to rhetoric and composition studies enshrined in so many textbooks. This orientation views the art of persuasion through the lens of an already established system of knowledge, an episteme, that promises an answer to every question. For Jarratt, the crucial difference between the fifth-century sophists and their fourth-century successors, Plato and Aristotle, is that "the sophists make possible an additional question—a question virtually unavoidable in the current critical climate: how does language create different answers to those questions at different moments in history?"[14] In other words, the sophists challenge the very idea of a universal episteme valid for all times, places, cultures, and individuals; they embody "a fundamental understanding of knowledge and values as historically contingent, a recognition of all discourse as 'rhetorical,' an integral relationship between theory, practice and the political sphere."[15] Consequently, recovering the sophistical spirit in education means engaging those points of conflict, uncertainty, and argumentation that inevitably channel the instinctive rhetorical impulses of individuals capable of reason. The continuing value of Aristotle's episteme remains undeniable, but whenever the disruptions of history threaten the serene confidence that the future will be like the past, the sophists provide the language and attitudes better suited to meet the flux of events that call for new visions of possibility.

The sophistical practice that Jarratt sees as most valuable in the classroom is the practice of *dissoi logoi*. This was the innovation of Protagoras, and it followed "a method of opposing one statement (logos) to another or drawing attention to such a contradiction in language or affairs." In one way, *dissoi logoi* represents a typical debating technique of arguing one side in order to better prepare the other side, but in a deeper way, it represents the embodiment of the democratic spirit itself. As Jarratt explains, "A reading informed by a democratic political agenda understands the process of discovering contradictory statements to be grounded in the sophistic belief that phenomena are characterized by constant change, and, further, that individual human perceptions are the only 'measure' of phenomena."[16] In other words, the practice of sophistical *dissoi logoi* is an extension of the attitude of sophistical humanism. Not only does it capture the multiplicity of human experience and interpretation, refusing the temptation to reduce the truth of things to a single perspective; it also accepts the political consequence of this multiplicity—conflict. However, "the recognition of this inevitability of conflict—in sophistical terms, a recognition of *dissoi logoi*—is not grounds for despair, but rather the starting point for creating a consciousness in students and teachers through which the inequalities generating those conflicts can be acknowledged and transformed."[17] This is precisely Dewey's faith as well. Jarratt's rereading of the sophists thus reveals the possibility of a democratic humanism in which pragmatist, sophist, and critical pedagogue work together to enliven and enrich the street-corner debates that keep alive the spirit of democracy in our everyday lives.

Dewey's review of Addams's work is perhaps one of the most explicitly rhetorical pieces of writing Dewey ever produced. Not only was his *intent* rhetorical, meaning that Dewey wished to use his review as an opportunity to influence the course of political affairs in his time, but the essay was also rhetorical in the object and orientation of his analysis. The object, *Peace and Bread*, was a rhetorical artifact written to praise the rhetorical activities of, in Addams's words, "a vigorous campaign among the doubting, making public opinion both for reasonable peace terms and for possible shortening of the war."[18] And Dewey's orientation to this object was as a rhetorical critic called upon to interpret its persuasive function both at the time of its initial publication and again in the context of postwar discussions about the new global order. In other words, Dewey produced a piece of rhetoric about the rhetorical strategies of a rhetorical artifact that describes a rhetorical phenomenon that is relevant to a contemporary rhetorical situation.[19] That Dewey does not use the term *rhetoric* only demonstrates that he too was influenced by the Platonic and antisophistical biases of the Western philosophical tradition, but it should not blind us from the fact that Dewey here is calling for a development of a rhetorical culture as the foundation for democratic practice and international peace.

Moreover, we can readily construct a definition of rhetoric consistent with Dewey's democratic humanism from the terminology of this essay alone. For him, *rhetoric is the timely art of warning and instructing free people to organize for political action through democratic institutions.* Let us look at each part in isolation. Rhetoric is *timely* because it speaks to the urgency of a problematic situation.[20] Rhetoric is an *art* because it is a product of reflective method and conscious design.[21] Rhetoric *warns* because it alerts us to dangers on the horizon that come from possible consequences of our choices, both direct and indirect.[22] Rhetoric *instructs* because it illuminates those paths forward that bring us closer to achieving our aims.[23] Rhetoric addresses those who are *free* because it solicits their voluntary assent rather than their forced obedience.[24] Rhetoric speaks to the *people* because it understands power as something that springs up between people rather than that emanates from leaders.[25] Rhetoric concerns itself with *organization* because it speaks to those who wish to act collectively outside of formal institutional structures.[26] Rhetoric inspires *political action* because it believes that collective participation is essential for managing the fact of historical change.[27] And rhetoric supports *democratic institutions* because it recognizes that political action must have organs for implementing that change if action is not to evaporate into thin air.[28] In a Deweyan reading, therefore, rhetoric is the art by which individuals make common cause with others in a changing world neither by force nor by manipulation but by their voluntary consent and collective action within a space of democratic freedom.

But we must begin a study of rhetoric not with its end but with its origin. Consistent with Dewey's naturalism, that origin is found in our biological matrix, which is to say the origin of language is in the gestures and cries of the animal world. And the fact is that "gestures and cries are not primarily expressive and communicative. They are modes of organic behavior as much as are locomotion, seizing and crunching. Language, signs and significance, come into existence not by intent and mind but by over-flow, by-products, in gestures and sound. The story of language is the story of the use made of these occurrences; a use that is eventual, as well as eventful."[29] Providing a naturalistic basis for rhetoric means to begin at this moment of overflow and study how rhetoric as an art grows out of the rhetorical quality of language.

The clue to rhetoric's development is found by investigating Dewey's assertion that the use of language is "eventual, as well as eventful." By "eventful," Dewey means anything that does not exist in isolation or in a single point but that deals with some qualitative interaction over time. For instance, the clucking of a hen to her chicks is an *event* insofar as it occurs in a moment in space and time marked by the continuous interaction of multiple elements together, but it is not *eventual*. What Dewey means by "eventual" is that which "presents something to be accomplished, to be brought about by the actions in which choice is manifested and made genuine."[30] From the perspective of an empathetic human observer, of course, the hen's clucking is akin to a human mother calling her children; we invest the hen with human emotions, desires, and aims and believe her to be self-conscious in her calling to her chicks. The reality is very different, however. The hen, in fact, clucks out of instinct and is not consciously aware of what she is doing; it is an innate impulse evolved as a sign to stimulate the activity of her chicks. As Dewey explains, "Animals thus behave in ways which have no direct consequences of utility to the behaving animal, but which call out certain characteristic responses, sexual, protective, food-finding (as with the cluck of a hen to her chicks), in other animals."[31] The effect of these coordinated instincts is, of course, beneficial for the chicks; they are able to feed and to be protected simultaneously. It may also be beneficial for the hen; it satisfies its maternal instinct and relieves it from stress. But these effects were not consciously intended by the hen or recognized by the chicks. They reacted purely to the instinctive signs that they are biologically hardwired both to interpret and to express.

The clucks of the hen are therefore *eventful* because they occur within temporal and spatial continuity of other events and objects, but they are not *eventual* because they are not coordinated by the mutual cognition of some common aim or purpose that influences their choices. Animals communicate, but their communication consists of an alternating sequence of signs that are all "overflows" of impulses rather than consciously crafted messages. That a more complex animal such as a dog might be trained to react differently to a gesture only means that its habitual reactions to certain signs may change, but it does not mean that the dog comprehends any more than the chicken the intentions or goals of its owner. In both cases, animal communication consists of an exchange of visible signs and their habitual or instinctual reactions; at no point do the animals ever become self-conscious of their own "eventual" intentions or those of other animals, including their humans.

The origin of language is thus not found in the signaling gestures and cries of animals; it is found in the *eventual* stance toward those gestures and cries that made its first appearance in the human consciousness. What this eventual stance required was a revolutionary change in the nature of stimulus. For the animal, the stimulus that elicits a reaction is the sound, action, touch, smell, or taste in its immediate, eventful qualitativeness; this quality acts as a primitive inference to which the animal instinctively or habitually responds. With the awaking of linguistic consciousness, however, the stimulus is transferred from *quality* to *intent*, from individual impulse to shared situation. A newborn baby is a bundle of instinctive reactions, but she becomes an infant when she becomes aware that the gestures and sounds of her parents acquire future meanings beyond their immediate qualitativeness. A newborn is comforted by a shushing sound that reproduces the familiar rhythms of the womb; a child is comforted by an awareness that her mother has promised to give her a candy if she behaves. Whereas the newborn's activity is "egocentric," absorbed in his immediate biological needs, the child's action is inclusive insofar as she puts herself "at the standpoint of a situation in which two parties share." For Dewey, this is the foundation of language—the symbolic construction of a shared standpoint to which two or more parties can respond as a common stimulus. The child thus does not react to some object of inference brought to mind on encountering a qualitative sign, such as the object of food inferred by a hen's clucking; rather, the child reacts to the eventual, future intent that she consciously attributes to the mother, an intent that then becomes communicated in a word. Thus the "heart of language is not 'expression' of something antecedent, much less expression of antecedent thought. It is communication; the establishment of cooperation in an activity in which there are partners, and in which the activity of each is modified and regulated by partnership."[32] Communication therefore allows us to respond to the *eventual* aims and purposes that grow out of a shared understanding of being within the same situation.

For Dewey, the method of rhetoric is thus to arouse and channel natural impulses so that they become directed toward achieving some eventuality.

An impulse, as we have already seen, is an outgoing expression of energy and power that arises in relationship to some qualitative situation. An impulse is a kind of drive, appetite, urge, or instinct. It is, in short, "original, unlearned activity." A newborn is hungry and opens his mouth; he is frightened and cries; he is restless and flails his arms. None of these things he does with rational purpose or because of cultural inheritance; it is the way that outgoing energy flows out of his body and into the world outside. As the newborn becomes an infant, however, he realizes that impulsive behavior can be modified for greater satisfaction; he begins to alter his actions in response to his social surroundings, learning what gives him greater control and reward. In this way, the infant comes to realize that "his impulses are merely starting points for assimilation of the knowledge and skill of the more matured beings upon whom he depends. They are tentacles sent out to gather that nutrition from customs which will in time render the infant capable of independent action. They are agencies for transfer of existing social power into personal ability; they are means of reconstructive growth."[33] The metaphor of "tentacles" is telling. Reminiscent of his criticism of the reflex arc concept in psychology, impulses are not merely reactions or reflexes; they are outgoing and intentional actions that reach *into* the environment, even if they do not necessarily know *why* they reach or what they reach *for*.

As we mature into adulthood, impulses are gradually formed into habits, which in turn become the basis of character, yet impulse remains. Because the world is not a block universe that ceases to stimulate us once our habits are in place, "the truth is that in every waking moment, the complete balance of the organism and its environment is constantly interfered with and as constantly restored. . . . Life is interruptions and recoveries." In other words, there are always moments in which our habits run aground and we are tossed once again into the turbulent sea of impulse in which we must rely again on unlearned activity to restore and recover ourselves. Dewey gives the example of an experienced traveler faring forth:

> We may consider him first at a moment where his activity is confident, straightforward, organized. He marches on giving no direct attention to his path, nor thinking of his destination. Abruptly he is pulled up, arrested. Something is going wrong in his activity. From the standpoint of an onlooker, he has met an obstacle which must be overcome before his behavior can be unified into a successful ongoing. From his own standpoint, there is shock, confusion, perturbation, uncertainty. For the moment he doesn't know what hit him, as we say, nor where he is

going. But a new impulse is stirred which becomes the starting point of an investigation, a looking into things, a trying to see them, to find out what is going on.

Impulse represents this stirring of outgoing energy that arises in response to shock, confusion, perturbation, and uncertainty. Whereas habit steers our thoughts and behaviors into well-worn paths in response to familiar phenomena, "impulse defines the peering, the search, the inquiry. It is, in logical language, the movement into the unknown, not into the immense inane of the unknown at large, but into that special unknown which when it is hit upon restores an ordered, unified action." In other words, impulse is always located in a specific event, a continuous moment of space and time that focuses our biological energies at a single, contingent point.[34]

The reason that rhetoric relies on impulse is that it is only through impulse that rhetoric acquires the force to direct individuals to new courses of thought and action. In a stable situation governed by habit, for instance, persuasion is rarely called for. In extreme cases of routine, for instance, habits shut out different possibilities; they act as "blinders that confine the eyes of mind to the road ahead." Even more subtle and flexible habits—such as those of the "hunter in the forest, the painter in his studio, the man of science in his laboratory"—still follow a method that confidently directs their observations, recollections, and judgments. While open to suggestions, their habits nonetheless process them according to familiar trains of thought and physical activity. Impulses are different. Whereas habits are organized, impulses are "chaotic, tumultuous and confused"; whereas habit incorporates all events and objects into a familiar structure, "impulse scatters and obliterates them with its restless stir."[35] This activity, to be sure, can be disruptive and dangerous, but it also provides the source of the novelty that rhetoric harnesses to adapt to changing conditions. As Dewey makes clear, "impulses are the pivots upon which the re-organization of activities turn, they are agencies of deviation, for giving new directions to old habits and changing their quality." This is particularly the case when dealing with "social transition and flux or with projects for reform, personal and collective." For Dewey, as long as we have an "interest in modifying existing institutions," then we should have an equal interest in the study of how impulses are aroused and directed.[36] From the perspective of the pedagogy of democratic humanism, this also means we must develop an interest in rhetoric.

Attentiveness to impulse brings us to the first attitude to consciously develop as a part of teaching rhetoric—that of *timeliness*. In the rhetorical tradition, timeliness is associated with the word *kairos*, a term used to refer to the "opportune moment," "due measure," or "right occasion."[37] But as a term of action, *kairos* also carried with it connotations of practical and moral excellence. In Greek mythology, the god Kairos was portrayed as a young man with wings on his feet standing on a razor's edge holding a scale in his hands. His power was therefore to make a choice at the right time to bring forth positive benefits that would have been lost had action been initiated at an earlier or later time. But the metaphor of the razor is misleading if it implies that timeliness exists in a single moment disconnected from the impulses and habits of individuals. There is no transcendent mystery or intuitive magic to timeliness; it acquires sensitivity to impulses and possibilities. For Dewey, "'present' activity is not a sharp narrow knife-blade in time. The present is complex, containing within itself a multitude of habits and impulses. It is enduring, a course of action, a process including memory, observation and foresight, a pressure forward, a glance backward and a look outward." And even more important, it "is of *moral* moment because it marks a transition in the direction of breadth and clarity of action or in that of triviality and confusion."[38] To be attentive to the timeliness of our actions thus means to grasp that moment within a continuous present in which impulses can be directed toward our imagined goods.

Perhaps nothing has more significance for the teaching of rhetoric than the insistence that we start not at the end but at the beginning. All too often, the teaching of rhetoric begins with the study of "great speeches," which represent not the initiation but the consummation of rhetorical form. This method presumes that we learn to speak well by imitating classical models that present us with eloquent praise of established virtues. Yet to marginalize the conflicts, contingencies, uncertainties, and fears from which rhetoric springs is to praise the flower while ignoring the soil. From a naturalistic perspective, this order is reversed. The accomplishment of rhetoric is not its ability to praise abstract virtue but its capacity to harness and direct impulses that exist in a continuous present. When Addams begins her book, for instance, she starts at the moment that war is declared in Europe, when America remained neutral. At this time, she notes, attitudes of the war were "divided into two spirited camps," their views expressed not only in speeches and lectures but in "newspaper cartoons and comments." Sometimes, when she would lecture on peace, she found "audiences of young people both large and eager." But other times, she encountered "students of the belligerent type who did not attend the lectures and occasionally a professor, invariably one of the older men, [who] rose in the audience to uphold the traditional glories of warfare."[39] It was into this divided state of public opinion that President Wilson would eventually step forward to declare war, but his declaration means nothing without understanding the clash of impulses that preceded it.

Timeliness, however, is aimless without its counterpart—*intelligence*. Within moments characterized by a clash of impulses, intelligence represents the readiness and capacity to draw from an equipment of established habits in order to define the contours of the situation. What this means, in other words, is that even when impulse dominates, habits still matter. What they provide are the resources for searching out the nature of a situation so one might constitute it as an object of thought capable of being described and communicated to others. As Dewey explains, "During this search, old habit supplies content, filling, definite, recognizable, subject-matter. It begins as vague presentiment of what we are going towards. As organized habits are definitely deployed and focused, the confused situation takes on form, it is 'cleared up'—the essential function of intelligence." For instance, Dewey continues his narrative of the lost traveler who encounters an unexpected obstacle. At this point, "habits which were interfered with begin to get a new direction as they cluster about the impulse to look and see. The blocked habits of locomotion give him a sense of where he was going, of what he had set out to do, and of the ground already traversed."[40] The product of this activity is thus the defining of a "situation" not as a *given* but as a *taken*, an accomplishment. To be intelligent is to be able to size up one's situation as a whole in a way that facilitates understanding and provides some leverage to be able to make effective judgments.

A rhetorical situation is thus one marked by urgency and uncertainty and whose resolution requires political discourse to facilitate collective moral judgments. To be *political* in this context means to solicit the voluntary participation of others to achieve some common aim; to be *moral* means to have a bearing on how we value individual conduct as a reflection of character and one's relationship with others. Notably, moral situations for Dewey are not ones in which we already know the good but struggle to do it; they are situations rather in which we are torn between competing goods: "From this point of view, uncertainty and conflict are inherent in morals; it is characteristic of any situation properly called moral that one is ignorant of the end and of good consequences, of the right and just approach, of the direction of virtuous conduct, and that one must search for them."[41] Add to these qualities a sense of timely *urgency* and one has all the characteristics of a rhetorical situation. When Dewey published his *Ethics* with James Tufts in 1932, for instance, he offered a perfect example of a rhetorical situation that spoke directly to the coming moral struggles of his age:

> Take . . . the case of a citizen of a nation which has just declared war on another country. He is deeply attached to his own State. He has formed habits of loyalty and of abiding by its laws, and now one of its decrees is that he shall support war. He feels in addition gratitude and affection for the country which has sheltered and nurtured him. But he believes that this war is unjust, or perhaps he has a conviction that all war is a form of murder and hence wrong. One side of his nature, one set of convictions and habits, leads him to acquiesce in war; another deep part of his being protests. He is torn between two duties: he experiences a conflict between the incompatible values presented to him by his habits of citizenship and by his religious beliefs respectively. Up to this time, he has never experienced a struggle between the two; they have coincided and reenforced one another. Now he has to make a choice between competing moral loyalties and convictions. The struggle is not between a good which is clear to him and something else which attracts him but which he knows to be wrong. It is between values each of which is an undoubted good in its place but which now get in each other's way. He is forced to reflect in order to come to a decision.[42]

The situation as Dewey presented it was not, of course, intended to demonstrate the nature of rhetoric; it was meant to highlight a moral debate within an individual's conscience concerning the nature of the good. Yet clearly the struggle within this individual is a product of a larger rhetorical situation constructed around the urgency of war. Driven by the need to recruit soldiers, political actors had appealed to the patriotic beliefs of the public and forced upon them the burden of judgment. For the pacifist, however, this was not a choice between patriotism and cowardice; it was a choice between patriotic and religious duty.

If our practical intelligence emphasizes the capacity to size up a situation according to its factual character, it is intelligence in the form of *conscientiousness* that stresses our attentiveness to how our actions have a bearing on the well-being of others. For Dewey, "conscientiousness is primarily the virtue of intelligence in regard to conduct. That is to say, it is the formed habit of bringing intelligence to bear upon the analysis of moral relations—the habit of considering what ought to be done."[43] Unfortunately, in ordinary usage, conscientiousness is inflected by the idealist tradition that concentrates attention on our own relationship to some abstract idea; it is not *other*-oriented but *self*-oriented. Dewey rejects this interpretation. For him, conscientiousness "is not an anxious prying into motives, a fingering of the inner springs of action to detect whether or not a 'motive' is good. Genuine conscientiousness has an objective outlook; it is intelligent attention and care to the quality of an act in view of its consequences for general happiness; it is not anxious solicitude for one's own virtuous state."[44] A rhetorical practice that expresses conscientiousness must thus begin with the care and concern for the other; it must demonstrate character by expressing a commitment to achieving the common good.

What that means in practice is to consciously define a rhetorical situation in such a way that transforms *impulses* into *motives*. Another common inheritance of the idealistic tradition is to assume that when people act, they always do so with a clearly defined prior intent and already articulated desire. In actual fact, as Dewey explains, a great deal of our actions are purely impulsive. In this way, we are no different from any living organism. For instance, hunger is not a motive; it is a natural instinct that arises without our conscious intent and that we act upon because it feels natural to do so. Therefore, "hunger primarily names an act or active process not a motive to an act. It is an act if we take it grossly, like a babe's blind hunt for the mother's breast." Impulses only become motives when the foresight of consequences and their social valuation is taken into account, either in reflection or in the act of judgment itself. Thus "when foresight enters, intent, purpose enters also, and with it a change of motive from innocent, because blind, impulse, to deliberate, and hence to virtuous or blameworthy interest in effecting a certain result." It is impulsive, for instance, for a baby to hunt for a mother's breast, but once a baby becomes an infant and starts reaching for candy, the praise and blame of a parent begins to make the child aware of the social consequences of his actions. Thus "he learns to influence his own conduct." Consequently, to look for motives, we should look *outside* ourselves rather than *inside* ourselves. Instead of "saying that a man requires a motive in order to induce him to act, we should say that when a man is going to act he needs to know *what* he is going to do—what the quality of his act is in terms of consequences to follow."[45] It is in this process of becoming aware of the context and consequences of our actions that we acquire our motives.

An analogous process occurs with rhetoric. In any situation dominated by a clash of impulses, collective deliberation and action require a definition of a situation that clarifies our possible motives and intentionally praises those that are desirable. Our motives, that is to say, are not abstract values and aims that dwell only in our moral imagination; they are rather our dispositions to respond to specific situations in a way that achieves predictable and desirable effects. As Dewey explains, "A motive is then that element in the total complex of a man's activity which, if it can be sufficiently stimulated, will result in an act having specified consequences."[46] The aim of rhetoric is to find a way to stimulate that activity by placing an individual *within* a situation in which that activity would be seen as praiseworthy. For instance, in the case of the young man struggling to find true good within the clash between his patriotic duty and his religious beliefs in a time of war, we find a competition between two rhetorical constructions of a situation. On the one hand, the young man sees himself as being nurtured by the state and hence obliged to come to its defense; the situation so defined stimulates the motive of loyalty, manifested perhaps in his volunteering for military service. On the other hand, he sees himself as being born a child of God, in fellowship with all other human beings; the situation thus defined stimulates the motive of love, manifesting in his refusal to support state-sponsored violence against another people. The motive that he chooses thus derives from his understanding of the nature of the situation he accepts. It is the virtue of conscientiousness that helps a speaker determine which situation will bring forth the most virtuous motives. When we teach the rhetoric of motives, therefore, one should begin not with a study of psychology but with a study of context. We understand people's motives, that is to say, by how they define the situation in which they acted; similarly, we motivate others by pointing out elements of a situation in which one motive over another seems appropriate.

Yet neither our grasp of a situation intellectually nor our sense of moral duty is sufficient in most cases to mobilize a public for collective action, particularly when confronted with the possibilities of suffering; to move people to action requires *passion*. By "passion," Dewey means a strong emotional desire for some absent object within a present situation. What the "object" of desire might be is infinitely variable; one might desire justice, a mate, a victory, a good night's sleep, the latest fashion, a joke, peace on earth, vengeance, or a vacation to Athens. What matters is that the object is desired, not for its own sake but because of how it relates to ongoing tensions and possibilities at the forefront of an individual's consciousness. Two characteristics of passionate desire stand out. First, desire is only aroused because of obstruction. Dewey writes that "desire is the forward urge of living creatures.

When the push and drive of life meets no obstacle, there is nothing which we call desire. There is just life-activity. But obstructions present themselves, and activity is dispersed and divided. Desire is the outcome." Second, desire is focused not on the object itself but on the object as it functions within some ongoing system of activities. Within that context, "the 'object' which then presents itself in thought as the goal of desire is the object of the environment *which, if it were present*, would secure a re-unification of activity and the restoration of its ongoing unity."[47] Dewey gives an example of the desire of a condemned man for the paper that carries his reprieve. He desires the paper not because he wishes to hold it or possess it but because it represents a means to his freedom. Thus the desire for the paper becomes synonymous with the passion for freedom itself; the two are one because they both represent the movement of a situation toward his release as a free man.

Of course, Dewey recognizes the dangers of passion, particularly political passions. Throughout his writings, he warned against the irrational inflaming of passions, noting that "mankind was ever subject to passion, dogma, self-interest, partisanship and propaganda."[48] That passion is included in this list lends considerable suspicion that Dewey, while a romantic in art, was a rationalist in politics. For instance, he not infrequently described passion in terms of an overwhelming desire that suffocates perspective and reason. Dewey describes how "the cue of passion . . . is to keep imagination dwelling upon those objects which are congenial to it, which feed it, and which by feeding it intensify its force, until it crowds out all thought of other objects. An impulse or habit which is strongly emotional magnifies all objects that are congruous with it and smothers those which are opposed whenever they present themselves." At its worst, passion leads straight to violence. In a telling example, Dewey notes how "a passionate activity learns to work itself up artificially—as Oliver Cromwell indulged in fits of anger when he wanted to do things that his conscience would not justify."[49] Here we find the familiar suspicion of passion as the source of all our political strife, a motive better suppressed and denied than cultivated and embraced.

Yet Dewey realized that the conflict between reason and passion is a false binary. Cultivated by idealists who would separate human beings from nature, the division between reason and passion became a way of distinguishing the merely biological self from its idealized form as a strictly rational soul. But for Dewey, it is a natural fact that "the intellect is always inspired by some impulse. Even the most case-hardened scientific specialist, the most abstract philosopher, is moved by some passion."[50] To be passionate about something does not necessitate being dogmatic, self-interested, or partisan; it means being viscerally moved by some object of desire. At issue is not the presence of *desire*, therefore, but the nature and function of the *object* desired: "In short, while there is conflict, it is not between desire and reason, but between a desire which wants a near-by object and a desire which wants an object which is seen by thought to occur in consequence of an intervening series of conditions, or in the 'long run.'" For instance, the impulse of fear might arouse a passion for flight or even for deception as a means of survival, yet "further thought may bring a man to a conviction that steadfastness and truthfulness insure a much larger and more enduring good."[51] The central point is that in each case, there is desire. The difference is in the object, scope, and quality of the desire. One desire lies close to impulses and instincts, while the other expands outward in space and time and includes the consideration of remote consequences on oneself and others. To decry passion is thus to condemn not only the selfish desire for survival but also the steadfastness and truthfulness that overcomes it.

To the degree that the art of rhetoric culminates in a committed and voluntary choice among alternatives, it must therefore provide not just a motive but arouse the passion that moves people to action. Recognizing a fact long stressed in the rhetorical tradition, Dewey argues that "no matter how elaborate and how rational is the object of thought, it is impotent unless it arouses desire."[52] To believe otherwise is to remove human beings from their natural context and act as if they are calculating machines. But to be a calculating machine is to be guided not by choice but by necessity, and to be ruled by necessity is the essence of antihumanism. Consequently, "there can be no separation morally of desire and thought because the union of thought and desire is just what makes an act voluntary."[53] To say that the culmination of rhetoric is *choice* is therefore to say that it is the sudden unification of reason and passion, of habit and imagination, and of reflection and action. Dewey goes on,

> What then is choice? Simply hitting in imagination upon an object which furnishes an adequate stimulus to the recovery of overt action. Choice is made as soon as some habit, or some combination of elements of habits and impulse, finds a way fully open. Then energy is released. The mind is made up, composed, unified. As long as deliberation pictures shoals or rocks or troublesome gales as marking the route of a contemplated voyage, deliberation goes on. But when the various factors in action fit harmoniously together, when imagination finds no annoying hindrance, when there is a picture of open seas,

filled sails and favoring winds, the voyage is definitely entered upon. This decisive direction of action constitutes choice.[54]

Importantly, the making of a choice does not necessarily mean that it is a *wise* choice. This feeling of open seas and filled sails may, as events progress, lead directly into those shoals, rocks, and troublesome gales. But regardless of its wisdom, for choice to exist at all requires a passionate commitment to follow some path that imagination sees before it. In the sphere of political discourse, it is rhetoric that both charts this path and stokes the breeze.

But the question of wisdom cannot be put aside. Everything that has been said up until this point, after all, applies equally to propaganda. For propaganda to function requires it to attend to the same qualities of human nature as do the highest flights of eloquence. An effective propagandist must obstruct habits, agitate impulses, construct situations, define motives, and arouse passions. In *Peace and Bread*, for instance, Jane Addams recounts the moment where she was confronted with the full power of wartime propaganda. From a personal perspective, she recalls how "after the United States entered the war, the press throughout the country systematically undertook to misrepresent and malign pacifists as a recognized part of propaganda and as a patriotic duty." But even more striking for her was the propaganda of the battlefield that systematically dehumanized its soldiers. In every country she visited, she writes, she encountered young soldiers who confessed that they were not able to enter into hand-to-hand fighting before they had been stimulated by propaganda: "To those who heard the address it was quite clear that it was not because the young men flinched at the risk of death but because they had to be inflamed to do the brutal work of the bayonet, such as disemboweling, and were obliged to overcome all the inhibitions of civilization."[55] Here is a type of "choice," to be sure, but one that leads straight to the slaughterhouse, the concentration camp, or the no-man's-land.

When faced with this terrible legacy of persuasion in the hands of the powerful, the central question for democratic humanism is how to cultivate a rhetoric that is not only passionate but also intelligent and humane. It would be tempting at this point for Dewey to retreat to the reductive rationalism of Plato and all who followed him, to imagine a rule by philosopher kings immune to the passions of the mob who could direct the ship of state with dispassionate objectivity. But he does not. Instead, he imagines a reason grounded in a wider, not a narrower, sympathy. The conclusion "is not that the emotional, passionate phase of action can be or should be eliminated in behalf of a bloodless reason. More 'passions,' not fewer, is the answer.

To check the influence of hate there must be sympathy, while to rationalize sympathy there are needed emotions of curiosity, caution, respect for the freedom of others." In contradistinction to bloodless conceptions of reason, Dewey envisions a *full-blooded* reason that seeks a higher unity through "a working harmony among diverse desires." In short, "reason" signifies neither a grasp of higher laws nor a capacity for detached mathematical calculation; instead, "'reason' as a noun signifies the happy cooperation of a multitude of dispositions, such as sympathy, curiosity, exploration, experimentation, [and] frankness."[56] For instance, the Wilson administration is not irrational simply because it advocates war; it is irrational because it suppresses all views to the contrary while denying the humanity of its enemy. By contrast, the rationality of Addams is not found in her resistance to war but in her capacity to feel passion for all those who suffer and to construct a vision of peace that will serve the interests of all.

It is therefore through the most important rhetorical attitude of all, that of *sympathy*, that we enlighten our passions and rationalize our motives. For Dewey, sympathy is not at all equivalent to the condescension of pity, which looks at others as mere objects; sympathy is a way of broadening our consciousness, both emotionally and empirically: "Sympathy widens our interest in consequences and leads us to take into account such results as affect the welfare of others; it aids us to count and weigh these consequences as counting for as much as those which touch our own honor, purse, or power." It does so by encouraging us to imagine perspectives outside of our own, to stimulate a train of thought whereby we envision the possible consequences of actions on those not ourselves. Sympathy is therefore a method of acquiring knowledge not accessible to our immediate experience: "To put ourselves in the place of another, to see from the standpoint of his purposes and values, to humble our estimate of our own claims and pretensions to the level they would assume in the eyes of a sympathetic and impartial observer, is the surest way to attain universality and objectivity of moral knowledge."[57] Dewey had already recognized the arts as providing this crucial function of developing sympathy with others through its universal language, but it is through rhetoric that this sympathy intersects with moral and political judgment and forces us to take responsibility for our choices. A rhetoric that refuses to put itself in the place of another is neither rational nor humane.

The way to cultivate both passion and sympathy in the teaching of rhetoric is thus to encourage students not only to dramatize their emotions in speech but to put those passions in conversation with the passions of others. This is no easy task, as the clash of passions is often the cause of turmoil and strife, but it is also the source of ultimate harmony and reconciliation. There is no way to truly rationalize speech except by adapting it to the recalcitrance of those who feel otherwise. In *Peace and Bread*, for instance, Addams recalls how even after the war, the international commitment to put an end to the widespread famines caused by years of devastation had waned as national leaders retreated to their own self-interests as millions of women and children starved. The Women's International League sent a representative to the second meeting of the League of Nations with the rhetorical message that it might be "a situation which might turn men's minds from war and a disastrous peace to great and simple human issues; in such an enterprise the government would 'realize the failure of national coercive power for indispensable ends like food for the people,' they would come to a cooperation born of the failure of force."[58] Here was a passion to serve a rational end, to expand the nationalistic passions of the great leaders into a wider passion for serving the common needs of humanity. Such an expansion of our consciousness comes about through sympathy provoked by imagining ourselves in the perspective of another.

And thus we return to the conflict between fascism and democracy. For the fascist, increased sympathy was the road to chaos; only by narrowing our sympathy to a clique could a nation be held together by the propaganda of the few. The fascist thus believes that "the truths which have the authority to direct social action are by right the possession of a small superior elite, and that the mass of human beings cannot be trusted to judge and to believe aright in moral matters; that if they are permitted to exercise freedom of mind their policies and decisions will be so swayed by personal and class interests that the final outcome will be division, conflict and disintegration."[59] For the democratic humanist, only by expanding the possibilities for sympathetic communication in logic, aesthetics, and rhetoric could a truly rational society be brought into being capable of regulating itself for the common good. For Dewey, "there is much to be said for the proposition that the essence and life blood of human society, that which makes our connections with one another genuinely social, not just physical, is the existence of *communication*—the fact that by means of language the net outcome of every experience, the meaning of every discovery, the occurrence of every fresh insight and stimulating outlook can be communicated to others, thereby becoming a common possession."[60] Nothing guarantees that this communication will be free of strife and turmoil, of division and dissension, but it is a tenet of the democratic faith that it is precisely by bringing these tensions into the open that we allow the opportunity to form common understandings on which social justice is built.

To teach rhetoric is thus to prepare individuals to take on the significant burden of democratic citizenship. Because the fact is that "the democratic road is the hard one to take. It is the road which places the greatest burden of responsibility upon the greatest number of human beings."[61] To take the hard road of democracy is not to passively consider the views of others but to participate in the active process in which heightened passions and clashing perspectives meet together within the deliberative public sphere in which the burden of judgment falls on everyone. As Jane Addams discovered, this is not at all an easy road. Often this exposed her to be targeted by propaganda and threatened with violence, yet she endured because she believed that the only alternative was to accept intolerance and war as permanent conditions of human existence. In her own words, she persevered because she was part of a movement that "believed that the ardor and self-sacrifice so characteristic of youth could be enlisted for the vitally energetic role required to inaugurate a new type of international life in the world. We realized that it is only the ardent spirits, the lovers of mankind, who can break down the suspicion and lack of understanding which have so long prevented changes upon which international good order depend."[62] That hope is undoubtedly a democratic one, but it is at the same time an expression of a rhetorical faith. That faith is in the capacity of language to invite others to respond with passionate intelligence to overcoming shared problems and to do so with the sympathy and humility that we all inhabit a common world.

CONCLUSION:
TEACHING DEMOCRATIC HUMANISM

> Art breaks through barriers that divide human beings, which are impermeable in ordinary association. This force of art, common to all the arts, is most fully manifested in literature. Its medium is already formed by communication, something that can hardly be asserted of any other art.
>
> —JOHN DEWEY, *ART AS EXPERIENCE*

Although the arts of democratic humanism are universal in scope and limited to no subject matter, it finds in literature the medium through which teachers can inspire students to develop an interest in and acquire mastery of all three arts conceived of as part of a unified whole. By "literature" I mean not only the traditional novel but all the many genres of literature that translate a complex environment of human relations into a dramatic narrative. Literature thus includes history, biography, journalism, poetry, mythology, and rhetoric. For instance, Dewey uses *Robinson Crusoe* to exemplify the function of logical inference, quotes from "Ode on a Grecian Urn" to teach us the nature of aesthetic experience, and interprets the biographical reflections in *Peace and Bread* to reveal to us our ethical responsibility as citizens in a global society. Literature opens up a shared imaginative space of possibilities in which all three arts work collaboratively to reveal new meanings.

For Dewey, these are all works of art formed by the medium of communication, whose effect is to break down the barriers that divide human beings. But they are also artifacts through which we can learn how logic, aesthetics, and rhetoric can work together as part of a humanistic "new trivium," a pedagogy whose aim is to cultivate the habits that make our judgments more intelligent, our experiences more deeply felt, and our practices more just. This does not deny the enduring value of teaching logic, aesthetics, and rhetoric each within its own disciplinary sphere; it simply recognizes the limitations inherent in teaching them in isolation. To be sure, laboratory courses in the sciences translate logic into the scientific method, seminars in art criticism and history provide a language of aesthetic taste and judgment, and public speaking and composition courses in rhetoric and communication cultivate skills in invention, arrangement, and delivery. Yet very rarely are these different methods considered three parts of a unitary whole, each a manifestation of a uniquely human capacity to invest experience with meaning and communicate it to others.

The advantage of using literature to teach the arts of democratic humanism is fourfold. First, literature represents a bounded universe of interconnected meanings that invites individuals from different backgrounds to enter into a shared imaginative space that is both complex but finite. For instance, what makes *Robinson Crusoe* such an ideal example for Dewey is precisely that Crusoe's "island" is limited enough that it can be reconstructed within a hypothetical diagram that contains multiple events, objects, and actors, each with certain properties and operating under specific relationships. Second, literature is composed of symbols whose meanings originated in the actual world of human experience, thus creating a connection between the bounded universe created in the imagination and the infinite universe of actual events. Literature thus can be used as a means of investigating real historical conditions, whether described by the text itself or discovered through an inquiry into the circumstances surrounding its production. For instance, *Peace and Bread* is a work of nonfiction literature that narrates the actual conditions of the war and postwar periods as well as the direct experiences of Jane Addams. Third, the patterns of experience that constitute works of literature—meaning here the adjustments that human beings make to recognizable and recurrent types of situations—can be abstracted from their specific context and used to interpret and influence situations in the present. To defend the pacifism of Jane Addams in the past is also to recommend it in the future. Lastly, literature is intrinsically enjoyable. Works of art such as literature draw us into their universes because of the pleasure that they bring, thus affecting the emotions, arousing the desires, and stimulating the curiosities that are necessary for any genuine act of thinking. For instance, a student might not initially care about the relationship between truth and beauty from a philosophical perspective until they actually are drawn into the worlds pictured on the Grecian urn. In sum, literature provides an intrinsically satisfying shared imaginary space in which students can playfully manipulate symbolic meanings, inquire into actual past events, identify and measure the value of emergent qualities, and advocate for future possibilities.

Following the triadic structure of this new trivium, a course dedicated to teaching the arts of democratic humanism will not only be divided into the three units of logic, aesthetics, and rhetoric but also involve three types of assignments: (1) history, (2) criticism, and (3) advocacy. A history assignment uses the literary text as an instigation inquiry into the nature of past events. These events include both those represented in the narrative as well as those events that may more indirectly have influenced the author's method of invention. For instance, a student might use logic to investigate the actual conditions of starvation during and after World War I, aesthetics to study the appearance of the actual Grecian urn that inspired John Keats, and rhetoric to define the conditions of the rhetorical situation faced by Jane Addams at the League of Nations. A criticism assignment looks at the text as a self-contained universe of meanings and determines their relationships to one another within the work of literature itself. For instance, a student might use logic to break down the reasoning process of those who advocated for the American entry into the war according to Addams, aesthetics to identify the nature of those qualities that so horrified or thrilled Robinson Crusoe, and rhetoric to understand how Crusoe persuaded himself and others within urgent moments of decision. Finally, an advocacy assignment asks students to use the work of literature as a resource to make an argument about past injustices, present values, or future judgments. A student might use logic to investigate the current relationship between war and starvation in the modern world, aesthetics to identify what is ugly in modern industrial society, and rhetoric to condemn the attitudes of colonialism that are continuous from Robinson Crusoe to the present.

Any syllabus would include four basic components: theory, exercises, literature, and creative assignments. First, students would be assigned theoretical and methodological readings intended to introduce students to the methods of logic, aesthetics, and rhetoric that are consistent with the values of democratic humanism. Second, they would be encouraged to engage in creative exercises alone or with other students to put these methods into practice and experiment with different forms of communication. Third, they would be asked to read three works of literature chosen to exemplify each of the three arts. Lastly, they would be given assignments modeled on the types of assignments outlined here:

1. Historical inquiry: Use the methods of logic to investigate a historical question raised by the work of literature. Highlight the specific

passage that evoked a feeling of doubt and then define your problem. Identify data in the text that you determine to be relevant to an answer. Create a hypothesis that would explain the presence of the data by positing the existence of some state of affairs—that is, some causal mechanism, circumstance, motive, event, or identity—that would account for these data. Use outside historical research to confirm or disconfirm this hypothesis and judge the significance of your findings.

2. Aesthetic criticism: Use the methods of aesthetics to investigate a conflict in "taste" either between two characters or within a single character that has a significant bearing on their judgments. Select specific moments in which characters encounter objects, events, or people and identify and name the qualities they perceive and the emotions that are aroused by those qualities. Provide an explanation, based on their past experiences, of why they may consciously perceive events in one way rather than another. Construct a definition of taste for these characters that helps us understand and predict their behavior in subsequent scenes.

3. Rhetorical advocacy: Use the methods of rhetoric to interpret a rhetorical situation in the work of literature and to construct a persuasive argument about a matter of pressing concern in the present. Select one or more scenes in which characters find themselves in a rhetorical situation. Diagram this situation and demonstrate how it bears on the motives of the actors involved. Using analogical reasoning, then show, through comparison and contrast, how this literary rhetorical situation can be used to interpret the characteristics of an active rhetorical situation today. Advance an ethical claim based on your analysis that encourages your reader to accept a certain view of the rhetorical situation that encourages the adoption of a specific motive and corresponding judgment.

The format of these assignments would also be varied in order to expose students to different communicative environments. For instance, teachers could assign the historical inquiry as a cooperative group investigation and presentation, the aesthetic criticism as an individual composition that would go through numerous drafts, and the rhetorical advocacy assignment as either a public speech or a kind of digital rhetoric that integrates public-speaking techniques and digital media. Finally, these major assignments would of course be complemented by numerous smaller exercises, group discussions, artistic improvisations, and out-of-class experiences during the semester. What is important is not that they understand all the specific terminology and techniques outlined in this book; this is designed for the teacher. What is important is that students acquire the spirit of the arts themselves and an intuitive and emotional understanding of how they work together to produce a richer and more intelligent shared experience.

For the sake of diagramming what these assignments might look like, a scene from *Robinson Crusoe* offers a perfect example of how teachers can draw from literature to instruct students in all three of the arts of democratic humanism. The action occurs more than a year after first seeing the footprint. One morning, he comes upon a grotesque scene on a beach. He writes in his journal that is impossible to "express the horror of my mind at seeing the shore spread with skulls, hands, feet, and other bones of human bodies; and particularly I observed a place where there had been a fire made, and a circle dug in the earth, like a cockpit, where I supposed the savage wretches had sat down to their human feastings upon the bodies of their fellow-creatures." Here he encounters a verification of his earlier inference concerning the existence of cannibals. With his worst fears confirmed and overcome with horror at what he sees, he decides it best to murder on sight anyone he takes to be a cannibal, arming himself with three pistols and his sword. But after a time, detachment sets in, and he starts a more genuine deliberation. He writes, "I began, with cooler and calmer thoughts, to consider what I was going to engage in; what authority or call I had to pretend to be judge and executioner upon these men as criminals." What follows is then one of the most provocative paragraphs in Daniel Defoe's book:

> When I considered this a little, it followed necessarily that I was certainly in the wrong; that these people were not murderers, in the sense that I had before condemned them in my thoughts, any more than those Christians were murderers who often put to death the prisoners taken in battle; or more frequently, upon many occasions, put whole troops of men to the sword, without giving quarter, though they threw down their arms and submitted. In the next place, it occurred to me that although the usage they gave one another was thus brutish and inhuman, yet it was really nothing to me: these people had done me no injury: that if they attempted, or I saw it necessary, for my immediate preservation, to fall upon them, something might be said for it: but that I was yet out of their power, and they really had no knowledge of me, and consequently no design upon me; and therefore it could not

be just for me to fall upon them; that this would justify the conduct of the Spaniards in all their barbarities practised in America, where they destroyed millions of these people; who, however they were idolators and barbarians, and had several bloody and barbarous rites in their customs, such as sacrificing human bodies to their idols, were yet, as to the Spaniards, very innocent people; and that the rooting them out of the country is spoken of with the utmost abhorrence and detestation by even the Spaniards themselves at this time, and by all other Christian nations of Europe, as a mere butchery, a bloody and unnatural piece of cruelty, unjustifiable either to God or man; and for which the very name of a Spaniard is reckoned to be frightful and terrible, to all people of humanity or of Christian compassion; as if the kingdom of Spain were particularly eminent for the produce of a race of men who were without principles of tenderness, or the common bowels of pity to the miserable, which is reckoned to be a mark of generous temper in the mind.[1]

In sum, Crusoe engages in a free play of ideas, drawing together propositions and promises from multiple sources. He considers the inscrutability of God's judgment; he acknowledges his own cultural bias in calling the "murderers"; he recognizes that within their moral code, the cannibals act with a clean conscience; he condemns Spanish colonizers for doing worse in the Americas; he admits the cannibals have done him no wrong; and he sees that the consequence of a frontal attack would be his own death. He thus concludes to act only in self-defense, thanking God for delivering him from sin in his resolve to use violence only if directly attacked himself.

Here we have a single episode in a work of literature that can stimulate multiple paths of inquiry into logic, aesthetics, and rhetoric. At the level of criticism, one can explore how Crusoe engages in his familiar process of drawing inferences and reasoning to conclusions, strongly reacts to the perception of aesthetic qualities of his surroundings, and composes a rhetorical argument that persuades himself to accept one course of action over another. At the level of history, Defoe's novel invites investigation into how eighteenth-century public opinion viewed the conduct of the Spanish in the Americas, the degree to which Crusoe reflects the aesthetic tastes of an agent of British colonialism, and the strategies by which Crusoe used the novel to advance dissenting religious doctrines that were consistent with Defoe's own Presbyterianism. At the level of advocacy, students might investigate the lingering effects of colonialism on former British colonies today, create an alternative aesthetic foundation for a competing moral code, and criticize similar hierarchal assumptions of cultural superiority in today's rhetoric of nationalism.

The spirit of these assignments is guided by the ideals of democratic humanism. Their aim is to inspire both teachers and students to acquire the virtues of inquiry, appreciation, and communication that are necessary to participate as equal members of a creative political culture. Perhaps the most surprising thing about these ideals is that they should be controversial at all. And yet they are, have been, and likely will always be so. What Dewey observed in 1930 could be said with as much force today in classrooms across the globe:

> When shall we realize that in every school-building in the land a struggle is also being waged against all that hems in and distorts human life? The struggle is not with arms and violence; its consequences cannot be recorded in statistics of the physically killed and wounded, nor set forth in terms of territorial changes. But in its slow and imperceptible processes, the real battles for human freedom and for the pushing back of the boundaries that restrict human life are ultimately won. We need to pledge ourselves to engage anew and with renewed faith in the greatest of all battles in the cause of human liberation, to the end that all human beings may lead the life that is alone worthy of being entitled wholly human.[2]

This struggle endures today against the rising movements of fascist antihumanism. And what makes this struggle so difficult and enduring is that these movements almost never declare themselves openly. Indeed, fascism never presents itself as anything but virtuous. This is its enduring power. It presents itself as the defender of universal ideas and values that transcend all distinctions of race, class, gender, and nationality and exist outside of nature to inspire and judge us. In the name of making us more human, it turns our eyes away from concrete human beings and toward that abstract form of being that captures the essence of humanity. From this point, all distinctions flow. To those destined for greatness, education turns their eyes toward the heavens so that their elected imaginations can catch a glimpse of universal ideals. Theirs is the training of the master class. To those destined to serve—almost always women and those classes, races, and religions deemed alien to the national spirit—education encourages them to forget their idle dreaming and learn the virtues of pious obedience and humble labor. Just how this master and servant relationship manifests itself differs in every society at each point in history, but the justification is always the same. For the antihumanists, the purpose of education is to be trained to fulfill the narrow purpose allotted to them. This purpose, in turn, is not created by the individual but determined by the established principles, distinctions, and abstractions that govern the traditional social order. In short, the characteristic trait of the antihumanist is fatalism. To exist is not to inquire, to feel, or to challenge; it is to rule or to obey.

Fascism is the fruit of antihumanism that springs forth whenever environmental disruptions threaten the privileges of an established hierarchical order. Through the symbolic magic that transforms masters into victims, the propaganda of fascism mobilizes preexisting antihumanist attitudes in order to scapegoat its ills and create a mass mobilization based on the fantasy of a unified order purged of everything impure. In an outburst of desperate passion, fascism tries to revive a dying order by becoming intolerant of everything that is not itself. Pedagogically, the result is the imposition of the education of the machine. It is an education that seeks to mass-produce an interchangeable type of citizen who says the same phrases, thinks the same thoughts, and performs the same acts—even if what they say, think, and perform together might change from week to week and hour to hour. What matters in fascist antihumanism is that the terror of difference and intelligent becoming is suffocated by a thick blanket of self-righteous being in which the future is a reproduction of a mythic past. Consequently, fascism turns us away from inquiry into our environment just at the point at which we need it most, thus condemning us to a mad race into oblivion. This is the prospect for our future if we do not come to terms with the magnitude of the planetary crisis we face.[3]

The lesson of democratic humanism is that progress, if it is to come, must appear because of the voluntary associations of individuals working together with passion and intelligence for a common end. The pedagogy of democratic humanism gives to these individuals the equipment for walking the hard road of democracy. But that democracy is a hard road does not mean that it precludes happiness. Quite the opposite. Democracy is a form of social life in which the richest form of happiness is possible, for if one learns anything from Dewey's work, it is that our most innovative revelations, our most moving encounters, and our most euphoric accomplishments must pass through turmoil, conflict, shock, and disarray before they achieve their consummation alongside those with whom we act. It is also to acknowledge that our most treasured and most meaningful experiences are shared experiences. The arts of democratic humanism provide the methods to bring about these experiences, methods that are universal not because they are transcendent but because they are capable of being shared. The responsibility of the teacher is to share them to any and all who wish to make their individual marks on the world as new beginnings, for none of us knows what the end of history might be, nor do we need to know. Our responsibility is to act in the present. Indeed, the present is all we will ever have. Dewey once wrote, in 1897, that he believed that the teacher is "the usherer in of the true kingdom of God."[4] This statement remained true for all his life and remains true today. One only has to keep in mind that the kingdom of God is not found *outside* of us but *between* and *within* us, a product of our communication with one another in our brief time acting together on the earth that is our common home. And cultivating the truth, goodness, and beauty inherent in the arts of democratic humanism is an essential part of what we need to know to be free.

NOTES

INTRODUCTION

1. Dewey and Watson, "Forward View," 536–37.
2. McDermott, *Drama of Possibility*, 35.
3. Ibid., 26.
4. Ibid.
5. Ibid., 29.
6. Ibid., 32.
7. Ibid., 35.
8. Dewey, "Critique of American Civilization," 133.
9. Ibid., 134.
10. Ibid., 134–36.
11. Two works in particular have influenced by understanding of fascism. See Griffin, *Modernism and Fascism*; and Paxton, *Anatomy of Fascism*.
12. Dewey, "Critique of American Civilization," 134–36.
13. Rockefeller, *John Dewey*, 444. For more on Dewey's political writings, see the biographies by Westbrook, *John Dewey and American Democracy*; and Ryan, *John Dewey and the High Tide*.
14. Dewey, "Does Human Nature Change?," 292.
15. Ibid., 293.
16. The pedagogy of democratic humanism follows in the pragmatic tradition of what Brian Jackson has given the name "paideweyan pedagogy," a phrase that points to the way that Dewey's work has been integrated with the tradition of ancient Greek paideia, or an education in the highest ideals of Greek culture. According to Jackson, placing Dewey in conversation with the rhetorical tradition "provides us with the framework for seeing rhetoric education as practical and theoretical instruction with the ultimate goal of providing students with a public dunamis" (Jackson, "Cultivating Paideweyan Pedagogy," 183). See also Jackson and Clark, *Trained Capacities*; Biesta and Burbules, *Pragmatism and Educational Research*; Hansen, *John Dewey and Our Educational Prospect*; Hickman and Spadafora, *John Dewey's Educational Philosophy*; Jackson, *John Dewey and the Lessons of Art*; Johnston, *Deweyan Inquiry*; Johnston, *Inquiry and Education*; and Simpson, Jackson, and Aycock, *John Dewey and the Art of Teaching*.
17. Dewey, "Democracy and Education," 301.
18. Ibid., 301.
19. Dewey, *Freedom and Culture*, 98.
20. McDermott, *Drama of Possibility*, 458–64.
21. Stengers, *In Catastrophic Times*.
22. Stengers, *Another Science Is Possible*, 146.

CHAPTER 1

1. Dewey, "Collapse of a Romance," 69.
2. Ibid., 69.
3. Ibid.
4. Ibid.
5. Ibid., 70.
6. Dewey, "Economic Situation," 128–29.
7. Dewey, "Collapse of a Romance," 70.
8. Aronowitz, *Against Schooling*, 9.
9. Ibid., 14.
10. Ibid., 18.
11. Ibid., 25.
12. Ibid., 18.
13. Ibid., 30.
14. Ibid., 49.
15. Ibid., 29.
16. Dewey, *Liberalism and Social Action*, 29.
17. Dewey, "Education for a Changing Social Order," 163.
18. Dewey, "Freedom," 248–49.
19. Ibid., 249.
20. Dewey, "Review," 338.
21. Dewey, "Presenting Thomas Jefferson," 220.
22. Dewey, "Future of Liberalism," 291.
23. Dewey, *Liberalism and Social Action*, 29.
24. Dewey, "Mr. Justice Brandeis," 238.
25. Dewey, "Education for a Changing Social Order," 163–64.
26. Dewey, *Individualism Old and New*, 49.
27. Dewey, "Social-Economic Situation," 68.
28. Dewey, "Philosophy," 119.
29. Dewey, *Schools of To-Morrow*, 359.
30. The following discussion has been influenced by my reading of Ellul, *Technological Society*; McLuhan, *Understanding Media*; and Hickman, *John Dewey's Pragmatic Technology*.
31. Dewey, *Experience and Nature*, 138.
32. Dewey, "Needed—a New Politics," 278.
33. Dewey, *Individualism Old and New*, 52.
34. Ibid., 47.
35. Ibid., 48.
36. Dewey, *Liberalism and Social Action*, 42.
37. Dewey, *Individualism Old and New*, 80.
38. Dewey, "Freedom," 247–48.
39. Dewey, *Liberalism and Social Action*, 7.
40. Ibid., 26.
41. Ibid., 11.
42. Ibid., 29–30.
43. Dewey, *Individualism Old and New*, 80–81.
44. Ibid., 81–82.
45. Ibid., 82–83.
46. Dewey, "Presenting Thomas Jefferson," 216.
47. Ibid., 220.

48. Dewey, "Crisis in Human History," 212 (emphasis in original).
49. Dewey, *Freedom and Culture*, 153.

CHAPTER 2

1. Dewey, "Fruits of Nationalism," 155–56.
2. Ibid., 155.
3. Dewey, "Crisis in Human History," 215.
4. hooks, *Teaching to Transgress*, 24.
5. Ibid., 32.
6. Ibid., 28.
7. Ibid., 37.
8. Ibid., 32.
9. Ibid., 148.
10. Ibid., 11.
11. Dewey, *Individualism Old and New*, 68.
12. Dewey, "What Humanism Means," 264–65.
13. Ibid., 265.
14. Dewey, "Crisis in Human History," 213.
15. Dewey, *Individualism Old and New*, 70.
16. Dewey, *Freedom and Culture*, 66.
17. Dewey, *Individualism Old and New*, 70–71.
18. Dewey, *Freedom and Culture*, 89.
19. Dewey, *Experience and Nature*, 142.
20. Dewey, *Art as Experience*, 182.
21. Dewey, *Experience and Nature*, 142.
22. Ibid., 21.
23. Dewey, *German Philosophy and Politics*, 178–79.
24. Dewey, *Freedom and Culture*, 90.
25. Dewey, "Crisis in Human History," 211.
26. Dewey, *Freedom and Culture*, 80.
27. Dewey, "One-World of Hitler's," 431–32.
28. Dewey, *Liberalism and Social Action*, 30.
29. Dewey, *Freedom and Culture*, 89.
30. Dewey, "What I Believe," 272.
31. Dewey, *Freedom and Culture*, 89.
32. Dewey, *Individualism Old and New*, 67.
33. Dewey, "Fruits of Nationalism," 156.
34. Ibid., 153–54.
35. Dewey, "One-World of Hitler's," 440.
36. Ibid., 436–37 (emphasis in original).
37. Dewey, *Freedom and Culture*, 153–54.
38. Ibid., 111.
39. Ibid., 176.
40. Ibid., 112.
41. Dewey, "One-World of Hitler's," 422.
42. Dewey, "Force, Violence, and Law," 213–14.
43. Dewey, "One-World of Hitler's," 424–25 (emphasis in original).
44. Dewey, "Future of Liberalism," 259.
45. Dewey, "One-World of Hitler's," 441.

CHAPTER 3

1. Dewey, "New Paternalism," 117–18.
2. Ibid., 118–21.
3. Ibid., 117.
4. Freire, *Pedagogy of the Oppressed*, 87.
5. Ibid., 74.
6. Ibid., 72.
7. Ibid., 66.
8. Ibid., 84.
9. Ibid., 88–89.
10. Dewey and La Follette, "Several Faults Are Found," 345–46.
11. Dewey, "*Mission to Moscow*," 289–90.
12. Ibid., 292.
13. Ibid.
14. Dewey, *Freedom and Culture*, 168.
15. Dewey, "Social-Economic Situation," 65.
16. Dewey and La Follette, "Several Faults Are Found," 345.
17. Pope, "'Mission to Moscow' Film," 93.
18. Pope, "Merit Seen," 12.
19. Dewey, "Imperative Need," 76.
20. Dewey, *Ethics*, 360–61.
21. Dewey, "New Party," 178.
22. Dewey and La Follette, "Several Faults Are Found," 347–49.
23. Dewey and La Follette, "Moscow Film Again Attacked," 354.
24. Dewey, *Art as Experience*, 187.
25. Dewey, "Democracy and Education," 297.
26. Dewey, "Fruits of Nationalism," 153–54.
27. Dewey and La Follette, "Several Faults Are Found," 346–48.
28. Dewey and La Follette, "Moscow Film Again Attacked," 352.
29. Dewey, *Liberalism and Social Action*, 50.
30. Dewey, *Ethics*, 361.
31. Dewey, "*Mission to Moscow*," 293.
32. Dewey, *Freedom and Culture*, 169.
33. Dewey, "Does Human Nature Change?," 289.
34. Dewey, "One-World of Hitler's," 436.
35. Dewey and La Follette, "Moscow Film Again Attacked," 350.
36. Dewey, *Individualism Old and New*, 69–70.
37. Dewey, *Freedom and Culture*, 168.
38. Dewey, "Basic Values," 275.
39. Dewey, "Social-Economic Situation," 101.

CHAPTER 4

1. Dewey, Letter from John Dewey to Alice Chipman Dewey, October 7, 1894.
2. Ibid.
3. Fishman and McCarthy, *John Dewey*, 220–21.
4. Ibid., 4–6.
5. Ibid., 225.
6. Rockefeller, *John Dewey*, 132.

7. Dewey, "Value of Historical Christianity," 531–32.
8. Dewey, "Emerson," 190; Dewey, "Comment," 135.
9. Dewey, "Emerson," 189–90.
10. Dewey, *Common Faith*, 36.
11. Ibid., 23.
12. Dewey, *Individualism Old and New*, 122–23.
13. Dewey, "Emerson," 192.
14. Dewey, *Experience and Nature*, 10.
15. Dewey, "Emerson," 189.
16. Dewey, "Revolt Against Science," 189.
17. Dewey, "Anti-naturalism," 54.
18. Dewey, *Experience and Nature*, 10–11.
19. Ibid., 13–14.
20. Dewey, "Emerson," 187.
21. Emerson, *Essays*, 84.
22. Dewey, *Experience and Nature*, 18.
23. Dewey, "Reflex Arc Concept," 97–98 (emphasis in original).
24. Dewey, *Human Nature and Conduct*, 97–98.
25. Ibid., 15–16.
26. Dewey, "Body and Mind," 25.
27. Dewey, *Public and Its Problems*, 235.
28. Dewey, "Character Training for Youth," 186.
29. Dewey, *Experience and Nature*, 137.
30. Dewey, *Construction and Criticism*, 316–17.
31. Dewey, *Experience and Nature*, 132.
32. See Burke, *On Symbols and Society*.
33. Dewey, "Crisis in Human History," 211.
34. Dewey, *Individualism Old and New*, 122–23 (emphasis added).
35. See Quine, *Ontological Relativity*.
36. Dewey, *Democracy and Education*, 19.
37. Ibid., 8–9.
38. See Arendt's discussion of homo faber in *Human Condition*.
39. Dewey, *Reconstruction in Philosophy*, 120.
40. Dewey, "What I Believe," 270.
41. Dewey, *Individualism Old and New*, 87.
42. For more on Aristotle's naturalism, see Poulakos and Crick, "There Is Beauty."
43. Dewey, *Individualism Old and New*, 88.
44. This reading reflects the insights of McLuhan's notion of technology as extension in *Understanding Media*.
45. Dewey, *Individualism Old and New*, 123.
46. Ibid., 58.
47. Dewey, "John Dewey Assails," 443.
48. Dewey, *Individualism Old and New*, 56–57.
49. Dewey, "Philosophy and Education," 297.
50. Dewey, *Democracy and Education*, 312.

CHAPTER 5

1. Dewey, "Address," 229–30.
2. Ibid., 226–29.

3. Ibid., 230.
4. Dewey, "Challenge to Liberal Thought," 265.
5. Dewey, *Liberalism and Social Action*, 39–40.
6. Giroux, *Giroux Reader*, 49–51.
7. Ibid., 51.
8. Ibid., 57.
9. Ibid., 56.
10. Ibid., 58.
11. Dewey, "World Anarchy," 205.
12. Dewey, "Dualism," 200.
13. Ibid., 203.
14. Dewey, "World Anarchy," 204–5.
15. Dewey, "What Is Democracy?," 471.
16. Dewey, "Religion and Morality," 177.
17. Dewey, *Freedom and Culture*, 156.
18. Dewey, "What Is Democracy?," 472.
19. Dewey, "Dualism," 202.
20. Dewey, "What Is Democracy?," 473–74.
21. See Burke, *Attitudes Toward History*.
22. Quoted in Dewey, *Freedom and Culture*, 174.
23. Dewey, *Freedom and Culture*, 175.
24. Dewey, *Public and Its Problems*, 368.
25. Dewey, *Freedom and Culture*, 176–77.
26. Ibid., 177.
27. Dewey, *Liberalism and Social Action*, 62.
28. Dewey, *Freedom and Culture*, 177.
29. Ibid., 187.
30. Dewey, *Liberalism and Social Action*, 14.
31. Ibid., 32.
32. Ibid., 28.
33. Ibid., 25.
34. Dewey, "Liberty and Social Control," 360–61 (emphasis in original).
35. Ibid., 362–63.
36. Dewey, *Freedom and Culture*, 79.
37. Dewey, *Liberalism and Social Action*, 30–31.
38. Ibid., 12.
39. Ibid., 31–32.
40. For more on this notion, see Habermas, *Structural Transformation*.
41. Dewey, *Liberalism and Social Action*, 35.
42. Ibid., 33.
43. Dewey, "Future of Liberalism," 292.
44. Dewey, "Education and Social Change," 416–17.
45. Dewey, "Social-Economic Situation," 76 (emphasis in original).

CHAPTER 6

1. Dewey, "Radio's Influence," 309.
2. Jaker, Sulek, and Kanze, *Airwaves of New York*, 65–66.
3. Dewey, "Radio's Influence," 309.
4. Hernández, *Pedagogy, Democracy, and Feminism*, 44–45.

5. Ibid., 50.
6. Ibid., 82.
7. Ibid., 91.
8. Dewey, "Review," 337.
9. Dewey, *Public and Its Problems*, 372.
10. For more on Dewey and Lippmann, see Carey, *Communication as Culture*; Crick, "Search for a Purveyor of News"; Jansen, "Phantom Conflict"; Tell, "Reinventing Walter Lippmann"; and Schudson, "'Lippmann-Dewey Debate.'"
11. Emerson, *Essays*, "Self-Reliance," 37.
12. Ibid., 34.
13. Dewey, "Review," 337–38.
14. Ibid., 340.
15. Dewey, "Practical Democracy," 217.
16. Dewey, "Review," 342 (emphasis in original).
17. Ibid., 340.
18. Ibid., 344.
19. Dewey, *Public and Its Problems*, 346.
20. Dewey, "Practical Democracy," 216.
21. Dewey, "Review," 344.
22. Dewey, *Public and Its Problems*, 350.
23. See Simonson, "Rhetoric for Polytheistic Democracy."
24. Dewey, "Three Contemporary Philosophers," 207.
25. Dewey, "Poetry and Philosophy," 123.
26. Dewey, *Public and Its Problems*, 370.
27. Ibid., 330.
28. Ibid., 332.
29. Ibid., 245–46.
30. Ibid., 345–46.
31. Ibid., 314.
32. Dewey, "Religion and Morality," 177.
33. Dewey, "How to Anchor Liberalism," 259–60.
34. Dewey, *Public and Its Problems*, 368.
35. Ibid.
36. Ibid.
37. Ibid., 362.
38. Dewey, "Science and Society," 52.
39. Dewey, "Education and Birth Control," 146–47.
40. Dewey, "What I Believe," 276.
41. Dewey, "Education and Birth Control," 147.
42. Ibid., 146.
43. Dewey, *Public and Its Problems*, 349–50.
44. Dewey, "Supreme Intellectual Obligation," 100.
45. Dewey, "New Party," 178.
46. Dewey, "Education for a Changing Social Order," 159.
47. Dewey, "Unity of Science," 273.
48. Dewey, "Education for a Changing Social Order," 159–60.
49. Dewey, "American Education," 97–98.
50. Dewey, "Democracy and Educational Administration," 219–20.
51. Dewey, "Education, the Foundation," 228.
52. Dewey, "American Education," 97.
53. Dewey, "Youth," 355.

CHAPTER 7

54. Dewey, "Irrepressible Conflict," 149.
55. Ibid., 151–52.

1. Dewey, *How We Think*, 202–3.
2. Dewey, *School and Society*, 106–7.
3. Defoe, *Robinson Crusoe*, 137–38.
4. Dewey, "Logical Objects," 91.
5. Ibid., 92.
6. Dewey, "Introduction," 342.
7. Dewey, "Logic of Judgments," 71.
8. Dewey, "Introduction," 321.
9. Shor, *Empowering Education*, 245.
10. Ibid., 35.
11. Ibid., 43.
12. Dewey, *Logic*, 3.
13. Shor, *Empowering Education*, 41.
14. Ibid., 36.
15. Ibid., 192.
16. Dewey, "Logic of Judgments," 71–72 (emphasis in original).
17. Dewey, "Logical Objects," 91.
18. Dewey, "Logic of Judgments," 70–72.
19. Dewey, *Logic*, 30.
20. Ibid., 28.
21. Ibid., 30.
22. Ibid., 32 (emphasis added).
23. Ibid., 34.
24. Ibid., 15 (emphasis in original).
25. Ibid., 67–68.
26. See Quine, *Ontological Relativity*.
27. Dewey, *Logic*, 57–58 (emphasis in original).
28. Dewey, "Logic of Judgments," 75.
29. Ibid., 76.
30. Ibid. (emphasis added).
31. Ibid., 76–77.
32. Dewey, *Quest for Certainty*, 99.
33. Ibid., 125.
34. Dewey, "Added Note," 366.
35. Ibid.
36. Dewey, *Quest for Certainty*, 129.
37. Dewey, *How We Think*, 202.
38. Dewey, *Logic*, 110 (emphasis in original).
39. Dewey, *How We Think*, 238.
40. Ibid.
41. Dewey, *Logic*, 228.
42. Dewey, *Experience and Nature*, 138.
43. Dewey, *How We Think*, 211.
44. Dewey, *Experience and Nature*, 151.
45. Dewey, "Introduction," 339 (emphasis in original).

46. Dewey, *Quest for Certainty*, 142–43 (emphasis in original).
47. Dewey, *Logic*, 113.
48. Dewey, *How We Think*, 239.
49. Ibid., 192–93.
50. Ibid., 195.
51. Ibid., 239 (emphasis added).
52. Dewey, *Logic*, 115 (emphasis in original).
53. Dewey, *Quest for Certainty*, 121.
54. Dewey, *How We Think*, 244.
55. Ibid., 254.
56. Ibid., 158.
57. Ibid., 160.
58. Dewey, *Experience and Nature*, 138.
59. Dewey, *How We Think*, 241.
60. Ibid., 332.
61. Dewey, *Logic*, 221.
62. Dewey, *How We Think*, 259.
63. Ibid., 263–64.
64. Ibid., 230.
65. Ibid., 232.

CHAPTER 8

1. Dewey, "Art as Our Heritage," 255.
2. Ibid., 256–57.
3. Dewey, *Art as Experience*, 348–49.
4. McDermott, "Introduction," xii.
5. Dewey, *Art as Experience*, 53.
6. Dewey, *Quest for Certainty*, 209.
7. Eberly, *Citizen Critics*, xi, 1–2.
8. Ibid., 9.
9. Ibid., 2.
10. Ibid., 179.
11. Keats, "Ode" (emphasis added).
12. Dewey, *Common Faith*, 23.
13. Dewey, *Art as Experience*, 38.
14. Dewey, *Psychology*, 363.
15. Ibid., 172–73.
16. Dewey, "Value of Historical Christianity," 533.
17. Dewey, *Art as Experience*, 38.
18. Ibid., 39 (emphasis in original).
19. Ibid., 39–40.
20. This is very similar to what William James extended in his concept of the "will to believe."
21. Dewey, *Art as Experience*, 40–41.
22. Ibid., 41.
23. Ibid., 10–11.
24. Dewey, "Qualitative Thought," 248.
25. Dewey, *Experience and Nature*, 82.
26. Dewey, "Postulate of Immediate Empiricism," 160–61.

27. Dewey, *Art as Experience*, 59–60 (emphasis in original).
28. Ibid., 48.
29. Dewey, "Appreciation and Cultivation," 113.
30. Dewey, *Art as Experience*, 59.
31. Ibid., 158.
32. Ibid., 18.
33. Ibid., 187.
34. Ibid., 22.
35. Ibid., 223–24.
36. Ibid., 270.
37. Ibid., 31.
38. Dewey, "Qualitative Thought," 259.
39. Dewey, *Art as Experience*, 169–70 (emphasis in original).
40. Ibid., 42–43.
41. Ibid., 22.
42. Ibid., 70.
43. Ibid., 271 (emphasis in original).
44. Ibid., 291.
45. Ibid., 248–49.
46. Ibid., 110.
47. Ibid., 270.
48. Dewey, *Construction and Criticism*, 139.
49. Ibid., 134.
50. Ibid., 139.
51. Dewey, *Democracy and Education*, 244.
52. Ibid., 246.
53. Dewey, *Quest for Certainty*, 209.
54. Dewey, *Experience and Education*, 29–30.
55. Dewey, "Meaning of Value," 76.
56. Dewey, "Qualitative Thought," 261–62.
57. Dewey, *Democracy and Education*, 246–47.
58. Dewey, *Ethics*, 433–34.
59. Dewey, *Construction and Criticism*, 127.

CHAPTER 9

1. Addams, *Peace and Bread*, 246.
2. Dewey, "Democratic Versus Coercive," 198.
3. Addams, quoted in ibid., 193.
4. Ibid. (emphasis in original).
5. Ibid.
6. Ibid., 196.
7. Addams, quoted in ibid.
8. Ibid., 194.
9. For more on Addams, see Danisch, *Pragmatism, Democracy*.
10. Dewey, "Democratic Versus Coercive," 195–96.
11. Ibid., 198.
12. Jarratt, *Rereading the Sophists*, 107.
13. Ibid., 116.
14. Ibid., xviii.

15. Ibid., xix.
16. Ibid., 103–4.
17. Ibid., 114.
18. Addams, *Peace and Bread*, 10.
19. For efforts to integrate Dewey within the field of rhetoric and communication, see Belman, "John Dewey's Concept"; Burks, "John Dewey"; Crick, *Democracy and Rhetoric*; Danisch, *Pragmatism, Democracy*; Johnstone, "Dewey, Ethics, and Rhetoric"; Fishman, "Explicating Our Tacit Tradition"; Fishman and McCarthy, "Teaching for Student Change"; Jackson and Clark, *Trained Capacities*; Mackin, "Rhetoric, Pragmatism"; Stroud, *John Dewey*.
20. See the essays in Sipiora and Baumlin, *Rhetoric and Kairos*, for an extensive treatment of kairos. Also see the extended discussion in rhetorical theory on the nature of the rhetorical situation, including Biesecker, "Rethinking the Rhetorical Situation"; Bitzer, "Rhetorical Situation"; Consigny, "Rhetoric and Its Situations"; Crick, "Rhetoric and Events"; Patton, "Causation and Creativity"; and Vatz, "Myth."
21. See Cole, *Origins of Rhetoric*, on how rhetoric developed as a self-conscious, rational art in ancient Greece.
22. To "warn" in this sense is a matter of argumentation and careful reasoning, much in the way outlined by Perelman and Olbrechts-Tyteca in *New Rhetoric*.
23. "Instruction" also means to inspire, guide, and direct through articulating an end-in-view. Weaver provides an inspiring and Platonic spin on instruction in *Ethics of Rhetoric*.
24. The relation of freedom to violence is eloquently explored in Crosswhite, *Deep Rhetoric*.
25. The centrality of citizen rhetoric in a democracy is emphasized in Hauser, *Vernacular Voices*.
26. In the language of rhetorical theory, the discourse of publics and counterpublics captures this sense of rhetorical organization. See Asen and Brouwer, *Counterpublics and the State*.
27. The function of rhetoric to guide us through periods of historical turmoil is captured in Burke, *Permanence and Change*.
28. The foundational analysis of the democratic ethos of rhetoric is in Farrell, *Norms of Rhetorical Culture*.
29. Dewey, *Experience and Nature*, 138–39.
30. Ibid., 33.
31. Ibid., 139.
32. Ibid., 140–41.
33. Dewey, *Human Nature and Conduct*, 67–68.
34. Ibid., 125–27.
35. Ibid., 123–24.
36. Ibid., 67.
37. Poulakos, "Kairos," 89.
38. Dewey, *Human Nature and Conduct*, 194–95.
39. Addams, *Peace and Bread*, 2.
40. Dewey, *Human Nature and Conduct*, 126–27.
41. Dewey, "Three Independent Factors," 280.
42. Dewey and Tufts, *Ethics*, 164–65.
43. Dewey, "Outlines," 364.
44. Dewey and Tufts, *Ethics*, 272–73.
45. Dewey, *Human Nature and Conduct*, 84–85 (emphasis in original).
46. Ibid., 84.

47. Ibid., 172–73 (emphasis in original).
48. Dewey, "Prospects," 201.
49. Dewey, *Human Nature and Conduct*, 136.
50. Ibid., 177–78.
51. Dewey and Tufts, *Ethics*, 187.
52. Dewey, *Human Nature and Conduct*, 187.
53. Ibid., 189.
54. Ibid., 134.
55. Addams, *Peace and Bread*, 134–36.
56. Dewey, *Human Nature and Conduct*, 136.
57. Dewey, *Ethics*, 302–3.
58. Addams, *Peace and Bread*, 219.
59. Dewey, "Religion and Morality," 177.
60. Ibid., 179 (emphasis in original).
61. Dewey, *Freedom and Culture*, 154.
62. Addams, *Peace and Bread*, 198.

CONCLUSION

1. Defoe, *Robinson Crusoe*, 153.
2. Dewey, "Philosophy and Education," 297–98.
3. One of the most powerful rhetorical statements in this regard is in Latour, *Down to Earth*. I borrow some of his language in the conclusion in order to establish a relation between Dewey and Latour that hopefully will bear fruit.
4. Dewey, "My Pedagogic Creed," 95.

BIBLIOGRAPHY

Addams, Jane. *Peace and Bread in Time of War.* New York: Garland, 1971.
Anderson, Benedict. *Imagined Communities: Reflections on the Origin and Spread of Nationalism.* Rev. ed. London: Verso Books, 2006.
Arendt, Hannah. *The Human Condition.* 2nd ed. Chicago: University of Chicago Press, 1998.
———. *The Promise of Politics.* New York: Schocken Books, 2005.
Aronowitz, Stanley. *Against Schooling: For an Education That Matters.* Boulder, CO: Paradigm Publishers, 2008.
Asen, Robert, and Daniel C. Brouwer. *Counterpublics and the State.* Albany: State University of New York Press, 2001.
Belman, Larry S. "John Dewey's Concept of Communication." *Journal of Communication* 27, no. 1 (1977): 29–37.
Bernays, Edward. *Propaganda.* New York: Ig, 1928.
Biesecker, Barbara A. "Rethinking the Rhetorical Situation from Within the Thematic of Difference." *Philosophy and Rhetoric* 22, no. 2 (1989): 110–30.
Biesta, Gert J. J., and Nicholas C. Burbules. *Pragmatism and Educational Research.* Lanham, MD: Rowman and Littlefield, 2003.
Bitzer, Lloyd F. "The Rhetorical Situation." *Philosophy and Rhetoric* 1, no. 1 (1969): 1–14.
Burke, Kenneth. *Attitudes Toward History.* Berkeley: University of California Press, 1959.
———. *Counter-Statement.* Berkeley: University of California Press, 1968.
———. *On Symbols and Society.* Edited by Joseph Gusfield. Chicago: University of Chicago Press, 1989.
———. *Permanence and Change: An Anatomy of Purpose.* Berkeley: University of California Press, 1965.
———. *The Rhetoric of Motives.* Berkeley: University of California Press, 1969.
Burks, Don M. "John Dewey and Rhetorical Theory." *Western Speech* 32, no. 2 (1968): 118–26.
Carey, James. *Communication as Culture: Essays on Media and Society.* New York: Unwin Hyman, 1988.
Cole, Thomas. *The Origins of Rhetoric in Ancient Greece.* Baltimore: Johns Hopkins University Press, 1991.
Consigny, Scott. "Rhetoric and Its Situations." *Philosophy and Rhetoric* 7, no. 3 (1974): 175–86.
Crick, Nathan. *Democracy and Rhetoric: John Dewey on the Arts of Becoming.* Columbia: University of South Carolina Press, 2010.
———. "Rhetoric and Events." *Philosophy and Rhetoric* 47, no. 3 (2014): 251–72.
———. "The Search for a Purveyor of News: The Dewey/Lippmann Debate in an Internet Age." *Critical Studies in Media Communication* 26, no. 1 (2009): 480–97.
———. "The Sophistical Attitude." *Quarterly Journal of Speech* 91, no. 1 (2010): 25–45.
Crosswhite, James. *Deep Rhetoric: Philosophy, Reason, Violence, Justice, Wisdom.* Chicago: University of Chicago Press, 2013.

Danish, Robert. *Pragmatism, Democracy, and the Necessity of Rhetoric.* Columbia: University of South Carolina Press, 2007.

Defoe, Daniel. *The Adventures of Robinson Crusoe.* London: S. O. Beeton, 1862.

Dewey, John. "An Added Note as to the 'Practical' in Essays in Experimental Logic." In *The Middle Works of John Dewey,* vol. 10, *1916–1917,* edited by Jo Ann Boydston, 366–69. Carbondale: Southern Illinois University Press, 1980.

———. "Address to the National Association for the Advancement of Colored People." In *The Later Works of John Dewey,* vol. 6, *1931–1932,* edited by Jo Ann Boydston, 224–30. Carbondale: Southern Illinois University Press, 1985.

———. *American Education Past and Future.* In *The Later Works of John Dewey,* vol. 6, *1931–1932,* edited by Jo Ann Boydston, 90–98. Carbondale: Southern Illinois University Press, 1985.

———. "Anti-naturalism in Extremis." In *The Later Works of John Dewey,* vol. 15, *1942–1948,* edited by Jo Ann Boydston, 46–62. Carbondale: Southern Illinois University Press, 1989.

———. "Appreciation and Cultivation." In *The Middle Works of John Dewey,* vol. 6, *1910–1911,* edited by Jo Ann Boydston, 223–27. Carbondale: Southern Illinois University Press, 1978.

———. *Art as Experience.* In *The Later Works of John Dewey,* vol. 10, *1933–1934,* edited by Jo Ann Boydston, 1–366. Carbondale: Southern Illinois University Press, 1987.

———. "Art as Our Heritage." In *The Later Works of John Dewey,* vol. 14, *1939–1941,* edited by Jo Ann Boydston, 255–57. Carbondale: Southern Illinois University Press, 1988.

———. "The Basic Values and Loyalties of Democracy." In *The Later Works of John Dewey,* vol. 14, *1939–1941,* edited by Jo Ann Boydston, 275–77. Carbondale: Southern Illinois University Press, 1988.

———. "Body and Mind." In *The Later Works of John Dewey,* vol. 3, *1927–1928,* edited by Jo Ann Boydston, 25–44. Carbondale: Southern Illinois University Press, 1984.

———. "Challenge to Liberal Thought." In *The Later Works of John Dewey,* vol. 15, *1942–1948,* edited by Jo Ann Boydston, 261–75. Carbondale: Southern Illinois University Press, 1989.

———. "Character Training for Youth." In *The Later Works of John Dewey,* vol. 9, *1933–1934,* edited by Jo Ann Boydston, 186–93. Carbondale: Southern Illinois University Press, 1986.

———. "The Collapse of a Romance." In *The Later Works of John Dewey,* vol. 6, *1931–1932,* edited by Jo Ann Boydston, 69–74. Carbondale: Southern Illinois University Press, 1985.

———. "Comment on 'Religion at Harvard.'" In *The Later Works of John Dewey,* vol. 17, *1925–1953,* edited by Jo Ann Boydston, 135. Carbondale: Southern Illinois University Press, 1990.

———. *A Common Faith.* In *The Later Works of John Dewey,* vol. 9, *1933–1934,* edited by Jo Ann Boydston, 1–59. Carbondale: Southern Illinois University Press, 1986.

———. *Construction and Criticism.* In *The Later Works of John Dewey,* vol. 5, *1929–1930,* edited by Jo Ann Boydston, 125–46. Carbondale: Southern Illinois University Press, 1984.

———. "Creative Democracy—the Task Before Us." In *The Later Works of John Dewey,* vol. 14, *1939–1941,* edited by Jo Ann Boydston, 224–30. Carbondale: Southern Illinois University Press, 1988.

———. "The Crisis in Human History: The Danger of the Retreat to Individualism." In *The Later Works of John Dewey,* vol. 15, *1942–1948,* edited by Jo Ann Boydston, 210–23. Carbondale: Southern Illinois University Press, 1989.

———. "A Critique of American Civilization." In *The Later Works of John Dewey*, vol. 3, *1927–1928*, edited by Jo Ann Boydston, 133–44. Carbondale: Southern Illinois University Press, 1984.

———. *Democracy and Education*. In *The Middle Works of John Dewey*, vol. 9, *1916*, edited by Jo Ann Boydston, 1–371. Carbondale: Southern Illinois University Press, 1980.

———. "Democracy and Educational Administration." In *The Later Works of John Dewey*, vol. 11, *1935–1937*, edited by Jo Ann Boydston, 217–25. Carbondale: Southern Illinois University Press, 1987.

———. "Democracy and Education in the World of Today." In *The Later Works of John Dewey*, vol. 13, *1938–1939*, edited by Jo Ann Boydston, 294–303. Carbondale: Southern Illinois University Press, 1988.

———. "Democratic Versus Coercive International Organization: The Realism of Jane Addams." In *The Later Works of John Dewey*, vol. 15, *1942–1948*, edited by Jo Ann Boydston, 192–98. Carbondale: Southern Illinois University Press, 1989.

———. "Does Human Nature Change?" In *The Later Works of John Dewey*, vol. 13, *1938–1939*, edited by Jo Ann Boydston, 286–93. Carbondale: Southern Illinois University Press, 1988.

———. "Dualism and the Split Atom." In *The Later Works of John Dewey*, vol. 15, *1942–1948*, edited by Jo Ann Boydston, 199–203. Carbondale: Southern Illinois University Press, 1989.

———. "The Economic Situation: A Challenge to Education." In *The Later Works of John Dewey*, vol. 6, *1931–1932*, edited by Jo Ann Boydston, 123–30. Carbondale: Southern Illinois University Press, 1985.

———. "Education and Birth Control." In *The Later Works of John Dewey*, vol. 6, *1931–1932*, edited by Jo Ann Boydston, 146–48. Carbondale: Southern Illinois University Press, 1985.

———. "Education and Social Change." In *The Later Works of John Dewey*, vol. 11, *1935–1937*, edited by Jo Ann Boydston, 408–20. Carbondale: Southern Illinois University Press, 1987.

———. "Education for a Changing Social Order." In *The Later Works of John Dewey*, vol. 9, *1933–1934*, edited by Jo Ann Boydston, 158–68. Carbondale: Southern Illinois University Press, 1986.

———. "Education, the Foundation for Social Organization." In *The Later Works of John Dewey*, vol. 11, *1935–1937*, edited by Jo Ann Boydston, 226–37. Carbondale: Southern Illinois University Press, 1987.

———. "Emerson—the Philosopher of Democracy." In *The Middle Works of John Dewey*, vol. 3, *1903–1906*, edited by Jo Ann Boydston, 184–92. Carbondale: Southern Illinois University Press, 1977.

———. *Ethics*. In *John Dewey: The Later Works*, vol. 7, *1932*, edited by Jo Ann Boydston, 1–463. Carbondale: Southern Illinois University Press, 1985.

———. *Experience and Education*. In *John Dewey: The Later Works*, vol. 13, *1938–1939*, edited by Jo Ann Boydston, 1–62. Carbondale: Southern Illinois University Press, 1988.

———. *Experience and Nature*. In *John Dewey: The Later Works*, vol. 1, *1925*, edited by Jo Ann Boydston, 1–401. Carbondale: Southern Illinois University Press, 1981.

———. "Force, Violence and Law." In *The Later Works of John Dewey*, vol. 9, *1933–1934*, edited by Jo Ann Boydston, 211–15. Carbondale: Southern Illinois University Press, 1986.

———. "Freedom." In *The Later Works of John Dewey*, vol. 11, *1935–1937*, edited by Jo Ann Boydston, 247–55. Carbondale: Southern Illinois University Press, 1987.

———. *Freedom and Culture*. In *The Later Works of John Dewey*, vol. 13, 1938–1939, edited by Jo Ann Boydston, 63–188. Carbondale: Southern Illinois University Press, 1988.

———. "The Fruits of Nationalism." In *The Later Works of John Dewey*, vol. 3, 1927–1928, edited by Jo Ann Boydston, 152–57. Carbondale: Southern Illinois University Press, 1984.

———. "The Future of Liberalism." In *The Later Works of John Dewey*, vol. 11, 1935–1937, edited by Jo Ann Boydston, 289–95. Carbondale: Southern Illinois University Press, 1987.

———. *German Philosophy and Politics*. In *The Middle Works of John Dewey*, vol. 8, 1915, edited by Jo Ann Boydston, 134–204. Carbondale: Southern Illinois University Press, 1980.

———. "How to Anchor Liberalism." In *The Later Works of John Dewey*, vol. 15, 1942–1948, edited by Jo Ann Boydston, 248–50. Carbondale: Southern Illinois University Press, 1989.

———. *How We Think*. In *The Middle Works of John Dewey*, vol. 6, 1910–1911, edited by Jo Ann Boydston, 105–354. Carbondale: Southern Illinois University Press, 1978.

———. *Human Nature and Conduct*. In *The Middle Works of John Dewey*, vol. 14, 1922, edited by Jo Ann Boydston, 1–230. Carbondale: Southern Illinois University Press, 1983.

———. "Imperative Need: A New Radical Party." In *The Later Works of John Dewey*, vol. 9, 1933–1934, edited by Jo Ann Boydston, 76–80. Carbondale: Southern Illinois University Press, 1986.

———. *Individualism Old and New*. In *The Later Works of John Dewey*, vol. 5, 1929–1930, edited by Jo Ann Boydston, 41–124. Carbondale: Southern Illinois University Press, 1984.

———. "Introduction to Essays in Experimental Logic." In *The Middle Works of John Dewey*, vol. 10, 1916–1917, edited by Jo Ann Boydston, 320–65. Carbondale: Southern Illinois University Press, 1980.

———. "'The Irrepressible Conflict.'" In *The Later Works of John Dewey*, vol. 6, 1931–1932, edited by Jo Ann Boydston, 149–52. Carbondale: Southern Illinois University Press, 1985.

———. "John Dewey Assails the Major Parties." In *The Later Works of John Dewey*, vol. 5, 1929–1930, edited by Jo Ann Boydston, 442. Carbondale: Southern Illinois University Press, 1984.

———. John Dewey to Alice Chipman Dewey, October 7, 1894. John Dewey Papers. Morris Library Special Collections Research Center, Southern Illinois University, Carbondale.

———. *Liberalism and Social Action*. In *The Later Works of John Dewey*, vol. 11, 1935–1937, edited by Jo Ann Boydston, 1–68. Carbondale: Southern Illinois University Press, 1987.

———. "Liberty and Social Control." In *The Later Works of John Dewey*, vol. 11, 1935–1937, edited by Jo Ann Boydston, 360–64. Carbondale: Southern Illinois University Press, 1987.

———. "Logical Objects." In *The Middle Works of John Dewey*, vol. 10, 1916–1917, edited by Jo Ann Boydston, 89–97. Carbondale: Southern Illinois University Press, 1980.

———. "The Logic of Judgments of Practice." In *The Middle Works of John Dewey*, vol. 8, 1915, edited by Jo Ann Boydston, 14–82. Carbondale: Southern Illinois University Press, 1980.

———. *Logic: The Theory of Inquiry*. In *The Later Works of John Dewey*, vol. 12, 1938, edited by Jo Ann Boydston, 1–528. Carbondale: Southern Illinois University Press, 1986.

———. "The Meaning of Value." In *The Later Works of John Dewey*, vol. 1, edited by Jo Ann Boydston, 69–77. Carbondale: Southern Illinois University Press, 1981.

———. "*Mission to Moscow* Reveals No New Evidence on Soviet Trials: Review of Joseph E. Davies's *Mission to Moscow*." In *The Later Works of John Dewey*, vol. 15, *1942–1948*, edited by Jo Ann Boydston, 289–94. Carbondale: Southern Illinois University Press, 1989.

———. "My Pedagogic Creed." In *The Early Works of John Dewey*, vol. 5, *1882–1898*, edited by Jo Ann Boydston, 84–95. Carbondale: Southern Illinois University Press, 1972.

———. "Needed—a New Politics." In *The Later Works of John Dewey*, vol. 11, *1935–1937*, edited by Jo Ann Boydston, 274–81. Carbondale: Southern Illinois University Press, 1987.

———. "The Need for a New Party." In *The Later Works of John Dewey*, vol. 6, *1931–1932*, edited by Jo Ann Boydston, 156–81. Carbondale: Southern Illinois University Press, 1985.

———. "The New Paternalism." In *The Middle Works of John Dewey*, vol. 11, *1918–1919*, edited by Jo Ann Boydston, 117–21. Carbondale: Southern Illinois University Press, 1982.

———. "The One-World of Hitler's National Socialism." In *The Later Works of John Dewey*, vol. 8, *1933*, edited by Jo Ann Boydston, 421–48. Carbondale: Southern Illinois University Press, 1987.

———. "Outlines of a Critical Theory of Ethics." In *The Early Works of John Dewey*, vol. 3, *1882–1898*, edited by Jo Ann Boydston, 237–390. Carbondale: Southern Illinois University Press, 1969.

———. "Philosophy." In *The Later Works of John Dewey*, vol. 3, *1927–1928*, edited by Jo Ann Boydston, 115–32. Carbondale: Southern Illinois University Press, 1984.

———. "Philosophy and Education." In *The Later Works of John Dewey*, vol. 5, *1929–1930*, edited by Jo Ann Boydston, 289–98. Carbondale: Southern Illinois University Press, 1984.

———. "Poetry and Philosophy." In *The Early Works of John Dewey*, vol. 3, *1882–1898*, edited by Jo Ann Boydston, Carbondale: Southern Illinois University Press, 1969.

———. "The Postulate of Immediate Empiricism." In *The Middle Works of John Dewey*, vol. 3, *1903–1906*, edited by Jo Ann Boydston, 158–67. Carbondale: Southern Illinois University Press, 1977.

———. "Practical Democracy. Review of Walter Lippmann's *The Phantom Public*." In *The Later Works of John Dewey*, vol. 2, *1925–1927*, edited by Jo Ann Boydston, 213–20. Carbondale: Southern Illinois University Press, 1984.

———. "Presenting Thomas Jefferson." In *The Later Works of John Dewey*, vol. 14, *1939–1941*, edited by Jo Ann Boydston, 201–33. Carbondale: Southern Illinois University Press, 1988.

———. "The Principle of Nationality." In *The Middle Works of John Dewey*, vol. 10, *1916–1917*, edited by Jo Ann Boydston, 337–44. Carbondale: Southern Illinois University Press, 1980.

———. "The Prospects of the Liberal College." In *The Later Works of John Dewey*, vol. 15, *1942–1948*, edited by Jo Ann Boydston, 20–204. Carbondale: Southern Illinois University Press, 1989.

———. *Psychology*. In *The Early Works of John Dewey*, vol. 2, *1887*, edited by Jo Ann Boydston, 1–366. Carbondale: Southern Illinois University Press, 1967.

———. "*The Public and Its Problems*: An Essay in Political Inquiry." In *The Later Works of John Dewey*, vol. 2, *1925–1927*, edited by Jo Ann Boydston, 235–374. Carbondale: Southern Illinois University Press, 1984.

———. "Qualitative Thought." In *The Later Works of John Dewey*, vol. 5, 1929–1930, edited by Jo Ann Boydston, 243–62. Carbondale: Southern Illinois University Press, 1984.

———. *The Quest for Certainty: A Study of the Relation of Knowledge and Action*. In *The Later Works of John Dewey*, vol. 4, 1929, edited by Jo Ann Boydston, 1–250. Carbondale: Southern Illinois University Press, 1984.

———. "Radio's Influence on the Mind." In *The Later Works of John Dewey*, vol. 9, 1933–1934, edited by Jo Ann Boydston, 309. Carbondale: Southern Illinois University Press, 1986.

———. *Reconstruction in Philosophy*. In *The Middle Works of John Dewey*, vol. 12, 1920, edited by Jo Ann Boydston, 77–204. Carbondale: Southern Illinois University Press, 1982.

———. "The Reflex Arc Concept in Psychology." In *The Early Works of John Dewey*, vol. 5, 1882–1898, edited by Jo Ann Boydston, 96–110. Carbondale: Southern Illinois University Press, 1972.

———. "Religion and Morality in a Free Society." In *The Later Works of John Dewey*, vol. 15, 1942–1948, edited by Jo Ann Boydston, 170–83. Carbondale: Southern Illinois University Press, 1989.

———. "Review of *Mr. Justice Brandeis*, edited by Felix Frankfurter." In *The Later Works of John Dewey*, vol. 9, 1933–1934, edited by Jo Ann Boydston, 237–39. Carbondale: Southern Illinois University Press, 1986.

———. "Review of Walter Lippmann's *Public Opinion*." In *The Middle Works of John Dewey*, vol. 13, 1921–1922, edited by Jo Ann Boydston, 337–44. Carbondale: Southern Illinois University Press, 1983.

———. "The Revolt Against Science." In *The Later Works of John Dewey*, vol. 15, 1942–1948, edited by Jo Ann Boydston, 188–91. Carbondale: Southern Illinois University Press, 1989.

———. *The School and Society*. In *The Middle Works of John Dewey*, vol. 1, 1899–1901, edited by Jo Ann Boydston, 1–112. Carbondale: Southern Illinois University Press, 1976.

———. *Schools of To-Morrow*. In *The Middle Works of John Dewey*, vol. 8, 1915, edited by Jo Ann Boydston, 205–406. Carbondale: Southern Illinois University Press, 1983.

———. "The Social-Economic Situation and Education." In *The Later Works of John Dewey*, vol. 8, 1933, edited by Jo Ann Boydston, 43–76. Carbondale: Southern Illinois University Press, 1987.

———. "The Study of Ethics: A Syllabus." In *The Early Works of John Dewey*, vol. 4, 1893–1898, edited by Jo Ann Boydston, 220–373. Carbondale: Southern Illinois University Press, 1971.

———. "The Supreme Intellectual Obligation." In *The Later Works of John Dewey*, vol. 9, 1933–1934, edited by Jo Ann Boydston, 96–101. Carbondale: Southern Illinois University Press, 1986.

———. "Three Contemporary Philosophers: William James, Henri Bergson, and Bertrand Russell." In *The Middle Works of John Dewey*, vol. 12, 1920, edited by Jo Ann Boydston, 205–52. Carbondale: Southern Illinois University Press, 1982.

———. "Three Independent Factors in Morals." In *The Later Works of John Dewey*, vol. 5, 1929–1930, edited by Jo Ann Boydston, 279–88. Carbondale: Southern Illinois University Press, 1984.

———. "To Those Who Aspire to the Profession of Teaching." In *The Later Works of John Dewey*, vol. 13, 1938–1939, edited by Jo Ann Boydston, 342–46. Carbondale: Southern Illinois University Press, 1988.

———. "Unity of Science as a Social Problem." In *The Later Works of John Dewey*, vol. 13, 1938–1939, edited by Jo Ann Boydston, 271–80. Carbondale: Southern Illinois University Press, 1988.

———. "The Value of Historical Christianity." In *The Later Works of John Dewey*, vol. 17, *1925–1953*, edited by Jo Ann Boydston, 529–34. Carbondale: Southern Illinois University Press, 1990.

———. "What Humanism Means to Me." In *The Later Works of John Dewey*, vol. 5, *1929–1930*, edited by Jo Ann Boydston, 263–66. Carbondale: Southern Illinois University Press, 1984.

———. "What I Believe." In *The Later Works of John Dewey*, vol. 5, *1929–1930*, edited by Jo Ann Boydston, 276–78. Carbondale: Southern Illinois University Press, 1984.

———. "What Is Democracy?" In *The Later Works of John Dewey*, vol. 17, *1925–1953*, edited by Jo Ann Boydston, 471–74. Carbondale: Southern Illinois University Press, 1990.

———. "World Anarchy or World Order?" In *The Later Works of John Dewey*, vol. 15, *1942–1948*, edited by Jo Ann Boydston, 204–9. Carbondale: Southern Illinois University Press, 1989.

———. "Youth in a Confused World." In *The Later Works of John Dewey*, vol. 11, *1935–1937*, edited by Jo Ann Boydston, 353–55. Carbondale: Southern Illinois University Press, 1987.

Dewey, John, and Suzanne La Follette. "Moscow Film Again Attacked." In *The Later Works of John Dewey*, vol. 15, *1942–1948*, edited by Jo Ann Boydston, 351–53. Carbondale: Southern Illinois University Press, 1989.

———. "Several Faults Are Found in *Mission to Moscow* Film." In *The Later Works of John Dewey*, vol. 15, *1942–1948*, edited by Jo Ann Boydston, 345–50. Carbondale: Southern Illinois University Press, 1989.

Dewey, John, and James H. Tufts. "Ethics." In *The Middle Works of John Dewey*, vol. 5, *1908*, edited by Jo Ann Boydston, 1–540. Carbondale: Southern Illinois University Press, 1978.

Dewey, John, and Goodwin Watson. "The Forward View: A Free Teacher in a Free Society." In *The Later Works of John Dewey*, vol. 11, *1935–1937*, edited by Jo Ann Boydston, 535–47. Carbondale: Southern Illinois University Press, 1987.

Eberly, Rosa A. *Citizen Critics: Literary Public Spheres*. Urbana: University of Illinois Press, 2000.

Ellul, Jacques. *Propaganda: The Formation of Men's Attitudes*. Translated by Konrad Kellen and Jean Lerner. New York: Vintage, 1965.

———. *The Technological Society*. Translated by John Wilkinson. New York: Vintage, 1964.

Emerson, Ralph Waldo. *The Essays of Ralph Waldo Emerson*. Cambridge: Belknap, 1987.

Farrell, Thomas. *Norms of Rhetorical Culture*. New Haven: Yale University Press, 1993.

Fishman, Stephen M. "Explicating Our Tacit Tradition: John Dewey and Composition Studies." *College Composition and Communication* 44, no. 3 (1993): 315–30.

———. *John Dewey and the Challenge of Classroom Practice*. New York: Teachers College Press, 1998.

Fishman, Stephen, and Lucille McCarthy. *John Dewey and the Philosophy and Practice of Hope*. Urbana: University of Illinois Press, 2007.

———. "Teaching for Student Change: A Deweyan Alternative to Radical Pedagogy." *College Composition and Communication* 47, no. 3 (1996): 342–66.

Freire, Paulo. *Pedagogy of the Oppressed*. New York: Continuum, 1993.

Giroux, Henry. *The Giroux Reader*. Edited by Christopher G. Robbins. Boulder, CO: Paradigm, 2006.

Griffin, Roger. *Modernism and Fascism: The Sense of a Beginning Under Mussolini and Hitler*. New York: Palgrave Macmillan, 2007.

Habermas, Jürgen. *The Structural Transformation of the Public Sphere: An Inquiry into a Category of Bourgeois Society*. Translated by Thomas Burger. Cambridge: MIT Press, 1989.
Hansen, David T., ed. *John Dewey and Our Educational Prospect: A Critical Engagement with Dewey's Democracy and Education*. Albany: State University of New York Press, 2006.
Hauser, Gerard A. *Vernacular Voices: The Rhetoric of Publics and Public Spheres*. Columbia: University of South Carolina Press, 1999.
Hernández, Adriana. *Pedagogy, Democracy, and Feminism: Rethinking the Public Sphere*. Albany: State University of New York Press, 1997.
Hickman, Larry A. *John Dewey's Pragmatic Technology*. Indianapolis: Indiana University Press, 1992.
Hickman, Larry A., and Giuseppe Spadafora, eds. *John Dewey's Educational Philosophy in International Perspective: A New Democracy for the 21st Century*. Carbondale: Southern Illinois University Press, 2009.
hooks, bell. *Teaching to Transgress: Education as the Practice of Freedom*. New York: Routledge, 1994.
Jackson, Brian. "Cultivating Paideweyan Pedagogy: Rhetoric Education in English and Communication Studies." *Rhetoric Society Quarterly* 37, no. 2 (2007): 181–201.
Jackson, Brian, and Gregory Clark, eds. *Trained Capacities: John Dewey, Rhetoric, and Democratic Practice*. Columbia: University of South Carolina Press, 2014.
Jackson, Philip W. *John Dewey and the Lessons of Art*. New Haven: Yale University Press, 1998.
Jaker, Bill, Frank Sulek, and Peter Kanze. *The Airwaves of New York: Illustrated Histories of 156 AM Stations in the Metropolitan Area, 1921–1996*. Jefferson, NC: McFarland, 1998.
Jansen, Sue Curry. "Phantom Conflict: Lippmann, Dewey, and the Fate of the Public in Modern Society." *Communication and Critical/Cultural Studies* 6, no. 3 (2009): 221–45.
Jarratt, Susan C. *Rereading the Sophists: Classical Rhetoric Refigured*. Carbondale: Southern Illinois University Press, 1991.
Johnston, James Scott. *Deweyan Inquiry: From Education Theory to Practice*. Albany: State University of New York Press, 2009.
———. *Inquiry and Education: John Dewey and the Quest for Democracy*. Albany: State University of New York Press, 2006.
Johnstone, Christopher Lyle. "Dewey, Ethics, and Rhetoric: Toward a Contemporary Conception of Practical Wisdom." *Philosophy and Rhetoric* 16, no. 3 (1983): 185–207.
Keats, John. "Ode to a Grecian Urn." Poetry Foundation. Accessed June 17, 2018. https://www.poetryfoundation.org/poems/44477/ode-on-a-grecian-urn.
Latour, Bruno. *Down to Earth: Politics in the New Climate Regime*. Hoboken, NJ: Wiley, 2017.
Mackin, James A., Jr. "Rhetoric, Pragmatism, and Practical Wisdom." In *Rhetoric and Philosophy*, edited by Richard A. Cherwitz, 275–302. Hillsdale, NJ: Erlbaum, 1990.
McDermott, John J. *The Drama of Possibility: Experience as Philosophy of Culture*. Edited by Douglas R. Anderson. New York: Fordham University Press, 2007.
———. Introduction to *The Later Works of John Dewey*, vol. 11, *1935–1937*, edited by Jo Ann Boydston, xi–xxxii. Carbondale: Southern Illinois University Press, 1987.
McLuhan, Marshall. *Understanding Media: The Extensions of Man*. Boston: MIT Press, 1994.
Patton, John. "Causation and Creativity in Rhetorical Situations: Distinctions and Implications." *Quarterly Journal of Speech* 65, no. 1 (1979): 36–55.

Paxton, Robert O. *The Anatomy of Fascism*. New York: Alfred A. Knopf, 2004.
Perelman, Chaim, and Lucie Olbrechts-Tyteca. *The New Rhetoric: A Treatise on Argumentation*. Notre Dame: University of Notre Dame Press, 1969.
Pope, Arthur Upham. "Merit Seen in Moscow Film: Detraction Is Regarded as Giving Aid to Nazi Propagandists." *New York Times*, June 12, 1943.
———. "'Mission to Moscow' Film Viewed as Historical Realism: Criticism of Much-Discussed Motion Picture Based on Ambassador Davies's Book, in Regarded as Not Wholly in Accord with Events So Far Known." *New York Times*, May 16, 1943.
Poulakos, John. "*Kairos* in Gorgias' Rhetorical Compositions." In *Rhetoric and Kairos: Essays in History, Theory, and Praxis*, edited by Phillip Sipiora and James S. Baumlin, 89–96. Albany: State University of New York Press, 2002.
Poulakos, John, and Nathan Crick. "There Is Beauty Here, Too: Aristotle's Rhetoric for Science." *Philosophy and Rhetoric* 45, no. 3 (2012): 295–311.
Quine, W. V. O. *Ontological Relativity and Other Essays*. New York: Columbia University Press, 1969.
Rockefeller, Steven C. *John Dewey: Religious Faith and Democratic Humanism*. New York: Columbia University Press, 1991.
Ryan, Alan. *John Dewey and the High Tide of American Liberalism*. New York: Norton, 1995.
Schiappa, Edward. *Protagoras and Logos: A Study in Greek Philosophy and Rhetoric*. Columbia: University of South Carolina Press, 2003.
Schudson, Michael. "The 'Lippmann-Dewey Debate' and the Invention of Walter Lippmann as an Anti-Democrat, 1986–1996." *International Journal of Communication* 2 (2008): 1031–42.
Shor, Ira. *Empowering Education: Critical Teaching for Social Change*. Chicago: University of Chicago Press, 1992.
Simonson, Peter. "A Rhetoric for Polytheistic Democracy: Walt Whitman's 'Poet of Many in One.'" *Philosophy and Rhetoric* 36, no. 4 (2003): 353–75.
Simpson, Douglas J., Michael J. B. Jackson, and Judy C. Aycock. *John Dewey and the Art of Teaching: Toward Reflective and Imaginative Practice*. Thousand Oaks: Sage Publications, 2005.
Sipiora, Phillip, and James S. Baumlin, eds. *Rhetoric and Kairos: Essays in History, Theory, and Praxis*. Albany: State University of New York Press, 2002.
Stengers. Isabelle. *Another Science Is Possible: A Manifesto for Slow Science*. Cambridge: Polity, 2018.
———. *In Catastrophic Times: Resisting the Coming Barbarism*. Paris: Open Humanities, 2015.
Stroud, Scott. *John Dewey and the Artful Life: Pragmatism, Aesthetics, and Morality*. State College: Penn State University Press, 2011.
Tell, Dave. "Reinventing Walter Lippmann: Communication and Cultural Studies." *Review of Communication* 13, no. 2 (2013): 108–26.
Vatz, Richard E. "The Myth of the Rhetorical Situation." *Philosophy and Rhetoric* 6, no. 3 (1973): 154–61.
Weaver, Richard M. *The Ethics of Rhetoric*. Davis, CA: Hermagoras, 1985.
Westbrook, Robert B. *John Dewey and American Democracy*. Ithaca: Cornell University Press, 1991.

INDEX

absence, 125, 131–33, 140, 143, 173
activity, 74
Addams, Jane, 177–83, 188, 195–98
aesthetics, 7, 55, 72, 146–76,
    199–207
American dream, 15
anarchy, 88
animism, 29, 35–36, 40–43, 109
antihumanism
    aesthetics and, 161, 170–72
    education and, 205–6
    fascism and, 4–8
    individualism and, 25–26, 65, 68
    nationalism and, 29, 39–41
    rhetoric and, 194
antinaturalism, 74, 79
Aristotle, 154, 181–82
Arnold, Matthew, 149
Aronowitz, Stanley, 12–14
art
    civilization and, 148–49, 175
    of individuality, 75, 79–80
    science and, 109, 114–15
    work of, 152–53, 159–69, 196, 199
atomic bomb, 87–89, 99
attitude, 5

beauty, 158–60, 174
becoming, 7, 91
belief, 131–31, 144

character, 75, 186
choice, 194–95
common sense, 125, 131, 140
communication, 72, 76–77, 184–85
    in art, 152, 169–70, 174
    democracy and, 90–93, 102, 108–9,
        197–98
    face-to-face, 112–14
    inquiry and, 142–43
community, 91–93
conformity, 24
confusion, 56–57
conscientiousness, 190–92

consciousness, 166–67
consequences, 135, 143
consummation, 165–67
corporate, 80
counter-memory, 87
courage, 171
Crusoe, Robinson, 2–3, 76, 124, 127–47,
    199–207
culture, 96, 129
    money and, 17–19

data, 138
deduction, 142
definition, 136, 146
democracy, 90–99, 105–10, 149, 173–75,
    197, 206–7
detachment, 133–35
doubt, 126, 130, 136–37, 144, 146
drama, 164–65, 168
dualism
    in art, 153, 156, 159–62
    in nature, 71, 73, 80, 127

Eberly, Rosa, 150–52
ecology, 72–73
Emerson, Ralph Waldo, 68–70, 73–76, 80,
    104–5, 108
emotion, 55–56, 106, 164, 192
Enlightenment, 94, 97
environment, 130, 156, 162, 164, 186
event, 138, 162, 184–85
experience, 73, 105, 143, 168
experimentalism, 135–36, 145

fascism, 1–8
    education and, 205–6
    elitism and, 197
    humanism and, 79
    individualism and, 29–30
    origins of, 89, 118
    propaganda and, 58
Fishman, Stephen M., 66–67
force, 42
form, 167–68

freedom
　in fascism, 38–39, 58
　liberalism and, 21, 90, 94, 123
　positive, 146–47
　rhetoric and, 180, 183
Freire, Paulo, 47–49

Geist, 36, 38, 43
Giroux, Henry, 85–87
global warming, 99, 206
God
　Crusoe and, 137, 204
　democracy and, 112
　early Dewey's notion of, 66–69, 129, 155
　fascism and, 42
　moral situation and, 192
　in rugged individualism, 12, 65
　teachers and, 204
Great Depression, 83–85, 148

habit, 74–75
　character as, 75
　human nature and, 4
　of inquiry, 123, 130–31, 136–37, 140
　rhetoric and, 186–91
happiness, 92
Hernandez, Adriana, 102–4
Hitler, Adolf, 5, 42–43, 53, 56–57
hooks, bell, 30–32
Hull House, 64–65
humanism
　antinaturalist interpretation of, 33, 35, 79
　democratic, 1–3, 68, 183, 195
　naturalism and, 65–66, 71, 75, 79
　pedagogy of, 6–8, 81, 150–51, 172, 176, 199–207
hypothesis, 136, 139–43, 146

idealism, 20, 139, 180
imagination, 169
　aesthetic, 149, 154–60
　idealistic interpretation of, 33, 154, 169
　inquiry and, 134, 139
immanence, 36, 65, 71
implication, 143
impulse, 74, 185–94
individualism, 12–27, 29, 38–39, 51, 96, 106
individuality, 63–82, 86
induction, 142
inference, 125–32
inquiry, 116, 126
　biological matrix of, 130–31, 137, 183
　cultural matrix of, 130–31, 137, 140

instrumentalism, 13, 78
intelligence
　cooperative, 82, 90, 96–99, 100–120
　fascist rejection of, 44
　habits of, 189–90
　human nature and, 79
intent, 185
intolerance, 41
intuitiveness, 170–71

Jarratt, Susan C., 181–82
Jefferson, Thomas, 15–16, 21, 24–25, 90–94, 104, 106
judgment
　in aesthetics, 150, 162, 173
　in logic, 136, 144–45
　in rhetoric, 179–80, 189–92, 189–91

Keats, John, 157–60, 174

laissez-faire
　individualism and, 23–25, 33, 38–39, 90
　liberalism, 21–22, 85, 95, 99
language, 75–77, 131–32, 139, 184–85
leader, 5, 29, 35, 40–44
liberalism, 21, 83–99
liberty, 94–95
Lincoln, Abraham, 100
Lippmann, Walter, 104–7, 113, 118
literature, 150–51, 199–207
locality, 91–93, 104–5, 111–12
logic, 6–7, 123–47
　aesthetics and, 161–62, 170
　pedagogy and, 199–207
logos, 17–18, 126

machine, 17–19, 78–77, 180
materialism, 19–20, 32–33, 71
McCarthy, Lucille, 66–67
McDermott, John J., 2, 6–7, 150
meaning, 133, 138
mechanization, 19
media, 101, 114
morality, 189–90
motives, 191–94
mysticism, 40–42

naming, 36, 75, 138–39, 146
National Association for the Advancement of Colored People (NAACP), 83–85
nationalism, 28–44, 79–80, 180, 197

naturalism
  cultural, 129
  humanistic, 65, 71–73
  in John Keats, 153, 156
  in rhetoric, 183–84
nature, human, 4, 25, 41, 77, 90, 113
negative capability, 158
neoliberalism, 13, 102

object, 138–39
observation, 136, 143–44, 146, 164
oversoul, 105

pacifism, 179–80, 195
passion, 192–95
paternalism, 45–46
patriotism, 40
perceptivity, 163–67
personality, 38, 42, 44
planning, 84–85, 97–98
Plato, 7, 153, 168, 180–81, 183, 195
playfulness, 134, 145
poetry, 149, 157
poiesis, 150
politics, 179, 189
power, 8
  democratic, 183
  education and, 1, 75, 129, 146
  individuality and, 65, 73, 75, 79, 186
  liberalism and, 95–96
  propaganda and, 50, 53
  technology and, 18, 78
pragmatism, 78, 92, 110, 123, 135
praxis, 47
presence, 125, 131, 140, 173
propaganda, 45–59, 89, 98, 100, 109, 115–16, 195
prophecy, 141, 154
public, 85, 102, 109–10, 152
publicity agents, 52–53
public opinion
  democratic, 45–46, 91, 98, 101–2, 110, 115
  Walter Lippmann and, 105–7
  propaganda and, 50–51, 57–58, 89, 106
public sphere, 97, 151, 180, 198
  literary, 151–52

quality, 19, 161–63, 185
quantification, 19
quantity, 19

racism, 40–41
radio, 46, 100

realism, 139, 143, 162–63, 180
reasoning, 136, 141–42, 156–58, 195–97
recognition, 143–44, 163–64
reflex arc, 73–74, 186
relations, 6–7, 23, 136, 173
religion, 33, 66, 69, 155
rhetoric, 7, 84, 177–207, 219
rhythm, 164–67
romanticism, 11, 20, 35, 153–54

scapegoating, 41
science, 77–79, 97, 109, 113–16, 126–27, 174
Shor, Ira, 126–27
sign, 131–33
situation
  problematic, 136–37
  rhetorical, 189–92
social movement, 97, 100, 117–20, 179
society, 21, 37, 76, 81
sophists, 126, 181–82
Stalin, Joseph, 40–41
standardization, 19
symbol, 131–32, 141–42
sympathy, 196–97

taste, 150–52, 171–72
teaching
  aesthetics, 150, 159, 164, 169–70, 173, 176, 199–207
  banking concept of, 48–49, 126
  border pedagogy, 85–87
  citizen critics, 151–52
  coming to voice, 30–32
  critical reading practice, 103–4
  democratic habits, 1–8, 75, 81, 102, 123, 136, 199–207
  dissoi logoi, 126, 182
  living in hope, 66–67
  logic, 123, 133, 136, 146, 199–207
  neoliberalism and, 11–13
  paideweyan pedagogy, 209
  problem-posing education, 48–49, 126–27
  rhetoric, 180, 187–88, 192, 196, 198–207
technology, 77–79, 97
temporality, 131–33, 162–65, 172
tension, 130
thinking, 75, 84, 134–38, 144, 172
timeliness, 187–89
transcendence, 128, 139–40, 142

trivium, 6, 199, 201
truth, 153–63, 174

value, 72, 149, 153
violence, 4–5, 40–44

warrant, 141
Whitman, Walt, 108–9
will to power, 74–75
words, 47, 54–55
Wordsworth, William, 167

RHETORIC AND DEMOCRATIC DELIBERATION

Other Books in the Series:

Karen Tracy, *Challenges of Ordinary Democracy: A Case Study in Deliberation and Dissent* / Volume 1

Samuel McCormick, *Letters to Power: Public Advocacy Without Public Intellectuals* / Volume 2

Christian Kock and Lisa S. Villadsen, eds., *Rhetorical Citizenship and Public Deliberation* / Volume 3

Jay P. Childers, *The Evolving Citizen: American Youth and the Changing Norms of Democratic Engagement* / Volume 4

Dave Tell, *Confessional Crises and Cultural Politics in Twentieth-Century America* / Volume 5

David Boromisza-Habashi, *Speaking Hatefully: Culture, Communication, and Political Action in Hungary* / Volume 6

Arabella Lyon, *Deliberative Acts: Democracy, Rhetoric, and Rights* / Volume 7

Lyn Carson, John Gastil, Janette Hartz-Karp, and Ron Lubensky, eds., *The Australian Citizens' Parliament and the Future of Deliberative Democracy* / Volume 8

Christa J. Olson, *Constitutive Visions: Indigeneity and Commonplaces of National Identity in Republican Ecuador* / Volume 9

Damien Smith Pfister, *Networked Media, Networked Rhetorics: Attention and Deliberation in the Early Blogosphere* / Volume 10

Katherine Elizabeth Mack, *From Apartheid to Democracy: Deliberating Truth and Reconciliation in South Africa* / Volume 11

Mary E. Stuckey, *Voting Deliberatively: FDR and the 1936 Presidential Campaign* / Volume 12

Robert Asen, *Democracy, Deliberation, and Education* / Volume 13

Shawn J. Parry-Giles and David S. Kaufer, *Memories of Lincoln and the Splintering of American Political Thought* / Volume 14

J. Michael Hogan, Jessica A. Kurr, Michael J. Bergmaier, and Jeremy D. Johnson, eds., *Speech and Debate as Civic Education* / Volume 15

Angela G. Ray and Paul Stob, eds., *Thinking Together: Lecturing, Learning, and Difference in the Long Nineteenth Century* / Volume 16

Sharon E. Jarvis and Soo-Hye Han, *Votes that Count and Voters Who Don't: How Journalists Sideline Electoral Participation (Without Even Knowing It)* / Volume 17

Belinda Stillion Southard, *How to Belong: Women's Agency in a Transnational World* / Volume 18

Melanie Loehwing, *Homeless Advocacy and the Rhetorical Construction of the Civic Home* / Volume 19

Kristy Maddux, *Practicing Citizenship: Women's Rhetoric at the 1893 Chicago World's Fair* / Volume 20

Craig Rood, *After Gun Violence: Deliberation and Memory in an Age of Gridlock* / Volume 21

www.ingramcontent.com/pod-product-compliance
Lightning Source LLC
Chambersburg PA
CBHW021942290426
44108CB00012B/931